DYING TO EAT

DYING
TO EAT

CROSS-CULTURAL
PERSPECTIVES ON
FOOD, DEATH, AND
THE AFTERLIFE

EDITED BY CANDI K. CANN

UNIVERSITY PRESS OF KENTUCKY

Scholarly publisher for the Commonwealth,
serving Bellarmine University, Berea College, Centre College of Kentucky, Eastern
Kentucky University, The Filson Historical Society, Georgetown College, Kentucky
Historical Society, Kentucky State University, Morehead State University, Murray
State University, Northern Kentucky University, Transylvania University,
University of Kentucky, University of Louisville, and Western Kentucky University.
All rights reserved.

Editorial and Sales Offices: The University Press of Kentucky
663 South Limestone Street, Lexington, Kentucky 40508-4008
www.kentuckypress.com

Library of Congress Cataloging-in-Publication Data

Names: Cann, Candi K., editor.
Title: Dying to eat : cross-cultural perspectives on food, death, and the afterlife /
    edited by Candi K. Cann.
Description: Lexington, Kentucky : University Press of Kentucky, [2018] | Includes
    bibliographical references and index.
Identifiers: LCCN 2017042895| ISBN 9780813174693 (hardcover : alk. paper) |
    ISBN 9780813174709 (pdf) | ISBN 9780813174716 (epub)
Subjects: LCSH: Food habits—Cross-cultural studies. | Death—Cross-cultural
    studies. | Funeral rites and ceremonie—Cross-cultural studies.
Classification: LCC GT2850 .D95 2018 | DDC 394.1/2—dc23

ISBN 978-0-8131-7851-6 (pbk. : alk. paper)

Dedicated to my mother, J. Arden Griffin

(1943–1997)

My recipe box is my shrine to your memory.

Contents

STARTERS

The Role of Food in Bereavement and Memorialization

Cooking and Corpses

The idea for this book emerged from the intersection of an interest in food from a personal perspective and an academic focus on the role of food in death and ritual practices. In modern society, food, life, and death have developed a rather precarious relationship with one another, as food consumption, class status, and notions of health are rapidly shifting, globalization is changing and increasing our food choices, and society is becoming more multicultural. Both death and food, in their rapidly changing states, must be examined and studied. The definition of death is not universal—some cultures see it as a process, others as a single moment. Some cultures view cardiopulmonary failure as death, whereas other cultures use brain death as their standard to define when death occurs. Similarly, food and foodways are not by any means universal. Food, like birth and death, has the ability to frame time, shape our days and the way in which we view and construct time, and regulate human experience. Through food, and the meal, social networks are formed and time is regulated.

Preparation of food is also important, as cooking is transformational: it is what turns food from mere sustenance into communal and social rituals. As Fernández-Armesto writes, "Everywhere, eating is a culturally transforming—sometimes a magically transforming—act. It has its own alchemy. It transmutes individuals into society and sickness into health."[1] The act of preparing food, followed by the act of consuming it, is similar in this way to the way death decays our bodies. We prepare dead bodies for public "consumption," through washing, purifying, embalming, or cremating them, preparing bodies to participate as corpses (or even as ab-

1

sent bodies) in public and social rituals of bereavement and loss. Similarly, we transform food into meals, preparing and altering food in the kitchen, changing raw materials into a synergetic meal. Cooking and corpses both transform and construct social rituals in which we come together and think about life, death, and life after loss; food is a mediating agent between heaven and earth and life and death.[2]

Death and Food: An Introduction

With some exceptions, studies conducted on food and death generally fall into one of the following categories: (1) food as a direct causation in preventing, prolonging, or causing death;[3] (2) food scarcity or abundance and its role in economic development or colonization (eco-critical studies of creating or preventing death);[4] (3) feasts and fasts and their relationships to saints, martyrs, and the general role of food (or absence of food) in religious asceticism and practices;[5] (4) explorations of dietary restrictions or food symbolism in religious texts and practices;[6] (5) anthropological and sociological explorations of food and foodways as a form of cultural identity;[7] and (6) food as a gender marker, in relationship to marginalized discourse and power.[8] *Dying to Eat* seeks to contribute to these various studies of the relationship between food and death by offering an interdisciplinary approach to the intersection of food and death, using a variety of disciplinary approaches, ranging from anthropological to religious to eco-critical, and arguing that the tensions between food and death are perhaps best explored through this interdisciplinary approach.

In recent years, popular literature and social media regarding food and death have placed food and death at center stage, as iconoclastic chefs herald their favorite meals in such books as the recent best seller *My Last Supper*, a coffee-table book rich with recipes, photographs, and stimulating conversation regarding what the last meal in life should be—a resplendent meal inducing a sensory experience, or comfort food that evokes one's childhood home. *My Last Supper* has an online website, a blog, and a continually growing audience, appealing to self-declared "foodies" and gourmet chefs alike and focusing on food as the main subject, where chefs highlight the role food has played in their lives.[9] Death in this book operates as a framing mechanism to allow food to play a central role in life and its meaning; food is presented as nourishing not only in substance but also in significance. Internet memes offer a similar focus on the last meal, but from a more sinister and depressing point of view, in the form of pictures of last meals requested by death-row inmates in various American prisons.[10] Death and food intersect here as an unspoken (and largely unexplored) discourse on power—both of the state over bodies that it nourishes, punishes, and then destroys, and of food, in its ability to evoke a sense of comfort, familiarity, and presence (through shared meals past). With these memes reaching several million Internet views and the book *My Last Supper* topping the *New York Times* best-seller list, it is evident that food plays an important and central role in contemporary society and culture.

Food is a central actor in funeral feasts, bereavement rituals, and memorialization practices, and it remains an enduring (and often overlooked) part of the material world of grief. Food has played a major role in funerary and ritualized funerary practices since the beginning of humankind. In the ancient Roman world, it was common practice to build tubes connecting the tops of the graves with the crypts themselves, and mourners would regularly pour food and drink offerings (mostly bread and wine) into these tubes, whose other end would be placed in the mouth of the corpse, in order to "feed" the dead while they waited for their afterlife. Similarly, early Christian mourners, remembering and honoring the dead, regularly feasted at graves, and it was common for cemeteries to contain kitchens to aid in the preparation of food for the graveside feasts that fed the dead while they waited for their resurrection.[11] By the seventeenth and eighteenth centuries, Christians in Great Britain commonly placed bread or cake on the corpse to absorb the sins of the deceased, to aid his or her journey to the afterlife. Some families even hired official "sin eaters," who, in exchange for a small amount of money, would eat the sins of the dead in order to expunge them. These corpse cakes were gradually replaced by the popular and communally shared funeral biscuits of the Victorian era, which were wrapped with printed prayers and poems meant to comfort gathered mourners, rather than to intercede on behalf of the dead.[12]

In Viking culture, funeral ale was consumed on the seventh day following a death to mark the passing of the deceased, and the heirs of the deceased were then ritually and formally recognized. Similarly, in Hindu Brahmin culture, sixteen rice balls (*pinda*) were traditionally offered every day over twelve days (five rice balls rather than one were offered on the last day) to ensure that the soul of the departed reached its destination. In

China, Japan, and Korea, it is customary to offer food not only to the bereaved but to the deceased; ritualistic foods are prepared and served at
particular times in order to remember and feed the dead. Food and drink
sustain us in life—why not also in death?

Funeral Feasting: An Act of Caring or Remembering?

Recent scholarship on bereavement has demonstrated that those who are
able to renegotiate continued bonds with the deceased are actually most
successful in moving forward without suffering complicated grief. Labeled
"continuing bonds theory,"[13] this scholarship challenges previous understandings of "attachment theories"[14] of grief, which view attachment to the
deceased as unhealthy, or even pathological. Examining the food practices
between the living and the dead reveal that continuing bonds have been
historically valuable and continue to occur in many cultures around the
world. As I argued in my last book, the Protestant worldview (along with
the medicalization and professionalization of death) has contributed to
the bifurcation of the realms of the living and the dead in contemporary
secular society, as well as an increasing incidence of disappearing corpses
from funerals and rituals regarding the dead.[15] This has, in turn, led to a
growing trend of disenfranchised mourning and views of attachment to
the dead as both unnatural and negative. As a result, grief has become
pathologized, bereavement leave has been shortened, and individuals have
been forced to create their own do-it-yourself rituals of mourning to give
expression to their grief.

　　Tony Walter, a scholar of death studies, argues that some cultures
"care for" the dead in their memorialization practices, whereas others "remember" the dead.[16] The function is quite different—"caring for the dead"
is a renegotiation of the status of the deceased person while allowing the
living to retain an active and participatory relationship with the dead in
their new state; "remembering the dead" is a renegotiation of life without
the deceased. The former, caring for the dead, can be said to be integral to
the recently accepted continuing bonds theory, which argues that to best
grieve, one must figure out a way in which one can continue to have a relationship with the deceased. Continuing bonds theory argues that developing a way to sustain a meaningful relationship with the dead (as opposed
to "moving on" or disengaging from the dead) may be a valuable and

meaningful part of the grieving experience. Though some of the most prominent continuing bonds scholars are American, ironically, continuing bonds theory has yet to influence scholars or grief therapists in the United States in the same way that it has across the Atlantic in the United Kingdom and Europe. Peter Brown writes in his latest book, *The Ransom of the Soul,* "The sense that the living could do something about the dead gave a much-needed sense of agency to the average believer. But it is here—in the vital link between the living and the dead—that one can sense the silent pressure of an entire society." The ways in which food functions as symbol and operates as a material conduit between the living and the dead reveal much about our culture, our worldviews, and our understandings of the afterlife.

Dining with the Dead

Feeding the dead, or "dining with the dead" (as the first section is titled), is more than simply remembering them; it is a way of reintegrating the dead back into our everyday lives. The first three chapters examine the role of food as a material conduit between the realms of the living and the dead. Emily S. Wu examines the meaning and symbolism of food in Chinese funerary rites, delving into the rich Confucian, Daoist, and Buddhist textual traditions to underscore her fieldwork observations of food as both boundary marker and boundary breaker. Wu connects the material remnants of the corpse with the symbolic functions of food, richly demonstrating the role of bone, pork, and wine in mediating the worlds of flesh—both living and decaying. Jung Eun Sophia Park's chapter examines the function of food in Korean funeral rituals and memorial festivities in Buddhism, Korean Catholicism, and memorial activities. Park gives the reader a rich descriptive analysis of the various foods and their meanings in honoring the Korean dead, in the food ritual of Young San Jae, describing how food is used as a way to connect the living with the dead ancestors. My own piece, "Sweetening Death: Sugar in the United States, Mexico, and China," presents a comparative analysis of the role of sugar and its transformation in funeral foods and remembrance rituals, documenting the ways the dead are perceived and understood as active or passive actors in their afterlives. Sugar, though widely available in the modern world, was initially used in memorialization and funereal practices because its being a luxury good bestowed a particular status on the dead, though it is now ironically a staple of the lower classes and a symbol of malnutrition. Through sugar, my chapter demonstrates and examines the distinction that Tony Walter makes between remembering the dead and caring for the dead. Like Joshua Graham in his chapter, I argue that perhaps we need to be more mindful of establishing ongoing relationships with the deceased, rather than simply expecting ourselves to "move on" and "recover from" grief. This chapter is an ideal transition to the second section of the book, as the comparison of food, bereavement, and memorialization rituals highlights a distinct difference between the function of food on the American table and its place in the Mexican or Chinese context: though in America food functions largely to aid the bereaved and reintegrate the grieving into their social network without the deceased, it functions to feed the dead in Mexico and China.

Eating After: Food and Drink in Bereavement and Remembrance

The second half of the book examines food's role in "remembering the dead," or "eating after" the funeral. In these five chapters, food and death center largely on rituals that focus on food and are conducted by the living in relationship to their conceptual and existential understandings of death, and what it means to face death in the midst of life. The reader will note that the contributions in this section discuss bereavement customs and the role of food in the gathering of the community following a death to renegotiate relationships *without* the deceased. Joshua Graham writes on the role of funeral foods in the American South, examining how these foods function in helping Southerners come to terms with their grief in light of the missing deceased. He examines the role of several foods and drinks (particularly the absence of alcohol) common in Southern Baptist culture at funeral repasts, and he questions the lack of current American scholarship on continuing bonds theory in American grieving customs.[17] Graham makes a compelling argument for its application in his chapter, while offering the reader a richly textured ethnography of contemporary American funeral feasts. Lacy Crocker and Gordon Fuller's chapter considers bagels as a symbol of the eternal return of life in the midst of death. They focus on the symbol of the eternal cycle of return, the bagel's roundness illustrating the wholeness of death as a completion of life. Their chapter reveals that the Jewish conception of death emphasizes the importance of life and seeks not to dwell in the shadows of death.[18] In these chapters there is a particular focus on food as a material artifact that provides social cohesion and communal identity; food provides the medium through which communal, ethnic, and religious identities are formulated, conveyed, and reinforced. David Oualaalou discusses the role of couscous in emphasizing Moroccan identity and mourning the dead. Couscous, through its ordinariness, and because it is an everyday staple, underscores the role of death as a part of life—as something not only unavoidable, but necessary to truly live as a Muslim. He also traces the shifting influences of class and status on these traditional mourning staples, noting that because of globalization and capitalism, Muslim funerals in contemporary Morocco are becoming less concerned with communal bereavement and are instead stressing the individual's life by means of expensive shows of wealth and class through more complicated and expensive foods.

Christa Shusko's chapter focuses on how alcohol-drinking rituals mimic the drinking of blood (a "blood" punch) in a male fraternity group. Shusko's chapter examines how the living face death and form community through food, albeit through male bonding rituals of consuming alcohol and reenacting illicit and horrific acts. Shusko contends that alcohol acts as both conduit and medium through which the living come to terms with death and the macabre. Unlike Graham, who argues that the absence of alcohol reinforces Protestant, and particularly Baptist, identity, Shusko points to the use of alcohol as a cohesive agent that brings the community together. Radikobo Ntsimane's chapter is an examination of the intersection of food and death among the Tswana and Zulu peoples in South Africa, discussing the function of funerals in feeding the living and the ways in which funerals can help socially and economically sustain a community. His analysis of the shift in the economic sustainability of funeral feasting in times of scarcity and widespread diseases such as AIDS in Africa is both valuable and important, providing a social and cultural critique that forces the reader to think about the function of funerals and their effects on the community. In this chapter the reader understands that the funeral attendants are dying to eat, both literally and figuratively.

Each author in this second section underscores the role of food and drink in reintegrating the community following the disruption of death. When people die, the survivors try to make sense of lives and deaths, give them meaning after the fact, and provide imposed narrative structures that interpret the value of a life. Meals are the narrative constructions of food—the story we want to tell with food, and an ordering of the foods so that they function to enhance not only sensory experience, but also shared social and ritual space. The cake on the American table functions like the Chinese soup at the end of the meal—it is a shared course meant to tie the participants of the meal together through the division of portions evenly across the table, which enhances and reinforces hospitality exchanges that shape identity and erase boundaries. To emphasize the meal is to recognize that food provides not only sustenance but also shared ritual space. The meal is eaten, and ended, in the way lives are narrated and constructed, and it is for this reason that the meal serves as the perfect metaphor for an understanding of the story of death and bereavement. Death has a tale to tell, and we should sit and share a meal as we listen to its story. It is with these last thoughts that I wish the reader bon appétit.

Notes

1. Felipe Fernández-Armesto, *Food: A History* (New York: Macmillan, 2001), 34.

2. Claude Lévi-Strauss, *The Raw and the Cooked,* trans. John Weightman and Doreen Weightman (New York: Harper & Row, 1975), 336.

3. Paul S. Mead, Laurence Slutsker, Vance Dietz, Linda F. McCaig, Joseph S. Bresee, Craig Shapiro, Patricia M. Griffin, and Robert V. Tauxe, "Food-Related Illness and Death in the United States," *Emerging Infectious Diseases* 5, no. 5 (1999): 607; Nancy Scheper-Hughes, *Death without Weeping: The Violence of Everyday Life in Brazil* (Berkeley: University of California Press, 1993).

4. Sidney Wilfred Mintz, *Sweetness and Power* (New York: Viking, 1985); Erik Millstone and Tim Lang. *The Atlas of Food: Who Eats What, Where and Why* (London: Earthscan, 2003); E. Valentine Daniel, Henry Bernstein, and Tom Brass *Plantations, Proletarians, and Peasants in Colonial Asia* (London: F. Cass, 1992).

5. Franz Xaver Weiser, *Handbook of Christian Feasts and Customs: The Year of the Lord in Liturgy and Folklore* (New York: Harcourt Brace, 1958); Caroline Walker Bynum, *Holy Feast and Holy Fast: The Religious Significance of Food to Medieval Women,* vol. 1 (Berkeley: University of California Press, 1987); Hester Goodenouch Gelber, review of Caroline Walker Bynum, *Holy Feast and Holy Fast: The Religious Significance of Food to Medieval Women, Modern Language Quarterly* 48, no. 3 (1987): 281–285; Caroline Walker Bynum, "Fast, Feast, and Flesh: The

Religious Significance of Food to Medieval Women," *Representations* 11 (Summer 1985): 1–25.

6. Arjun Appadurai, "Gastro-Politics in Hindu South Asia," *American Ethnologist* 8, no. 3 (1981): 494–511; Ravindra S. Khare, ed., *The Eternal Food: Gastronomic Ideas and Experiences of Hindus and Buddhists* (Albany: State University of New York Press, 1992).

7. Mary Douglas, *Food in the Social Order* (New York: Routledge, 2014); Mary Douglas and Jonathan Gross, "Food and Culture: Measuring the Intricacy of Rule Systems," *Social Science Information/Sur les sciences sociales* 20, no. 1 (1981): 1–35; Mary Douglas, "Deciphering a Meal," *Daedalus* 101, no. 1 (1972): 61–81; James L. Watson and Melissa L. Caldwell, eds., *The Cultural Politics of Food and Eating* (Malden, Mass.: Blackwell, 2005); Douglas Brownlie, Paul Hewer, and Suzanne Horne, "Culinary Tourism: An Exploratory Reading of Contemporary Representations of Cooking," *Consumption Markets & Culture* 8, no. 1 (2005): 7–26; Carole Counihan and Penny Van Esterik, *Food and Culture: A Reader* (New York: Routledge, 2013); Susan Zlotnick, "Domesticating Imperialism: Curry and Cookbooks in Victorian England," *Frontiers: A Journal of Women Studies* 16, nos. 2–3 (1996): 51–68. Though the subject is not explored in this book, it is important to note that not only are the dead fed, but they are also themselves, at times, eaten. Cannibalism, and cannibalistic behavior, has been exhibited across a wide variety of species, and across cultures and time. For more, see Peggy Reeves Sanday, *Divine Hunger: Cannibalism as a Cultural System* (New York: Cambridge University Press, 1986).

8. Janet Theophano, *Eat My Words: Reading Women's Lives through the Cookbooks They Wrote* (New York: Palgrave Macmillan, 2002); Jessamyn Neuhaus, "The Way to a Man's Heart: Gender Roles, Domestic Ideology, and Cookbooks in the 1950s," *Journal of Social History* 23, no. 3 (1999): 529–555; Rafia Zafar, "The Signifying Dish: Autobiography and History in Two Black Women's Cookbooks," *Feminist Studies* 25, no. 2 (1999): 449–469.

9. Melanie Dunea, *My Last Supper* (Edinburgh: A&C Black, 2007). The website is www.mylastsupper.com.

10. Two such examples are Alan White, "12 Pictures of Death Row Prisoners' Last Meals," Buzzfeed, February 18, 2014, www.buzzfeed.com/alanwhite/12-pictures-of-death-row-prisoners-last-meals#.p00bPx5mb, accessed October 3, 2015; and Tom Butler, "17 Death Row Requests You Won't Believe Were Made," What Culture, http://whatculture.com/offbeat/17-death-row-requests-you-won-39-t-believe-were-made, accessed October 3, 2015.

11. Brown argues that this was primarily because the early "Christians died for the Resurrection, not for the immortality of their souls. . . . Good souls enjoyed what Tertullian called a *refrigerium interim*—a refreshing period of rest in the other world, as delightful as the cool water and of food shared, in shady bowers, with boon companions"; Peter Brown, *The Ransom of the Soul: Afterlife and Wealth in Early Western Christianity* (Cambridge: Harvard University Press, 2015), 10–12.

12. These biscuits sometimes also served as announcements of the death: printed notices accompanied the cookies and were sent out to the friends and family of the dead. For more on this, see Hoag Levins, "The Story of Victorian Funeral Cookies: Revisiting a Centuries' Old Mourning Tradition," Historic Camden County, September 12, 2011, http://historiccamdencounty.com/ccnews153.shtml, accessed January 4, 2017.

13. Dennis Klass, Phyllis R. Silverman, and Steven Nickman, *Continuing Bonds: New Understandings of Grief* (Washington, D.C.: Taylor & Francis, 2014); Nigel P. Field, Beryl Gao, and Lisa Paderna, "Continuing Bonds in Bereavement: An Attachment Theory Based Perspective," *Death Studies* 29, no. 4 (2005): 277–299. Field et al. are careful to nuance continuing bonds theory in relation to grief and assert that it depends on the *types* of attachment bonds developed that determine the healthiness of the grief displayed. (My thanks to Tony Walter for pointing this out to me.)

14. John Bowlby, *A Secure Base: Clinical Applications of Attachment Theory* (Hoboken, N.J.: Taylor & Francis, 2005).

15. See Candi Cann, *Virtual Afterlives: Grieving the Dead in the Twenty-first Century* (Lexington: University Press of Kentucky, 2014).

16. Tony Walter, "Communicating with the Dead," in *Encyclopedia of Death and the Human Experience,* ed. Clifton D. Bryant and Dennis L. Peck (Los Angeles: Sage Publications, 2009), 216–219.

17. Briana L. Root and Julie Juola Exline, "The Role of Continuing Bonds in Coping with Grief: Overview and Future Directions," *Death Studies* 38, no. 1 (2014): 1–8; Margaret S. Stroebe, Georgios Abakoumkin, Wolfgang Stroebe, and Henk Schut, "Continuing Bonds in Adjustment to Bereavement: Impact of Abrupt versus Gradual Separation," *Personal Relationships* 19, no. 2 (2012): 255–266.

18. Because this book addresses the tension between food and death, rather than dying, the tensions between food and *dying* are not addressed. It is important to note, however, that in contemporary medical culture, there is a failure by many medical personnel (and the families of the dying) to see the harmful side effects of food and drink as the dying patient nears death. For example, it is not beneficial for dying patients to be fed solid food, as bowel movements in the last days of life often become extremely painful. Additionally, there are more and more studies that reveal the benefits of keeping dying patients hydrated at only 70 percent hydration rates, which decreases pain and makes the last days of life much more comfortable. Perhaps future studies of food and dying can examine this more deeply from a cultural, social, and psychological standpoint. For more on this, see John E. Ellershaw, Jane M. Sutcliffe, and Cicely M. Saunders, "Dehydration and the Dying Patient," *Journal of Pain and Symptom Management* 10, no. 3 (1995): 192–197; Joyce V. Zerwekh, "Do Dying Patients Really Need IV Fluids?" *AJN: The American Journal of Nursing* 97, no. 3 (1997): 26–30; Zheng-Bo Huang and

Judith C. Ahronheim, "Nutrition and Hydration in Terminally Ill Patients: An Update," *Clinics in Geriatric Medicine* 16, no. 2 (2000): 313–325.

Bibliography

Appadurai, Arjun. "Gastro-Politics in Hindu South Asia." *American Ethnologist* 8, no. 3 (1981): 494–511.

Bowlby, John. *A Secure Base: Clinical Applications of Attachment Theory.* Hoboken, N.J.: Taylor & Francis, 2005.

Brown, Peter. *The Ransom of the Soul: Afterlife and Wealth in Early Western Christianity.* Cambridge: Harvard University Press, 2015.

Brownlie, Douglas, Paul Hewer, and Suzanne Horne. "Culinary Tourism: An Exploratory Reading of Contemporary Representations of Cooking." *Consumption Markets & Culture* 8, no. 1 (2005): 7–26.

Butler, Tom. "17 Death Row Requests You Won't Believe Were Made." What Culture. http://whatculture.com/offbeat/17-death-row-requests-you-won-39-t-believe-were-made, accessed October 3, 2015.

Bynum, Caroline Walker. "Fast, Feast, and Flesh: The Religious Significance of Food to Medieval Women." *Representations* 11 (Summer 1985): 1–25.

———. *Holy Feast and Holy Fast: The Religious Significance of Food to Medieval Women.* Berkeley: University of California Press, 1987.

Cann, Candi K. *Virtual Afterlives: Grieving the Dead in the Twenty-first Century.* Lexington: University Press of Kentucky, 2014.

Chizhik, Avital. "Passover's Perennial No-Show," *Tablet,* April 3, 2102. www.tabletmag.com/jewish-life-and-religion/95853/passover's-perennial-no-show, accessed October 27, 2015.

Counihan, Carole, and Penny Van Esterik. *Food and Culture: A Reader.* New York: Routledge, 2013.

Daniel, E. Valentine, Henry Bernstein, and Tom Brass. *Plantations, Proletarians, and Peasants in Colonial Asia.* London: F. Cass, 1992.

Douglas, Mary. "Deciphering a Meal." *Daedalus* 101, no. 1 (1972): 61–81.

———. *Food in the Social Order.* New York: Routledge, 2014.

Douglas, Mary, and Jonathan Gross. "Food and Culture: Measuring the Intricacy of Rule Systems." *Social Science Information/Sur les sciences sociales* 20, no. 1 (1981): 1–35.

Dunea, Melanie. *My Last Supper.* Edinburgh: A&C Black, 2007.

———. *My Last Supper.* www.mylastsupper.com, accessed October 5, 2015.

Ellershaw, John E., Jane M. Sutcliffe, and Cicely M. Saunders. "Dehydration and the Dying Patient." *Journal of Pain and Symptom Management* 10, no. 3 (1995): 192–197.

Field, Nigel P., Beryl Gao, and Lisa Paderna. "Continuing Bonds in Bereavement:

An Attachment Theory Based Perspective." *Death Studies* 29, no. 4 (2005): 277–299.

Gelber, Hester Goodenouch. Review of Caroline Walker Bynum, *Holy Feast and Holy Fast: The Religious Significance of Food to Medieval Women. Modern Language Quarterly* 48, no. 3 (1987): 281–285.

Holtzman, Jon D. "Food and Memory." *Annual Review of Anthropology* 35 (2006): 361–378.

Huang, Zheng-Bo, and Judith C. Ahronheim. "Nutrition and Hydration in Terminally Ill Patients: An Update." *Clinics in Geriatric Medicine* 16, no. 2 (2000): 313–325.

Khare, Ravindra S., ed. *The Eternal Food: Gastronomic Ideas and Experiences of Hindus and Buddhists.* Albany: State University of New York Press, 1992.

Klass, Dennis, Phyllis R. Silverman, and Steven Nickman. *Continuing Bonds: New Understandings of Grief.* Washington, D.C.: Taylor & Francis, 2014.

Levins, Hoag. "The Story of Victorian Funeral Cookies: Revisiting a Centuries' Old Mourning Tradition," Historic Camden County, September 12, 2011. http://historiccamdencounty.com/ccnews153.shtml, accessed January 4, 2017.

Lévi-Strauss, Claude. *The Raw and the Cooked.* Translated by John Weightman and Doreen Weightman. New York: Harper & Row, 1975.

Mead, Paul S., Laurence Slutsker, Vance Dietz, Linda F. McCaig, Joseph S. Bresee, Craig Shapiro, Patricia M. Griffin, and Robert V. Tauxe. "Food-Related Illness and Death in the United States." *Emerging Infectious Diseases* 5, no. 5 (1999): 607–625.

Millstone, Erik, and Tim Lang. *The Atlas of Food: Who Eats What, Where and Why.* London: Earthscan Publications, 2003.

Mintz, Sidney Wilfred. *Sweetness and Power.* New York: Viking, 1985.

Neuhaus, Jessamyn. "The Way to a Man's Heart: Gender Roles, Domestic Ideology, and Cookbooks in the 1950s." *Journal of Social History* 23, no. 3 (1999): 529–555.

Root, Briana L., and Julie Juola Exline. "The Role of Continuing Bonds in Coping with Grief: Overview and Future Directions." *Death Studies* 38, no. 1 (2014): 1–8.

Sanday, Peggy Reeves. *Divine Hunger: Cannibalism as a Cultural System.* New York: Cambridge University Press, 1986.

Scheper-Hughes, Nancy. *Death without Weeping: The Violence of Everyday Life in Brazil.* Berkeley: University of California Press, 1993.

Stroebe, Margaret S., Georgios Abakoumkin, Wolfgang Stroebe, and Henk Schut. "Continuing Bonds in Adjustment to Bereavement: Impact of Abrupt versus Gradual Separation." *Personal Relationships* 19, no. 2 (2012): 255–266.

Theophano, Janet. *Eat My Words: Reading Women's Lives through the Cookbooks They Wrote.* New York: Palgrave Macmillan, 2002.

Walker, Harlan, ed. *The Meal: Proceedings of the Oxford Symposium on Food and Cookery, 2001.* Trowbridge, U.K.: Prospect Books, 2002.

Walter, Tony. "Communicating with the Dead." In *Encyclopedia of Death and the Human Experience,* edited by Clifton D. Bryant and Dennis L. Peck, 216–219. Los Angeles: Sage Publications, 2009.

Watson, James L., and Melissa L. Caldwell, eds. *The Cultural Politics of Food and Eating.* Malden, Mass.: Blackwell, 2005.

Weiser, Franz Xaver. *Handbook of Christian Feasts and Customs: The Year of the Lord in Liturgy and Folklore.* New York: Harcourt Brace, 1958.

Weller, Robert P. *Resistance, Chaos and Control in China: Taiping Rebels, Taiwanese Ghosts and Tiananmen.* Seattle: University of Washington Press, 1994.

White, Alan. "12 Pictures of Death Row Prisoners' Last Meals," Buzzfeed, February 18, 2014. www.buzzfeed.com/alanwhite/12-pictures-of-death-row-prisoners-last-meals#.p00bPx5mb, accessed October 3, 2015.

Zafar, Rafia. "The Signifying Dish: Autobiography and History in Two Black Women's Cookbooks." *Feminist Studies* 25, no. 2 (1999): 449–469.

Zerwekh, Joyce V. "Do Dying Patients Really Need IV Fluids?" *AJN: The American Journal of Nursing* 97, no. 3 (1997): 26–30.

Zlotnick, Susan. "Domesticating Imperialism: Curry and Cookbooks in Victorian England." *Frontiers: A Journal of Women Studies* 16, nos. 2–3 (1996): 51–68.

Part 1

Dining with the Dead

I

Chinese Ancestral Worship
Food to Sustain, Transform, and Heal the Dead and the Living

Emily S. Wu

Introduction

In a small kitchen the women drip sweat as heat emanates from the stovetop and a noisy exhaust vent goes at full force. Foods that have been offered to the ancestors—a whole boiled chicken (its head and claws intact), a whole deep-fried fish, and a strip of boiled pork belly—are cleared from the ancestral shrine and moved into the kitchen. Foods for the clan ancestors are cooked but minimally processed, barely edible to start with, and especially stale and tasteless after sitting on the ancestral shrine for hours. Rather than disposing of the meat offerings, frugal Han Chinese take them back into the kitchen to make them into dishes to serve at the family gathering that follows. Twice-Cooked Pork is one such dish. By slicing the pork and adding an oil-invigorated bean paste and aromatic vegetables, the pork is given new life as part of a sizzling, rice-downing dish for the living family. Food is shared between the dead and the living, but in different forms—the boiled pork for worship that is bland yet essential to the final dish, and the resulting rich and appetizing dish. This transformation encapsulates how the dead ancestors and living descendants relate to each other in Han Chinese communities.

This chapter explores how in Han Chinese[1] ancestral worship, food is used as an important agent to transcend the boundary between the living and the dead. The postmortem ancestral "body" consists of physical bone remains that need to be properly stored and maintained, wooden tablets

HUIGUO ROU (TWICE-COOKED PORK)

1 lb. (½ kg) boiled pork belly, cut into ⅛-inch slices
1 pot water
2 tbsp cooking oil
¼ cabbage, cut in large chunks

Seasonings:
1 tbsp spicy fermented bean paste
1 tsp chopped garlic
2 stalks leek, julienned
1 tbsp rice wine
1 tbsp soy sauce
1 tsp sugar, or to taste

After worshipping family ancestors, carefully pack the pork from grave offerings to take home, or transport the pork from the offering table in front of the ancestral shrine to the kitchen. (If you are starting from raw pork belly, the pork needs to be boiled until cooked through—but not falling apart—then sliced.)

Boil a pot of water, and add 1 tablespoon of the oil.

Blanch the cabbage in the water for a few minutes, until it is still a little crunchy. Take the cabbage out of the pot and strain. There is no need to squeeze, but try to strain as much water as possible.

On high heat, pour the other tablespoon of cooking oil into a wok. When the oil starts to smoke slightly, add the spicy fermented bean paste and stir vigorously until the fragrance of the bean paste is released. Add the garlic and leek to the wok, taking care to stir the oil–bean paste mixture so it does not burn and stick to the bottom of the wok. When the leek and garlic are evenly coated by the oil–bean paste mixture, add the rice wine and soy sauce and sauté until the leek is tender. Add sugar to taste. Add cabbage and pork, give everything a quick stir, and transfer to a serving plate to serve.

Three sacrificial meats and fruits for ancestors, offered by a member in Pusa's temple committee. (Photo by the author)

with the ancestors' names inscribed to reinforce their identities, and spirits that can be evoked through proper rituals and, most important, nourished and healed with food. Through the act of offering food by the living, the ancestors are consistently and continually revived and included in the community. Properly worshipped ancestors serve as the living community's proxy in maintaining a connection with the larger flow of the universe, connecting it not only physically and spatially with the land, but also temporally across generations and through reincarnations.

Relationships with the Ancestors

A twelfth-century Chinese Neo-Confucian scholar Zhu Xi (or Chu Hsi) explains the relationship between living people and their ancestors as the continuation of the same *qi,* or cosmic force: "By the scale of heaven and earth, there is only one qi. By the scale of one individual [human] body, my qi is my ancestors' qi, it is also only one qi. Therefore, whenever we are emotionally moved (*gan*), there is always response (*ying*) [between us]."[2]

Qi is the shared substance in the universe, and it is concretely physical even in the states that are not humanly tangible. Contrary to the popular (and especially Western) misunderstanding that qi is an energetic, metaphysical, or even purely theoretical thing, in this classical Chinese worldview, qi is the basic makeup of all things in the world, from things with form (solid, liquid, gas) to things without form (natural phenomena, spirits, and even thoughts). The connection that Zhu describes here transcends two dimensions of human connection through qi—the physical (biological and genetic) blood relationship between the ancestor and the descendants, and the emotional vibration between the two because of the shared qi.

The *Book of Burial,* a classic that was written sometime around the third century C.E., puts the qi connection in much more "solid" terms: "[We] humans beget our bodies from our parents. When the bones [of the ancestors] are filled with qi, the bodies of the descendants are endowed. The Classics say: When qi is emotionally moved (*gan*), it responds (*ying*); the prosperity of the ghosts extends to the people."[3]

Notice that the *Book of Burial* also uses the term *ganying,* which I have translated separately as "emotionally moved" (*gan*) and "response" (*ying*). Robert Sharf appropriately renders *ganying* as "sympathetic resonance," which addresses both the emotional and the visceral aspects of the qi con-

nection.[4] It is crucial to recognize that there is *always* a physical implica-
tion to the ancestor-descendent connection. The description of ancestral
bones being "filled with qi" is not meant to be symbolic or poetic; in the
Chinese tradition, it is imperative to properly maintain and sustain the
bones of the ancestors. The bones, as the physical remains of the ancestors,
continue to be connected with the descendants. Furthermore, if they are
properly buried (or in the words of the *Book of Burial,* properly "stored")
in the earth, the vibrancy of the life force in nature "endows" the descendants. Such qi endowments affect all dimensions of human life experiences—physically, emotionally, financially (yes), and even spiritually. This
is the foundational reason for the unceasing popularity of geomancy, or
fengshui, in Chinese culture. Whereas *fengshui* is often understood outside
the Chinese community as home decluttering or aesthetic interior design,
it was at first a set of strategies for finding the best location for burial. The
terms *feng* (wind) and *shui* (water) indicate the goal of finding sites that
have ideal airflow and moisture level for the "storage" of ancestral bones.

Food to Sustain: Bones to Store and Tablets to Call

Proper burial and maintenance of ancestral bones are so important that
the practice of reburial is common in Chinese communities. The practice
of bone picking and professional bone-picking masters (*jiangushi*) can be
found in southern coastal provinces of China and Taiwan, and in Chinese
diasporas in Malaysia and Singapore.[5] In the North American Chinese
diasporic communities, reburial entails shipping the picked bones back to
the ancestral hometown of the deceased in China, so that the body of the
deceased can be reunited with the rest of the clan ancestors.[6]

In communities where reburial is practiced, the body is exhumed five
to ten years after the first burial.[7] An auspicious day is selected, one whose
astrological alignment is suitable for the deceased.[8] The coffin is reopened,
and the bone-picking master inspects the remains. The ideal condition is
achieved when the flesh has decomposed completely and cleanly, leaving
only bones that can be easily picked up to be placed into a bone urn.

This is why the *fengshui* of the burial site is so important: if the burial
site is too dry, the body can mummify intact rather than decomposing
into separate bones. If the site is too damp, the dampness (or sometimes
water damage) and mold growth can also affect the decomposition process

negatively; the decomposition may be incomplete, or the bones may start to disintegrate as well. Finally, bones can be damaged or lost at sites that are subject to the intrusion of plant roots and animals—and the incomplete skeletal body can have detrimental effects on the rest of the living family.[9]

The bone-picking master assesses the condition of the remains and proceeds accordingly. If the body is ready for positioning in the bone urn for reburial, the master carefully removes the bones from the casket, washes them with wine, dries the bones under the sun, sorts and arranges the bones in anatomical order, then places them in the urn. The urn can be reburied into the same site; more often it is placed in a clan grave with the clan's other bone urns. This practice of reburial in the clan grave makes worship easier for the descendants, effectively ensuring that no ancestor in the lineage is neglected in regular and proper worship of the ancestors.

If the remains are not in the ideal condition for reburial, then the master takes appropriate remedial measures. Sometimes holes need to be drilled in the sides of the coffin to allow air, moisture, and probably microbes from the soil to enter the coffin. The coffin is then reburied to continue with the decomposition process; other times lime powder or other drying materials are poured into the coffin to regulate the moisture of the remains. Occasionally the master may have to manually remove the remaining flesh from the bones, so that the bones can be placed in the urn and relocated without waiting any further.[10]

Properly stored ancestral bones serve as an essential basis for the continuing connection between the deceased and their descendants. The energetic quality of the bones has direct effects on the well-being of the descendants. This connection must be frequently reinforced using proper rituals. Zhu Xi instructs: "Skillfully and solemnly perform the ritual with [animal] fat to worship [ancestral] qi. Offer fragrant wine for libation to call forth the souls [of the ancestors]. That is to become one with the ancestors."[11] The offering of food and wine is essential to the process of conjuring the spirits of the ancestors, for the purpose of their "becoming one" with their descendants.

Grave-site worship, whether it is at an individual grave or at a clan grave for all the ancestral bone urns, entails first the living family's paying respect to the land protector (there is usually a small shrine built as part of the grave for him), and then food and flowers are offered. Important items in worship—animal fat and alcohol—have not changed much since the days of Confucius (551–479 B.C.E.), whose ritual practices (which he attributes to the old traditions from the Zhou Dynasty before him) Zhu Xi later tried to revise and standardize. The historian Wendy Rouse lists the offering by Cantonese mourners in a San Francisco Chinatown funeral in 1888: "whole roast pigs, chicken, soup, rice, cakes, and other food and drink items remained at the gravesite until evening for the spirits' delight."[12] The anthropologist Rubie Watson describes the spread she observed in Hong Kong in 1977: five roast pigs, incense, candles, rice, wine, cakes, and a steamed chicken.[13] Cooked pork and chicken, preferably whole (sometimes pork is offered in a large uncut piece), are also preferred animal offerings in the Hakka- and Hokkien-speaking community worships I observed in Taiwan. Sometimes a whole pan-fried fish is also offered, so that there are three meats on the offering table, a parallel presentation to the traditional Confucian offering of the three sacrificial meats. There are no strict rules regarding the other food items, although a few cooked dishes, cooked rice, some sweets, and fruits are generally also offered, as they are considered components of a proper family meal.

Food to Transform: The Karmic Economy of Ancestral Worship

Worship of the ancestors can be performed at grave sites, at clan shrines, in temples, and at home. The offerings at the clan shrines are similar to grave-site offerings, for the clan shrine is another location where the ancestral spirits can be conjured to congregate. At the grave site, the ancestral bones serve as the objects of qi connection; in the ancestral shrine, the ancestral tablets are proxy objects for the qi evocation. Properly constructed ancestral tablets are much more than wooden tablets with the names of the ancestors written on them; they are physical objects in which the ancestral souls reside and from which they can be evoked.[14] Some families choose to worship their ancestors in community temples, some of which dedicate rooms in which families have their own family plaque (sometimes also a plaque for a deceased individual).[15] On important seasonal festival days, the families can visit the temples with food offerings to worship their family or individual plaques. In diasporic communities this arrangement is very popular; temples with ancestral shrine rooms can be found in large Chinese communities in the United States. Ching Chong

Temple (Daoist) and Narras Temple (Buddhist) in San Francisco's Chinatown offer this service. Hsi-Lai Temple in Los Angeles and City of Ten Thousand Buddhas in Ukiyah, California, are more sizable Buddhist temples, and they have dedicated buildings for the storage of bone urns as well.

Some families have smaller shrines at home for more regular worship. The home ancestral tablets also represent ancestors from the entire lineage, but in terms of naming individual ancestors, they include the closest immediate family members. One small tablet is placed on the home shrine, alongside statues of Daoist deities and Buddhist bodhisattvas (I have seen one shrine that includes a picture of Mother Mary and Baby Jesus) that the family worships. On the front side of the tablet, the surname lineage is named; for example, the tablet on my home shrine reads, "All Ancestors of the Wu Family from XX County." On the backside of the tablet, names of the most recent ancestors are written or carved; again, my home tablet includes the names of my grandparents and my father. Some families also have photos of these immediate ancestors on the shrine, usually within three generations.

Kenneth Brashier categorizes ancestors as "permanent progenitors in the distant past and recent forebears enjoying only a temporary existence," and what he calls a "structured amnesia" distinguishes the two types of ancestors: "[one] began at the recent tangible past, the remembered ancestors, the believable history. This sense of historicity flows backwards and ultimately breathes some life into the mythic ancestor, lending him some degree of veracity. In turn, that mythic ancestor with his super-abundance of spirituality and associations with heaven pushes forward a sense of the sacred, ultimately infecting the most recent and profane generations of the dead with some degree of saintliness."[16]

Food offerings directly reflect the type of ancestors one worships. At a clan grave or shrine, where the "saintly" type of distant ancestors of the larger social entity congregate, animals are offered whole, cooked but usually minimally processed. On the other hand, the "profane," or those immediate ancestors of whom the family still has memory, are offered more processed, home-cooked dishes.[17]

My grandfather, who is almost ninety years old and still the most avid ancestral worshiper in my Taiwanese family, makes sure that on my late grandmother's annual death memorial, she is offered her favorite Buddha-

Jumps-over-the-Wall (*Fo-tiao-qiang*): a thick savory stew, steamed in a sealed ceramic pot, consisting of deep-fried pork ribs, taro chunks, napa cabbage, dried scallops, dried chestnuts, quail eggs, and, most important, a piece of shark fin on top. Besides the stew, my grandfather asks other family members to bring a few of their favorite home dishes. The worship is intimate; first all the family members offer burnt incense to invite family ancestors and my grandmother to enjoy the food. After about half of the incense sticks are burnt, a few of the family members go outside into the front yard to burn some paper money—these are produced especially for the deceased—as a gift for my grandmother to collect. Then the family sits around the dining table to enjoy the food that we had offered to my grandmother about thirty minutes before.

In a *Li Jiao* (Teachings of Principles)[18] shrine in Taipei, where the community teaches Confucianism, Daoism, and Buddhism as a unified historical lineage and fully integrated set of teachings, I discussed ancestral worship with the resident spirit medium, Pusa.[19] On the day I visited, the shrine had a temporary folding table set up with food offerings, including what is commonly called *sansheng siguo* (three meats and four fruits): whole boiled chicken, whole fried fish, and a large piece of boiled pork belly, as well as a pineapple, persimmons, oranges, and bell fruits. Also on the table were glasses of rice wine, a small pot with two sticks of burning incense, and a packet of raw rice.

This syncretic shrine worships deities from across the three traditions, and so its shrine tables were arranged in the order of celestial hierarchy—Shakyamuni Buddha, the Jade Emperor, and other higher-level deities were on tables toward the center of the shrine. Deities in descending ranks were placed on tables closer to the outside door. The popular teenage deity *Nazha* stood on top of the outermost permanent table, and the tiger god, who is closest in rank to land protectors, sat under the table. The food offerings were placed even closer to the door.

I guessed that the recipients of the offering were general or distant ancestors of one of the followers, but Pusa corrected me and said that only deities are worshipped with the three sacrificial meats, which were presented whole. On the other hand, she asserted, ancestors should be worshipped with five home-cooked dishes and cooked rice. Her explanation of the difference had a very human basis:

When we worship ancestors, they don't come just one by one, but
many will come all at the same time. It's harder to share the food
when the food is not cut into smaller pieces. If there is a woman
ancestor you have in mind, especially moms, who were traditionally
the last to eat at the dinner table, often there would not be enough to
eat at the ancestral worships. If that is something to consider, we could
specifically take a little bit of food from the offerings onto a plate, and
let it be known that the plate is dedicated to the woman ancestor. That
way she can also enjoy the food.[20]

Wanting to know more about her understanding of spirit categories (after
all, she communicates with them professionally), I shared my guess of the
offering's being for general and distant ancestors, and she nodded her head
and said, "Oh, that could also make sense." She continued, "I have some
Hakka clients who insist that their ancestors have become deities after
they passed, so they offer only sacrificial meats, and no cooked dishes."
    Pusa's remark is consistent with Arthur Wolf's classic continuum of
the differentiation between ancestors and ghosts: "At one end of this continuum are ancestors whose tablets are placed in the position of honor at
the left of the altar; at the other, we find the despised ghosts whose offerings are set outside the back door."[21] As a spirit medium, Pusa sees clients
who encounter obstacles in life, and if the challenges are related to conflicts with spirits, she can communicate and mediate. From her experience
working with the spirits, she categorizes spirits by what they would accept
as offerings: "Ghosts and vengeful spirits coming after specific enemies
usually request lotus flowers and money, not so much food. Ancestors are
usually the ones requesting food. Karmic connections between nonfamil-
ial folks can be settled mostly with merits and money in the form of lotus
flowers and paper money, while ancestors require food, like asking for a
family dinner."
    The offering of food and money is the giving of material goods to an-
cestors and a direct spiritual exchange. We offer my grandmother her favorite home dishes and money to spend; in turn, she is happy, and her
satisfaction resonates to positively affect the qi of the living family. In the
Li Jiao shrine, where the Buddhist ideas of karmic merits and reincarnations are incorporated, there is also a more complicated way the spiritual
economy is conceptualized. Pusa adds a Buddhist twist to her interpreta-

tion of effective ancestor worship: "People in the same family often reincarnate back into the family. So very often we are our own ancestors, and worshiping them is really worshiping ourselves. This explains why ancestor worship could bring more wealth and fortune to ourselves, but we are essentially forwarding them back to ourselves. Paying respect to ancestors is the same idea. For some people, once they understand that prostrating to the ancestors is really prostrating to themselves, they feel okay about doing it."

Then she ended with some food for thought, in a tone that I believe Zhu Xi would have appreciated: "We all come from the same place anyway. There is no differentiation."

Food to Heal: Mulian and the Aogao Porridge

The story of Mulian comes from Buddhist sources but was transformed as it became infused with Confucian moral lessons. Maudgalyayana, later transliterated as Mulian in Mahayana sutras and vernacular narratives, was one of Sakymuni Buddha's most venerated disciples. He was known for his supernatural abilities, one of which was the ability to travel to other realms; *Mahāvatsu* (Great Events) records his visits to the realm of hell and reports his experiences to Buddha upon his return.[22] Despite his powers, he was attacked and murdered by fanatic rivals. In an East Asian Mahayana Buddhist rendering of the story, Mulian's violent death was not due to an inability to predict the event. On the contrary, he intentionally chose not to avoid his fateful demise, so that he could descend into hell and teach the suffering souls there. In some retellings of the tale, he joined Bodhisattva Ksitigarbha (dizang pusa) in vowing to liberate all suffering souls from hell. Mulian is sometimes mistaken for or merged with Ksitigarbha in vernacular narratives because of this compassionate collaboration.[23]

In the Chinese iteration of this story, when Mulian descended to hell, he went to visit his mother, who was suffering as a hungry ghost. Mulian, an ever-so-filial son, tried to use his supernatural powers to offer food to his starving mother. No matter how many times he tried, however, as soon as any food touched his mother's lips, it would burst into flame and burn into ashes. In hopeless devastation, Mulian cried loudly and asked his teacher for help. Sakyamuni Buddha supposedly gave Mulian a solution, but there are two versions of what that solution was.

The first version is described in the *Ullambana Sutra* (also known as *Buddha Speaks of Sutra of Ullambana;* in Chinese, *Foshuo Yulanpen Jing*): "The Buddha told Maudgalyayana, "The fifteenth day of the seventh month is the Pravarana Day for the assembled Sangha of the ten directions. For the sake of fathers and mothers of seven generations past, as well as for fathers and mothers of the present who are in distress, you should prepare an offering of clean basins full of hundreds of flavors and the five fruits, and other offerings of incense, oil, lamps, candles, beds, and bedding, all the best of the world, to the greatly virtuous assembled Sangha of the ten directions."[24]

In this version of the solution, the offerings were not to Mulian's mother, but to "the greatly virtuous assembled Sangha of the ten directions." Here is some intricate karmic math for the reader to understand how this process works: offering food and necessities to the virtuous is in itself an extremely virtuous act, and the merits of the act can be forwarded not just to Mulian's mother but to "fathers and mothers of seven generations past, as well as for fathers and mothers of the present who are in distress," and thereby liberate them all from suffering.

The second version reflects a Chinese folk perception of the bureaucracy in hell. Instead of presenting a puja-type offering, as in the first version, here Mulian was instructed to cook porridge with dried fruits and grains. The dark color of that porridge would trick the prison guards in hell into believing that it was already burned, and Mulian's mother could finally consume the porridge and be liberated from eternal hunger. In parts of Fujian province in southern China, a festival called *Aojiu jie* is dedicated to this version of Mulian's story. *Aojiu,* or *Aogao* in the Fuzhou dialect, is phonetically synonymous to "gunk" or "dirt." It is customary to cook this glutinous rice porridge with peanuts, dried jujube dates, dried longan (an Asian fruit somewhat similar in consistency and taste to lychee), and water chestnuts; brown sugar is added to give a darker color to the porridge. Sometimes lotus seeds, ginko nuts, sesame seeds, walnuts, and red beans are also added. On the lunar date of January 29, families cook *Aogao* porridge in the morning. The day's festivity starts with worshipping family ancestors with this porridge and other food offerings, respectfully presenting the porridge to living family elders, and eating this porridge together.

The healing properties of *Aogao* porridge can be understood to apply on three levels for the family members involved—the dead ancestors, the living elders, and the younger descendants. First, for ancestors (such as Mulian's mother) whose souls are suffering in a hungry ghost state, it is the only nourishment they can consume, and it thus liberates them by directly addressing the source of suffering. Second, since the well-being of the ancestors affects the well-being of the living descendants, once the ancestors are in a better state of being (and when they can be sustained with regular worship), the descendants also benefit from the healing process. Third, the items added to the porridge have known healing properties for the living. The basic ingredients of the sweet porridge—glutinous rice, peanuts, jujube dates, longan, and brown sugar—are known for their warming, nourishing qualities in traditional Chinese medicine. In fact, porridge made with glutinous rice, brown sugar, and dried longan is a popular dietary prescription for seniors in the wintertime. The other common additions—seeds, nuts, and beans—are also ones that are commonly used for their healing and nourishing properties. Walnuts and sesame seeds are especially good for the elders in that they promote kidney function and brain health. Lotus seeds and red beans are also used medicinally for toning the digestive system and calming the spirit (for example, in promoting better sleep).

Besides the medicinal quality of the ingredients in the *Aogao* porridge, its dark color has medicinal implications. The color black energetically corresponds with the mode of storing. In the traditional Chinese medical view of human anatomical functions, the kidneys are responsible for storage—kidneys are where *jing,* a highly refined form of qi that effectively nourishes and fuels the body, can be stored. In turn, having enough *jing* is directly reflected by the health of the bone marrow.[25] This perspective of the bones as being directly related to the amount of *jing* stored in the living person is analogous to the aforementioned understanding that ancestral bones serve as vessels of familial qi (which resonates and affects those who share blood relations) and also channels for earthly qi (which, with proper burial fengshui, can benefit the descendants).

The *Yijing* (Book of Changes, a classic divination text) scholar Wang Ming-hsiong speculates that anorexia can be interpreted as a living condition of the hungry ghost state, and so by reverse logic, anorexic patients might be able to consume dark-colored food more easily than lighter foods.[26] I once encountered an anorexic woman in Taiwan who was told by a folk Daoist spirit medium that her condition was caused by a group of hungry ghost spirits hovering around her. In this particular case, the medium explained that in a previous lifetime this woman had been a bandit and a ruthless killer. Many of her victims died young and unmarried and were therefore ineligible for ancestral worship. These vengeful, homeless, and hungry spirits (unsustained and unfed by their families) finally found their way to her, and they actively fed on her life energy and thrived on seeing her deteriorate physically. It was recommended to her that she try to consume more dark-colored food to better sustain these spirits, and ultimately herself as well.[27] Without more substantial data to support the actual efficacy of dark-colored food for healing anorexia, it is still important to recognize the cultural influence of the Mulian narrative on making food offerings to deceased spirits, especially when those spirits are in conditions in which healing needs to take place before regular sustaining worship can be sufficient.

Concluding Remarks

The anthropologist James Watson observes Chinese ancestral offerings in transactional terms: "A central feature of Chinese funerals and postburial mortuary practices is the transfer of food, money, and goods to the deceased. . . . In return the living expect to receive certain material benefits, including luck, wealth, and progeny."[28] Though on the surface the ritualistic practice of ancestral worship seems utilitarian, Chinese ancestral worship is much more complex than merely appeasing the ancestral spirits. There is a conceptual parallel between the living and the dead, which is translated into how families prepare their food offerings for their ancestors. An early Canadian newspaper article documents how a young man from Hong Kong, working as a servant in turn-of-the-twentieth-century Victoria, British Columbia, explained Chinese funerary food-offering practices: "'You see,' replied he quickly, taking up a cup, and holding it in front of a lamp so that a sharp shadow was thrown on to the white tablecloth. 'You see that,' pointing to the shadow, 'dead men all the same that, he eat all the same that [shadow] of food and wine, I this,' flicking the cup with his finger; "if I no get all the same this, food and wine, me pretty soon die quick.'"[29]

Xinzhong Yao also elegantly articulates the continuous reciprocal, if not intimate, relationship between the ancestors and their descendants:

> A sense of eternity can be obtained through the continuity of the family in which each generation is treated as a necessary link in the family chain and every life is considered a contribution to the huge enterprise that was initiated by the ancestors and continued by their descendants. Confucians taught that through the performance of their duties in the family, the young would obtain a sense of moral responsibility, the elderly gain respect, the dead live in the hearts of their descendants and the newborn be given a mission. In these ways an individual would last as long as his family lasted, and would acquire a sense of eternity in the midst of temporal life.[30]

While this Confucian model of continuity and interdependency through inevitable qi connection and sympathetic resonance (*ganying*) is fundamental, more factors need to be considered in fully understanding this relationship. Through his analysis of ancient Chinese ritual practices, Mu-chou Poo argues that the Chinese cosmological view was this-world oriented and pertained more to the personal wellness of the living;[31] in other words, self-agency had always been given negotiation space in the power structure between the dead and the living.

The introduction of Buddhist ideas of reincarnation and karma into the Chinese system provided alternative considerations for mobility— whether it is within the social hierarchy and power structures in the context of this lifetime, or in the larger scheme of unfixed identities and relationships in the context of many lifetimes. Chinese ancestral worship today must be considered as having two intertwining models underlying the ritualistic acts: First there are the qi connections, as well as the spiritual economy that arises from the day-to-day accounting of karmic merits and (possibly) deductions. Although the formal ritual of offering food to ancestors is unidirectional, and in a respectful manner people ask for blessings from the ancestors in return, I argue that the intertwining ideological models that are basic to the practice allow for dynamic interactions rather than simple exchange.

Through the conceptual understanding of "oneness" with the ancestors, living blood descendants use ritual offerings of food to establish a community that includes the dead ancestors and to sustain such familial relationships. In this inclusive community, the ancestors continue to serve social roles long after their physical deaths.

Notes

1. In my study I use Han Chinese as an ethnic and cultural category, which grounds its general life ideology and cosmology in a mixture of Confucian, Daoist, and Buddhist traditions, which includes communities inside and outside the geographic region of the People's Republic of China. My sources and ethnographic examples focus on the Han Chinese communities in Taiwan and the Fujian Province in southern China. Christians in these communities do not practice folk ancestral worship rituals and will not be considered here.

2. See section 54 of "Gui-shen [Ghosts and Deities]" in Zhu Xi, *Zhuzi Yulei* [Classified Dialogues of Master Zhu], ed. Li Jingde, circa 1270 C.E., http://ctext. org/zhuzi-yulei/3/zh. For an introduction to *Zhuzi Yulei* and a translation of the text, see Daniel Gardner, *Learning to Be a Sage: Selections from the Conversations of Master Chu, Arranged Topically* (Berkeley: University of California Press, 1990).

3. From *Zangshu* [Book of Burial], author unknown, but the work is often attributed to the Daoist mystic Guo Pu. The English translation provided here is my own. For more historical background and an English translation of *Book of Burial*, see Juwen Zhang and Guoliang Pu, *A Translation of the Ancient Chinese: The Book of Burial (Zang Shu) by Guo Pu (276–324)* (Lewiston, Maine: E. Mellen Press, 2004).

4. For a more substantial discussion on the concept of *ganying,* see Emily Wu, *Traditional Chinese Medicine in the United States: In Search of Spiritual Meaning and Ultimate Health* (Lanham, Md.: Lexington Books, 2013), 184–186. For a historical analysis of how the Chinese religious context transformed the meaning of the term, see Robert Sharf, *Coming to Terms with Chinese Buddhism: A Reading of the Treasure Store Treatise* (Honolulu: University of Hawai'i Press, 2005), 82–88.

5. See He Bin, *Jiangzhe Hanzu sangzang wenhua* [Funerary Culture of Han Ethnics in Jiang-Zhe] (Beijing: Minzu University of China Press, 1995). For practices in Hakka communities, see Zhou Qing, Hong Fulian, and Chen Yaotang, *Taiwan minjian binsang lisu huibian* [Collection of Folk Funerary Customs in Taiwan] (Kao-hsiung: Fuwen Publishing, 2005).

6. See Sue Fawn Chung and Priscilla Wegars, eds., *Chinese American Death Rituals: Respecting the Ancestors* (Lanham, Md.: AltaMira Press, 2005); Lani Ah Tye Farkas, *Bury My Bones in America: The Saga of a Chinese Family in California, 1952–1996: From San Francisco to the Sierra Gold Mines* (Nevada City, Calif.: Carl Mautz, 1998).

7. People who died under the age of sixteen, or sometimes before they have married and produced their own descendants, are not reburied and included in the clan ancestral grave. See Zeng Xicheng, *Taiwan kejia wenhua yanjiu* [Studies

of Hakka Culture in Taiwan] (Taipei: National Taiwan Library, Taiwan Branch, 1999). Zeng records the custom that the remains of adults are usually buried for five to ten years before bone picking, and the longer the person has lived, the more time the bones should spend in the ground before reburial.

8. See Hong Minlin and Hong Yingsheng, *Taiwan Minsu Tanyuan* [Exploring the Sources of Taiwanese Folk Customs] (Taichung: Taiwan Provincial Government Information Department, 1992), and Xu Fuquan, *Taiwan minjian chuantong sangzang yijie yanjiu* [Study of Traditional Folk Funerary and Burial Rituals and Customs in Taiwan] (Taipei: Xu Fuquan, 2003). Both works are of the opinion that besides choosing an astrologically appropriate date according to the birthday of the deceased, reburials are usually done in dryer seasons of the year, so that the bones can be properly sunned and dried during the bone-picking process.

9. In the Confucian view, the completeness of one's body directly reflects one's moral character, which although it should not be a concern after one's death, in terms of energy the state of the body would still affect the moral vibration of the family as a whole. It is also considered unfilial for one to not take proper care of one's body, which is endowed by one's parents and ancestors. The moral and energetic consequences of missing body parts result in low rate of organ donation, as well as the custom of persevering amputated limbs for proper burial later.

10. See Zhang Jianzhi, "Sige jiangushi shengming jingyan zhi yanjiu [The Research of the Life Experience of Four Professionals Who Pick Up Bones from Graves]" (master's thesis, Nanhua University, 2011).

11. See section 63 of "Gui-shen [Ghosts and Deities]" in *Zhuzi Yulei*. Translation is my own.

12. Wendy L. Rouse, "'What We Didn't Understand: A History of Chinese Death Ritual in China and California," in Chung and Wegars, *Chinese American Death Rituals*, 34.

13. Rubie Watson, "Remembering the Dead: Graves and Politics in Southeastern China," in *Death Ritual in Late Imperial and Modern China*, edited by James L. Watson and Evelyn Sakakida Rawski (Berkeley: University of California Press, 1988), 221.

14. As part of proper ritual for the deceased, the soul of the deceased is carefully tended immediately after death until the funeral that takes place forty-nine days later. Family members are reminded constantly to call for the newly deceased to stay close and not be lost. Before a wooden tablet can be acquired, a paper tablet with the name of the deceased is used for the soul to "reside in." When one is killed in an accident outdoors, it is a common practice in Taiwan for the family to be instructed to take to the site of the accident a piece of clothing worn by the deceased and a bamboo stick with twigs and leaves still attached. The family members call the name of the deceased to come home with them, the clothing and bamboo stick functioning as a place for the soul to travel in. Mudangs in Korea

have a similar practice; in their death rituals, they construct an intricate paper effigy for the soul of the deceased to temporarily stay in.

15. Historically, Confucianism, Daoism, and Buddhism coexist in Chinese society as the main Three Teachings, and it is completely acceptable for people to simultaneously attend and support temples across the religious traditions. It is often the case that in Daoist temples, followers also worship some Buddha and Buddhist bodhisattvas, and Buddhist temples include popular Daoist deities on their shrines. Such services as providing a place for families to worship their ancestors are offered in both Daoist and Buddhist temples.

16. Kenneth Brashier, *Ancestral Memory in Early China* (Cambridge: Harvard University Press, 2011), 64, 65.

17. Stuart Thompson calls this categorization of spirit beings by differentiating the level of processing in the food offerings the "semantics of food." See Stuart Thompson, "Death, Food, and Fertility" in Watson and Rawski, *Death Ritual in Late Imperial and Modern China,* 71–108.

18. This syncretic faith community traces its founding back to the Ming Dynasty and claims to rival the popularity of the Heaven and Earth Society (Tiandi Hui), which was deeply involved in the Heavenly Kingdom Movement in the Qing Dynasty. Currently, it is one of the many syncretic faith communities in Taiwan. My fieldwork in this community is still in its early stage, but some of my observations and conversations with members of the community are informative for this general discussion of ancestor worship.

19. Personal communication with Pusa, December 21, 2014.

20. Ibid.

21. Arthur Wolf, "Gods, Ghosts, and Ancestors" in *Religion and Ritual in Chinese Society,* ed. Arthur Wolf (Stanford: Stanford University Press, 1974), 147.

22. See Emile Senart, *Mahāvastu avadānam: Le Mahâvastu: Texte Sanscrit publié pour la première fois et accompagné d'introductions et d'un commentaire* (Tokyo: Meicho-Fukyū-Kai, 1977).

23. Dizang temples in Taiwan label the main deity in their shrine as Mulian Zunzhe, the Venerable Mulian. In the monk Hsuan-Hua's retelling of the story of Mulian, he explains that Mulian took the vow of Bodhisattva Ksitigarbha to liberate all beings in hell, and therefore Mulian *was* Ksitigarbha. See Ven. Hsuan-Hua, "Mohe Mujianlian Zunzhe [Venerable Mohe Mujianlian]," in Fotuo shida dizi zhuan [Biography of Buddha's Ten Disciples], www.drbachinese.org/online_reading/sf_others/10_Disciples/Mahamaudgalyagana/Mahamaudgalyagana.htm, accessed September 13, 2016.

24. English translation quoted from Buddhist Text Translation Society, "The Buddha Speaks to the Ullambana Sutra," www.cttbusa.org/ullambana/ullambana .asp, accessed June 13, 2016. The original full text in Chinese can be found as part of the Buddhist Canon, *Taishō shinshū daizōkyō* 16, no. 685, www.cbeta.org/result/normal/T16/0685_001.htm, accessed September 13, 2016.

25. Paul Unschuld, *Huang Di Nei Jing Su Wen: Nature, Knowledge, Imagery in*

an *Ancient Chinese Medical Text* (Berkeley: University of California Press, 2003), 132–133.

26. Personal communication with Wang Ming-hsiong, April 13, 2002.

27. Personal communication, July 29, 2015. Interviewee wishes to remain anonymous.

28. James Watson, "The Structure of Chinese Funerary Rites: Elementary Forms, Ritual Sequence, and the Primacy of Performance," in Watson and Rawski, *Death Ritual in Late Imperial and Modern China,* 9.

29. Florence Baillie-Grohman, "The Yellow and White Agony: A Chapter on Western Servants," in *Fifteen Years' Sport and Life in the Hunting Grounds of Western America and British Columbia,* ed. William A. Baillie-Grohman (London: Horace Cox, 1900), 338–339.

30. Xingzhong Yao, *An Introduction to Confucianism* (New York: Cambridge University Press, 2007), 204.

31. Mu-chou Poo, *In Search of Personal Welfare: A View of Ancient Chinese Religion* (Albany: State University of New York Press, 1998), 215.

Bibliography

Baillie-Grohman, Florence. "The Yellow and White Agony: A Chapter on Western Servants." In *Fifteen Years' Sport and Life in the Hunting Grounds of Western America and British Columbia,* edited by William A. Baillie-Grohman. London: Horace Cox, 1900.

Brashier, Kenneth. *Ancestral Memory in Early China.* Cambridge: Harvard University Press, 2011.

Buddhist Text Translation Society. "The Buddha Speaks to the Ullambana Sutra." www.cttbusa.org/ullambana/ullambana.asp, accessed September 16, 2016.

Chung, Sue Fawn, and Priscilla Wegars, eds. *Chinese American Death Rituals: Respecting the Ancestors.* Lanham, Md.: AltaMira Press, 2005.

Farkas, Lani Ah Tye. *Bury My Bones in America: The Saga of a Chinese Family in California, 1952–1996: From San Francisco to the Sierra Gold Mines.* Nevada City, Calif.: Carl Mautz, 1998.

Gardner, Daniel. *Learning to Be a Sage: Selections from the Conversations of Master Chu, Arranged Topically.* Berkeley: University of California Press, 1990.

He Bin. *Jiangzhe Hanzu sangzang wenhua* [Funerary Culture of Han Ethnics in Jiang-Zhe]. Beijing: Minzu University of China Press, 1995.

Hong Minlin and Hong Yingsheng. *Taiwan Minsu Tanyuan* [Exploring the Sources of Taiwanese Folk Customs]. Taichung: Taiwan Provincial Government Information Department, 1992.

Poo, Mu-chou. *In Search of Personal Welfare: A View of Ancient Chinese Religion.* Albany: State University of New York Press, 1998.

Rouse, Wendy L. "'What We Didn't Understand': A History of Chinese Death

Ritual in China and California." In *Chinese American Death Rituals: Respecting the Ancestors,* edited by Sue Fawn Chung and Priscilla Wegars, 19–45. Lanham, Md.: AltaMira Press, 2005.

Senart, Emile. *Mahāvastu Avadānam: Le Mahâvastu: Texte Sanscrit publié pour la première fois et accompagné d'introductions et d'un commentaire.* Tokyo: Meicho-Fukyū-Kai, 1977.

Sharf, Robert. *Coming to Terms with Chinese Buddhism: A Reading of the Treasure Store Treatise.* Honolulu: University of Hawai'i Press, 2005.

Thompson, Stuart. "Death, Food, and Fertility." In *Death Ritual in Late Imperial and Modern China,* edited by James L. Watson and Evelyn Sakakida Rawski, 71–108. Berkeley: University of California Press, 1988.

Unschuld, Paul U. *Huang Di Nei Jing Su Wen: Nature, Knowledge, Imagery in an Ancient Chinese Medical Text.* Berkeley: University of California Press, 2003.

Watson, James. "The Structure of Chinese Funerary Rites: Elementary Forms, Ritual Sequence, and the Primacy of Performance." In *Death Ritual in Late Imperial and Modern China,* edited by James L. Watson and Evelyn Sakakida Rawski, 3–19. Berkeley: University of California Press, 1988.

Watson, Rubie. "Remembering the Dead: Graves and Politics in Southeastern China." In *Death Ritual in Late Imperial and Modern China,* edited by James L. Watson and Evelyn Sakakida Rawski, 203–227. Berkeley: University of California Press, 1988.

Wolf, Arthur. "Gods, Ghosts, and Ancestors." In *Religion and Ritual in Chinese Society,* edited by Arthur Wolf, 131–182. Stanford: Stanford University Press, 1974.

Wu, Emily S. *Traditional Chinese Medicine in the United States: In Search of Spiritual Meaning and Ultimate Health.* Lanham, Md.: Lexington Books, 2013.

Xu Fuquan. *Taiwan minjian chuantong sangzang yijie yanjiu* [Study of Traditional Folk Funerary and Burial Rituals and Customs in Taiwan]. Taipei: Xu Fuquan, 2003.

Yao, Xingzhong. *An Introduction to Confucianism.* New York: Cambridge University Press, 2007.

Zeng Xicheng. *Taiwan kejia wenhua yanjiu* [Studies of Hakka Culture in Taiwan]. Taipei: National Taiwan Library, Taiwan Branch, 1999.

Zhang, Juwen, and Guoliang Pu. *A Translation of the Ancient Chinese: The Book of Burial (Zang Shu) by Guo Pu (276–324).* Lewiston, Maine: E. Mellen Press, 2004.

Zhang Jianzhi. "Sige jiangushi shengming jingyan zhi yanjiu [The Research of the Life Experience of Four Professionals Who Pick Up Bones from Graves]." Master's thesis, Nanhua University, 2011.

Zhou Qing, Hong Fulian, and Chen Yaotang. *Taiwan minjian binsang lisu huibian* [Collection of Folk Funerary Customs in Taiwan]. Kao-hsiung: Fuwen Publishing, 2005.

2

The Eating Ritual in Korean Religiosity
Young San Jae for the Dead and for the Living

Jung Eun Sophia Park

Introduction

Eating is one of the most crucial elements in defining a worldview. The ways in which food is prepared, consumed, and disposed of reflects and shapes a culture, describing and interpreting various aspects of life, including death itself. Food is an organic material that sustains physical life, yet at the same time it can symbolize the divine nature that is life-giving and ever-loving for all humans or sentient beings. Food gives life to the consumer by being consumed; food becomes subsumed into the eater. In Korea, the Young San Jae meal is deeply related to death directly and indirectly; it emphasizes new life through transformation, connection, and joy, over decay, separation, and bereavement. Ritual space, as an antistructure, can deconstruct existing emotional and social structures.[1] In this ritual space the boundaries between the living and the dead, the secular and the sacred, the human and the divine, become thin, and the participants experience reunion with the dead. Meals in a death ritual help actualize a space for bonds and connection between the living and the dead, as well as endorse the notion of communion in the shared cosmos.

For Koreans, one of the most important filial duties is to observe ancestral rites that ensure the continuum of life through the family line, and ritual food is the universal element in any ritual. In Korean myths, gods and goddesses were human beings first, who, after distinct and adventurous lives, became divinities themselves, unlike the Christian concept of God.[2] Thus, worship of the ancestors and gods can coexist in Korean reli-

---

YAK-KWA (FRIED HONEY CAKE)

1 cup flour
1 tbsp honey
dash of sesame oil
vegetable oil

Mix the flour with honey and sesame oil. Shape this paste in a flower-shaped pastry tin (or other traditionally shaped tin). Sauté the shaped paste in the vegetable oil in a hot frying pan for ten minutes. These oil-and-honey pastries can be decorated by adding flowers to them.

---

giosity and in traditional religion, and it is the syncretistic thread of Korean religiosity.[3] Yet it would be fair to say that the meal is the central part of death rites of all religions in Korea as an expression of communion and connection with ancestors. Eating rituals for the dead, including food preparation, eating, and even food storage, are some of the most common and overlooked religious rituals in Korea. In this chapter I describe the importance of eating rituals in Korea, especially in terms of the connection with ancestors. As a case study, I examine the Buddhist eating ritual of Young San Jae, comparing the Eucharist, Confucian rites, and Shamanic eating rituals. In doing so, I will demonstrate how the eating ritual creates communion between the ancestor and the sacred.

Korean Eating Rituals for Dead Ancestors

In Korea it is common to prepare and serve food in veneration ceremonies for ancestors. All participants, in most cases descendants of the dead ancestor, then eat the food together during or after worship. The major religions in Korea tend to include some element of eating in their rituals. For example, during Confucian rites for ancestor veneration, one of the male elders drinks rice wine or *Soju* as a part of the ritual called *Eumbok*. In the shamanic ritual *Kut,* the shaman—as the embodied spirit of the government official who loves women, money, and liquor—drinks rice wine and shares it with all the participants. One of the most striking parts of *Kut* is the segment of *KoonWoong*. Here the word *KoonWoong* designates a collective group of soldiers who died during the war. The shaman invokes young

BEAN PASTE SOUP (MILD)

1 block soft tofu
1 zucchini
2 tbsp soybean paste
4 cups water
1 small onion, thinly sliced
1 small chili pepper, thinly sliced
½ cup sliced mushrooms
Green onions, chopped (for garnish)

Cut the block of tofu and the zucchini into half-inch cubes. Put the soybean paste and water into a pot and stir well until mixed. Cover and boil over medium-high heat for 5 minutes. Add the tofu, zucchini, onion, chili pepper, and mushrooms. Boil for an additional 5–7 minutes. Sprinkle chopped green onions on top before serving.

ancestors who died on the field of war. Because Korea experienced several wars in the twentieth century, such as the Second World War and the Korean War, it is not difficult to find families who have lost young ones in war. Thus, in almost every Hamgyoung Province *Kut,* which originated with northern shamanic traditions in Siberia and Mongolia, the food segment and ritual are crucial. The shaman, possessed by the souls of angry young soldiers, becomes violent in mixing fruit and rice cake with the blood of chickens, and he subsequently devours them. In this case, the hungry souls who are invoked in the ritual are supposed to eat food and release their heavy emotions, such as fury and fear, which the young soldiers would have experienced on the battlefield. Releasing these emotions helps the young soldiers move forward to a more peaceful afterlife.

In Christianity the primary eating ritual centers on the Eucharist, one of the most crucial parts of the Mass in the Catholic Church. The Eucharist recalls the death of Jesus as well as his Resurrection, by reenacting Jesus' final dinner with his disciples. Thus, in the moment of eating the bread and drinking the wine, the past and the future become one moment in the present. By consuming the bread, Catholics believe that they are subsumed into the body of Christ. It is common for Korean Catholics to celebrate Mass almost every day for the remembrance of the souls of each family. Often, Korean Catholics offer a Mass on the anniversaries of the

---

KIMCHI (Fermented Cabbage)

1 head cabbage
5 tbsp kosher salt
Sauce: 1 head garlic, peeled and minced, 1 bunch green onions, diced,
    1 tbsp ground red pepper, and ½ tsp ginger paste

Thoroughly clean the cabbage and then chop into two-inch squares. In a big bowl, place a layer of cabbage and salt it liberally with the kosher salt. Repeat the layering with all the cabbage and the remaining salt. Wait about two hours, until the cabbage becomes limp. Meanwhile, mix the garlic, green onions, ground red pepper, and ginger paste to make the sauce. Thoroughly rinse the cabbage of the salt and then mix with the sauce in a large bowl. Make sure all the cabbage is coated with the sauce. Store in jars or other containers. Kimchi does not need to be refrigerated until opened.

---

deaths of their ancestors. For many, daily Mass has replaced ancestor veneration ceremonies, which were performed in Confucian, Buddhist, and shamanic traditions. Also, on big holidays, such as *Chuseok* (Harvest Festival) and *Sul* (New Year's Day), Catholic churches prepare food to offer at a special Mass for the souls of the departed, ancestors of parishioners in particular. In this way, Korean Catholics are able to maintain their identities as both Christians and Koreans, while remembering the dead through food.

Sometimes it is unclear whether rituals are Buddhist or shamanist because of the syncretic nature of Korean religiosity. In fieldwork students are often confused because typical shamanic deities are also worshipped in Buddhist temples, and vice versa. It is often said, "Koreans have a shamanic gut, a Buddhist heart, a Confucian head, and a Christian body."[4] Within this syncretic world, one of the common elements is the eating ritual for ancestors. Eating as a way to reconnect with dead ancestors is a core element of Korean religiosity.

In Korea every household, no matter its religious affiliation, practices the ritual of ancestor veneration, and the act of preparing and eating food for the dead is a part of the whole ritual. This phenomenon comes from the Korean understanding of the ancestral body as a celestial body, and the notion that food can operate as a conduit between ancestors and their descendants through the body. Food functions as a medium through which the descendants encounter ancestors, and, as a consequence, they are connected. In Korean religiosity, food for the soul, for that of the ancestor in particular, is considered to be the following: (1) feeding the soul physically and spiritually during the ritual as a duty of filial obligation; (2) providing travel food for the journey to the other world after the ritual; (3) receiving blessings from the ancestor, who is now part of the celestial body; and (4) offering hospitality to any other souls who might come. Also, food offered during the eating ritual is shared not only with family members, but with anyone who wants food. This idea supports a larger cultural assumption regarding the function of food, which emphasizes the communal dimensions of food and eating. Thus, food in rituals serves as a genuine symbol of the virtues of compassion and love, of sustaining the life force, communal relationships, and community.

In Korea food functions as an important element of death rituals, which include funerals, anniversary rites of ancestor veneration, and holidays. Koreans remember their ancestors with food, and, in so doing, they express respect and love. Douglas J. Davies, in *Death, Ritual and Belief: the Rhetoric of Funerary Rites,* argues that in most East Asian cultures, kinship provides a strong sense of individual and group identity, embracing the living and the dead simultaneously, and this death ritual, especially the eating ritual, is a paragon.[5] Any ritual related to death includes a belief in reconnection or reunion with the dead, and both eating and food function as a medium through which the living and the dead are deeply united.[6]

Growing up in Korea, I often witnessed food placed on the threshold or at the front gate of the house. The offerings were composed of simple foods, such as a bowl of rice, rice wine, and rice cake, along with money and traditional Korean straw shoes. Koreans believe that the souls of the dead, especially parents and ancestors, visit their families on holidays and on the anniversaries of their deaths for reunion. Thus, the families prepare food for the dead to eat during their visit, as well as more food, money, and shoes for the soul's return journey to the other world. Even in the modern, high-tech society of Korea, almost every household (with the occasional exception of more conservative Protestant families) performs this ancestor rite. Catholics allow family ancestor veneration as a part of enculturation.[7] Jacques Derrida asserts that life is reconfigured through a relationship to death. There is a sense that one can never go beyond death; instead, life continues in the sustained presence of death in life.[8] In this way, the eating ritual manifests the intertwined nature of the dead and the living and provides a strong foundation for both individual and group identities. The following section focuses on Young San Jae, the Buddhist eating ritual, as an example of connection and communion between the living and the dead.

Young San Jae

In Korea, Young San Jae is one of the most significant eating rituals for the dead, and it is performed on June 6, Korea's Memorial Day. This ritual symbolically reenacts the last festival that the historical Buddha had with his disciples. The word *Jae* signifies rituals that include the teaching of the dharma (the decree of Buddha), which sustains the spiritual body and the offering of food while supporting the physical body.[9] The word *Jae* also indicates that this ritual aims to help the souls of the dead. Therefore, Young San Jae is a solemn eating ritual for the dead or for the benefit of the souls of the dead. The ritual is famous for visual art, dance, and chants, and it was registered on the United Nations Educational, Scientific and Cultural Organization (UNESCO) Representative List of Intangible Cultural Heritage of Humanity.[10]

Young San Jae literally means "the Mount Young ritual." Mount Young describes Young Chi Mountain, a mythic place where the Buddha died after teaching the dharma, more specifically the Lotus Flower Sutra, or the *Yeon Wha Kyoung*. This scripture is one of the most important scriptures in Mahayana Buddhism, and it is popular throughout East Asia, particularly Korea. According to legend, when Siddhartha taught the dharma, the entire universe was elated so that flower petals fell like rain and birds sang chants. The Yeon Wha Kyoung says that the first historical Buddha enjoyed dinner with his disciples and then went to Nirvana. In reenacting that historical moment, however, Young San Jae is always present, no matter where or when the Buddha is present.[11]

Every year on June 6, one of the most traditional Buddhist temples, Bong Won Sa, celebrates Young San Jae. Chun Tae Jong, one of the denominations of Korean Buddhism, is famous for its rituals for the dead, such as *49 Jae* and *Cheondo Jae*. In Buddhism it is believed that when a person dies, the soul wanders the Earth for forty-nine days, after which the soul should move into the afterlife. In relation to this time frame, Buddhists perform a ritual, *Cheondo Jae,* to help the soul move into Nirvana on the forty-ninth day after death. This allows the soul to leave its limbo state and move into a more permanent afterlife state, ideally extinction, or Emptiness. If performed appropriately, this death ritual is believed to help ancestors attain the ideal postmortem status.[12] Monks are experts in ritual drumming, dancing, and chanting, and ordinary Buddhists rely on their skills to guide their ancestors to Nirvana. On the other hand, Jo Kye Jong, another main denomination, is famous for its monks' teaching and philosophy on Emptiness but lacks excellence in performing the rituals. In the death ritual, how the message is narrated and communicated is crucial, and the Young San Jae is one of the most highly aesthetic and skillful rituals to convey the teaching of Emptiness in Buddhism. Although I agree with the theory of the death ritual that emphasizes the importance of rhetoric, nonverbal communications such as dancing, chanting, and the act of eating in Yong San Jae function as strong media through which the meaning of the death ritual can be amplified.

Young San Jae is one of Korea's most beautiful and solemn rituals, and it includes sacred dance, song, and drumming. In its emphasis on dancing and chanting, this ritual is distinct from Zen Buddhist traditions and other Mahayana Buddhist sects that negate any visual images and embodiment and seek Emptiness through sitting mediation or speculation. Young San Jae, in contrast, contains all kinds of visual arts and performances, and its lineage stems from the early Shilla Dynasty of the seventh century C.E. This feast is considered one of the most powerful ways to empower the soul so that it gains Nirvana. The Young San Jae is similar to the Last Supper of Jesus in Christianity in that this ritual embodies the friendship between Buddha and his disciples and embodies the teaching of Buddha, namely enlightenment through the practice of the middle path. Unlike the current minimalistic Catholic practice of the Eucharist, however, the Young San Jae ritual continues to include a huge eating ritual for the dead; its unique nature comes from Koreans' spiritual connection with their ancestors. In this ritual, souls are officially invited to come eat the offered food. Many Buddhists believe that their ancestors come to hear Buddha's teaching as well as to enjoy the food during the ritual. Thus, this magnificent ritual, called the *49 Jae,* operates as a communal

ritual for the dead.[13] Young San Jae reenacts the Buddha's teaching at
Young Chi Mountain while simultaneously guiding souls to the West
Land if they are lost. At Young San Jae, all participants—such as monks,
practitioners, and the souls of the dead—listen to the artistic teachings of
the dharma and appreciate the Buddha's mercy. Through this ritual, the
descendants and the ancestors are spiritually united, and participants consequently experience the continuation of life through their family lineage,
as a response to human mortality.[14]

All the chants are in the vernacular Korean language and rhythm, including a transliteration of Chinese and Sanskrit. Thus, Young San Jae is
also an example of a native Korean Buddhist ritual. Buddhist scholars,
such as Chae Hye Ryeon, emphasize that this ritual integrates Korean
popular religiosity and is an example of Buddhism's enculturation, which
originated in India and came to Korea through China.[15] This is a unique
Korean Buddhist ritual, which focuses on food and the souls of the dead,
as well as the intertwined nature of the living and the dead. Unlike the
West and its thanatology, Asia—and Korea in particular—pays more attention to the merit of the ancestor than the grieving process of the survivors.[16] It is true, however, that through the ritual, the embodied teaching
of enlightenment gives descendants space to process their grief and to gain
relief. After the ritual, I often hear participants saying, "I feel released because my late mother is in Nirvana."

Preparation for Young San Jae

The preparation for this huge ritual is very complex and communal. A
monk who is in charge of the whole ritual uses a written manual. One of
the most fundamental elements in the preparation for this ritual is cleansing. First, the entire temple must be cleaned, and then the gathering
ground is decorated with beautiful and auspicious items, such as paper
lotus flowers and fish, which are carefully selected. Paper flowers represent the petals that fell on Mount Young Chi when the Buddha taught
the dharma. Lotus flowers symbolize the wisdom of the dharma, and the
fish represent the diligent Buddhist who is always awake. Second, to wel-
come the souls, the special altar for souls is filled with flowers. Lamps in
the shape of a coin are held by participants to pay the debt that the souls
might have accumulated through their lives. The most important prepa-

ration for the souls of the dead, however, is to construct a bathing room. This room aims to cleanse them of bad karma, so that they can go to the main site of the ritual and listen to the dharma. A poster is put on the wall that states, "Forget about human sentience and emotions so that you can gain wisdom. If you finish your bathing, come to the ground where the ritual is performed, and listen to the chants. Through your being a participant in the ritual, I wish for you to go to the West Land."[17] This message summarizes why and how the souls are invited into this solemn ritual.

All the participants prepare for this magnificent ritual by offering money and by cleansing their hearts through remembering the five precepts: (1) not to destroy any life; (2) not to tell a lie; (3) not to steal from other people; (4) not to have love affairs outside marriage; and (5) not to drink any liquor.[18] Very often lay practitioners fast, take a cold shower early in the morning, and abstain from sexual intercourse, even conjugal intercourse. More positively, they try to give to charity or release living things into the wild.[19] Because the purpose of this ritual is to aid their ancestors in going to the West Land, the descendants offer money and new clothing for them. In addition, monks who perform any dances, play musical instruments such as drums, cymbals, flutes, and bells, or chant the dharma prepare for their sacred performances and cleanse their tools by citing mantras. A critical aspect of Young San Jae, however, is the preparation and consumption of food. Religious precepts are strongly expressed through foods and the ways of preparing, distributing, and eating them.[20] In this solemn ritual, Buddha, monks, and all participants—including the souls of the dead—eat the sacred food. Food preparation for the eating ritual is processed in three tiers: the first for Buddha or dharma; the second for the souls; and the third for all the monks.

Out of a spirit of devotion, food preparation for the Buddha follows a most solemn procedure. Monks who are in charge of the food prepare six items: burning incense, lamps, flowers, delicacies, tea, and rice. In the preparation of the food, at least twenty-two jobs are listed.[21] It is fair to say that one of the most important duties of preparation involves the food offering to the Buddha. Food delicacies are offered in an artistic way: monks tower the delicacies on small plates and each plate of delicacies looks like a pillar with an artistic design. These tower-shaped offerings signify deep wishes of dedication, blessing, and invocation. The most basic unit is composed of three towers of offerings: one composed of nuts and fruits from a tree; one consisting of oil-and-honey pastries; and the last one made of rice cakes. The delicacies from trees—chestnuts, Chinese dates, dried persimmons, pine nuts, and walnuts—are built up by the monks using the different colors of the nuts and fruits to achieve attractive designs. Honey is used as the "glue" between these nuts and fruits to shape them into a tower. In addition, they add fruits that are yellow-orange, such as persimmons, tangerines, and melons, to the tower. The second pole, of oil-and-honey pastries, often contains *Yak-kwa* (fried honey cake). On the third plate, monks offer thin rice cakes (*Dduk*), which are made of sticky rice and plain rice with bean powder or pine powder. At the center of the offering board, monks offer rice that is cooked with clean water.

In my fieldwork at Bong Won Temple in Seoul, Korea, the temple designated for the preservation of Young San Jae, I found that the only difference between the offerings to Buddha and those to the souls of the deceased is the height of the towers of food offerings.[22] For example, the towers of delicacies offered to ancestors were shorter than those offered to Buddha. Many anthropologists, such as Mary Douglas, Marshall Sahlins, and Pierre Bourdieu, argue that food functions as an indicator of social class and power. The culinary complexity reflects the mode of insiders and outsiders.[23] The offered food is composed of very simple foods such as rice, kimchi, and other vegetables. This selection of food demonstrates Buddha's teaching of simplicity, but, at the same time, it invites everyone, regardless of social class.

Posted on the wall of the altar for the souls of the dead are cards on which the names of the souls and their dates of birth and death are written. These name cards indicate that the souls are invited to this ritual. After bathing or being cleansed, the souls are allowed to enter the site of the ritual, and each invited soul can enjoy the food as well as the teaching. Here the major difference is that Buddha and the living sentient beings eat rice, but the souls of the dead eat noodles. Also, unlike the altar for ancestor veneration in Confucianism, the Buddhist altar contains no plates of meat or fish, or cups for liquor. Instead of liquor, tea and a sweet drink made from fermented rice are offered. There is also no meat or fish for the souls of the dead in the shamanic ritual, and both liquor and a sweet drink made from fermented rice, called *Kamju,* are used, but tea is not offered. The tea ceremony is unique to Buddhism. The eating ritual is both simple and inclusive, as it comprises simple foods, excludes no persons, and minimizes differences between divine and secular and the living and the dead. This is done though each religion maintains its unique components of the rituals for ancestors. Also, this eating ritual emphasizes the equality of human beings, who are all mortal. Food operates as a dialectic revealing the tension that exists between the "clean" purity of the organic life-giving force and the "messy" nature of inevitable decay. Food provides great pleasure and necessary energy, but it also includes dirt. Food forever threatens contamination and bodily impurity, but it is necessary for survival and is a source of pleasure. As Deborah Lupton incisively states, "Food is a metonym of the mortality of human flesh, the inevitable entropy of living matter."[24] Thus, the eating ritual reveals the important Buddhist teaching about impermanence and staying in the moment as a way to enter into Nirvana or eternal bliss.

Procedure of Young San Jae

The whole procedure of Young San Jae is very complicated in its chanting and dancing. Thus, only the essential aspects will be introduced here, divided into three parts: the introduction, the teaching, and the eating ritual.[25] The introduction entails proclaiming the beginning of the solemn ritual, inviting, and welcoming. The ringing of a huge bell signals the beginning of the ritual, in which the Buddhas,[26] bodhisattvas, and other spirits are beseeched to come and join the ceremony.

Welcoming the souls of the dead follows. They are the main guests in this special ritual but cannot enter the main site because they are not yet cleansed. So in the bathing room, the monks chant and dance to guide the invited souls to cleanse their minds by letting go of all attachments and emotions. Through this symbolic bathing, these souls become purified and can then come to the site of Young San Jae. Then, the *Young San Do* (a painting of the scene on Mount Young Chi where the Buddha taught the dharma) is carried outside in a procession, guided by a leader and followed by the monks and the lay people who are participating in the ritual. This represents the appearance of the Buddha at the ceremony. Once the painting is placed at the center of the site, the monks cleanse the site with water while chanting, which symbolizes the cleansing of the mind. This time, water symbolizes wisdom or the dharma. After these chants, all the monks are seated around the painting, at which point the invited souls join together to listen to the dharma.

The second part, teaching the dharma, starts with reciting the goal of this ritual, which is to help the souls of the dead be guided to the West Land. The monks chant the mystical incantation to Avalokitesvara, the bodhisattva of compassion, to relieve the sentient beings of their sufferings. During the incantations, two monks dance. One of the most spectacular dances is the cymbal dance, which is famous for its joyful and masculine body movements. Then the dharma drum dance is performed, in the hope that the sound will awaken all sentient beings, including animals and fish, to the Buddhist wisdom.

After that, the "six offerings" ritual is performed. Although these offerings are already prearranged at the altar of Buddha, the chants describe the monks offering six items to the Buddha. In these chants, the monks wish the six offerings to be transformed into the source of enlightenment for all living things. After this offering ceremony, the teaching of the Lotus Sutra is performed, in which the main theme is Emptiness. This section is very similar in structure to the Catholic Mass, in which the readings and homily are based on the scripture, and an offering is made. In the Catholic liturgy, however, after listening to the scripture, the entire congregation makes its offering to God. The third part is the eating ritual and transferring the merit of the rituals to the souls and the participants' ancestors. Whereas the second part reenacts the feast of the Buddha at Mount Young Chi, this eating ritual is for the monks, who receive the food and then teach the dharma as a response to the offered food. This is called *Shik Tang Jak Bup,* where *Jak Bup* means ritual; it is a teaching composed of music and dance aimed at enlightenment. Thus, this eating ritual is different from other food offerings or eating. *Shik Tang Jak Bup* is called the dharma eating ritual. As the final segment of the eating ritual, the ceremony transfers the merits of the whole ritual: the merits are supposedly transferred to the monks and lay participants as well, but mainly to the souls of the dead. At this point, the Buddhas and bodhisattvas are sent off. After seeing them off, the monks burn the offered money and clothing for the souls of the dead, as a way to transfer all the merits to the souls.[27] The clothing signifies enlightened identity, and the money symbolizes travel fare to paradise. Burning clothing is also used in shamanic rituals as a gesture of closure in the sending off of the soul.

Shik Tang Jak Bup (The Eating Ritual)

The eating ritual is at the center of the Young San Jae, and eighteen monks are in charge of this segment. Here the monks eat rice, soup, vegetables, and pickled cabbage, *kimchi*. The process of eating and washing the bowl is highly refined, and in it the wish for the soul to gain enlightenment is embodied. Eating is an action not just to nourish the body, but also to transform oneself into the body of dharma. This eating ritual emphasizes the importance of food as a source for gaining enlightenment, since eating functions as a gateway to enlightenment for all sentient beings and the souls of the dead.

The edible contents of the eating ritual are clean water, rice, soup, side dishes, seasoning sauce, and tea. Monks who are in charge of the food arrange the sauce in the middle and put rice, soup, and side dishes on both sides. Clean water is used for washing the dish both before and after eating. At the end, the monks collect all the water used for washing the dishes and throw it away as a means of giving food to hungry ghosts (beings who live in hell, struggling with hunger; they suffer from hunger no matter how much they eat). In the Buddhist tradition, all the food given to a person must be eaten thoroughly. After eating, a monk uses only water to clean the dishes; the temples do not use any chemicals, such as detergent, to wash the dishes or utensils. In this ritual, the "dirty" water, which is not actually very dirty, is poured to the ground, especially for the hungry ghosts.

The rice is called *Magi*. When the rice is cooked, the monks offer it to Buddha and take it to this eating ritual. This reenacts the mythic event on Young Chi Mountain, which was a feast with Buddha. As the disciples of Buddha ate with Buddha, so also do the monks, consuming the rice that was offered at the altar of Buddha. The soup is a bean paste soup, without any meat, and is made in one of two ways: one is mild and watery, seasoned with salt, and contains spicy radish, potatoes, and tofu; the other is thick and made with Chinese cabbage. The side dishes are *kimchi,* spicy radish *kimchi,* vegetables, fried tangleweed, mung-bean pancakes, and pan-fried squash slices. In cooking these side dishes, the chefs specifically refrain from using green onion, garlic, ginger, rocambole, and Chinese chives, because it is believed that these five herbs cause sexual desire and anger. For seasoning, the monks use only soy sauce and red pepper. These foods give the fundamental energy with which all human beings and other living things, as well as everything in the universe, are enlightened. Before the foods are cooked, the culinary monks chant. Because the feast is so big, many female volunteers join the monks in cooking the food.

Procedure of the Eating Ritual

This eating ritual includes all the people in the temple. According to the *Sukmoon Eibum* (Ritual Manual), it offers food to all Buddhas and bodhisatvas, and all kinds of ghosts who dwell in hell.[28] The physical serving is limited to the monks, however. The eating ritual begins with striking the bell eighteen times. All the monks come to the site and sit in a rectangle with their own Balwoo, which is a set of portable containers for water, rice, soup, and side dishes. Because eating is an act of cultivating as well as sustaining life, these four items are essential tools for prayer and cultivation.[29] After sitting at the site, monks who are in charge of striking the bronze gong, bells, drum, and *Moko* (a fish-shaped wooden drum) strike their instruments as a gesture symbolic of waking up all creatures. Then the monks recite and dance on the teaching of Emptiness. After providing the people and the souls of the dead with spiritual food—the teaching of Emptiness—they sit at the site.

Next, the monks chant while opening up their Balwoo. They stand up, chanting the Heart Sutra (Prajñāpāramitā-hrdaya-sūtra) in Korean.[30] When they complete this chant, the novice monks carry the food and distribute it to each monk. In front of the food, the monks recite the mantra that helps them reach wisdom and virtue. The monks then sit on the assigned ground and recite the prayer, "When we see the food fills the Balwoo, let us all wish together that the dharma will be filled with the whole world. Once we receive this sweet food, let us all wish together that we will be free from attachment through the temperance of food." After this prayer, the monks lift the Balwoos above their heads, offering them to the Three Gems, which are the Buddha, the dharma, and the monks. The monks put the Balwoos on the table and recite a mantra, reminding themselves that they should be enlightened first before helping the world. Here all chants emphasize that even one drop of water includes the life of millions.

Once the bell rings, the monk in charge of the procedure says, "Eat the food," at which time the monks begin to eat. After checking that all the monks have begun to eat, the leader rings the bell as a reminder of all the chants. When the meal is almost over, the monk rings the bell six times. After the participating monks have finished the food, the young serving monks bring the water to clean the Balwoos. While cleansing the Balwoos and wrapping them up, they recite the mantra, which will help all creatures and the souls of the dead reach the West Land. In closing, all the monks stand up and salute one another by saying, "Be the Buddha." After deep bows to lay practitioners, they leave the eating ritual. Once the monks leave the ritual site completely, the lay practitioners begin their meal. While the solemn ritual proceeds, most participants walk around the temple and specifically the altar for the dead. It is natural to cry and even bid farewell to the dead. As the ritual closes, some families become saddened and highly emotional, while other families remain calm. Because the ritual is communal, each individual family does not have to deal with all the preparation. Rather, they follow the guidance of ritual professionals, pour out their emotions, and remember their permanent bond in the teachings of the Buddha.

Closing Remarks

Ritual creates a liminal space where the boundary between the living and the dead and the secular and the sacred is blurred. In the food rituals for the dead, Koreans experience reunion with ancestors, and food functions as the medium. The food symbolizes the life-giving love of god and that of ancestor, while it represents the descendant's respect and piety. Here food demonstrates the communal nature of the ritual. Ritual food should be simple so that everyone can participate in the ritual and so that the ritual space is inclusive and open to everybody. In Korean society, most people do not talk about the dead or ancestors often, but the death ritual remains a crucial cultural aspect of Korean society, and all religions include death rituals such as the funeral, ancestor veneration days, New Year's remembrance or veneration, and the Full Moon Festival. All these rituals are centered on eating. The Buddhist eating ritual, Young San Jae, is an example that shows how important it is for Koreans to be reunited with ancestors and provide food for their ancestors. This eating ritual helps the ancestors attain enlightenment and Nirvana, and helps practitioners fulfill their filial obligation while reconnecting with their ancestors' bodies. Offered food can be an expression of participants' loyalty to Buddha and to their ancestors simultaneously. Finally, this huge ritual is communal. Hundreds of people gather to perform the ritual at one time in the ritual space, and myriads of dead souls are invoked and invited to the site. A solemn ritual feast of eating, Young San Jae emphasizes the connections between the living and the dead, and both the living and the decedents share in an opportunity to listen to the dharma, the Buddha's message, together. Food becomes an expression of gratitude and filial piety, as well as a medium through which descendants offer the teaching of the dharma to their ancestors. This ritual is not an individual one but one of the whole Buddhist community, which cherishes the three treasures, Buddha, the dharma, and the community.

Notes

1. Catherine Bell, *Ritual Theory, Ritual Practice* (Oxford: Oxford University Press, 1992), 27.

2. Jung Eun Sophia Park, *Border-Crossing Spirituality: Transformation in the Borderland* (Eugene, Ore.: Wipf and Stock, 2016).

3. Christianity has different views, but I do not deal with this topic here because it is beyond the scope of this chapter.

4. Paul S. Chung, *Martin Luther and Buddhism: Aesthetics of Suffering*, 2nd ed. (Eugene, Ore.: Pickwick Publications, 2008), 191.

5. Douglas J. Davies, *Death, Ritual and Belief: the Rhetoric of Funerary Rites* (New York: Continuum, 2002), 101.

6. Kenneth J. Doka, "Spirituality: Quo Vadis?" in *Death, Dying, and Bereavement: Contemporary Perspectives, Institutions, and Practices,* ed. Judith M. Stillion and Thomas Attig (New York: Springer Publishing, 2015), 17.

7. The Second Vatican Council encouraged local churches to embrace their cultural heritage. See Austin Flannery, "Church in the Modern World," in *Vatican Council II: The Conciliar and Post Conciliar Documents,* ed. Flannery, rev. ed. (Boston: St. Paul Books & Media, 1992), 962.

8. Jacques Derrida, "Living On," in *Deconstruction and Criticism,* ed. H. Bloom et al. (New York: Continuum, 1979), 76.

9. Sang Hyeon Sim, *Young San Jae* (Seoul: National Research Institute of Cultural Properties, 2003), 73.

10. "UNESCO & Heritages," www.unesco.or.kr/heritage/ich/korich_young-san.asp, accessed January 15, 2015.

11. Sim, *Young San Jae,* 9.

12. Davies, *Death, Ritual and Belief,* 102.
13. Mahayana Buddhism teaches that people go to the Pure Land to the West, paradise, after death.
14. Davies, *Death, Ritual and Belief,* 6.
15. Sim, *Young San Jae,* 10–12. See also Hye Ryeon Chae, *Young San Jae and Beom Pae: Theory and Analysis* (Seoul: Kookhak Zaryowon, 2011), 36.
16. For the contemporary Western approach to death, or thanatology, see Stillion and Attig, *Death, Dying, and Bereavement.*
17. Sim, *Young San Jae,* 98. The West Land, or western paradise, as it is often called, is symbolic of a Buddhist heaven where faithful practitioners go following their deaths, and from which one can become enlightened and reach Nirvana.
18. Pa Keung Seon Baik, *Jakbupkwikam [Ritual Collection],* trans. Doojai Kim (Seoul: Dong Kook University Press, 2010), 81–83.
19. In Korea people buy fish or other captured living creatures that are destined to be killed and release them back into nature. This is an expression of charity toward other living things. But recently, because of environmental issues, this is no longer encouraged.
20. William K. Powers and Marla M. N. Powers, "Metaphysical Aspects of an Oglala Food System," in *Food in the Social Order: Studies of Food and Festivities of Three American Communities,* ed. Mary Douglas (1973; repr., New York: Rutledge, 2003), 45–46.
21. Sim, *Young San Jae,* 123–125.
22. I performed my field research on Young San Jae in 2013–2015. I completed interviews with the monks in charge of this ritual as well as other monks who dwelled in this temple.
23. Mary Douglas, "Standard Social Uses of Food: Introduction," in Douglas, *Food in the Social Order,* 17–19.
24. Deborah Lupton, *Food, the Body and the Self* (London: Sage Publications, 1996), 3.
25. This description follows Bongwon Temple's performance of the ritual.
26. The reason I use the plural form of Buddha is that in Mahayana tradition, there are many different Buddhas who represent certain aspects of Buddha's nature.
27. Paper money and paper clothing, rather than real money and clothing, which are usually bought at specialty stores for the dead or in Buddhist temples, are burned here as symbolic replacements for money and clothing that might be needed in the afterlife.
28. Baik, *Jakbupkwikam,* 81–83, 220–224.
29. Won Ki Pak, "The Aesthetic World of Young San Jae and the Meaning of the Chants," *Journal of Comparative Literature of East and West* 23 (December 2010): 130.
30. Prajñāpāramitā-hrdaya-sūtra is a summary of the Mahayana Buddhist teaching. The translated version is called the Heart Sutra and is composed of

260 Chinese characters. See Woon Hu, *The Dictionary of Buddhism* (Seoul: Dong Kook University Press, 2003).

Bibliography

Baik, Pa Keung Seon. *Jakbupkwikam* [*Ritual Collection*]. Translated by Doojai Kim. Seoul: Dong Kook University Press, 2010.

Chae, Hye Ryeon. *Young San Jae and Beom Pae: Theory and Analysis.* Seoul: Kookhak Zaryowon, 2011.

Chung, Paul S. *Martin Luther and Buddhism: Aesthetics of Suffering*, 2nd ed. Eugene, Ore.: Pickwick Publications, 2008.

Davies, Douglas J. *Death, Ritual and Belief: The Rhetoric of Funerary Rites.* New York: Continuum, 2002.

Derrida, Jacques. "Living On." In *Deconstruction and Criticism*, edited by H. Bloom et al., 62–142. New York: Continuum, 1979.

Doka, Kenneth J. "Spirituality: Quo Vadis?" In *Death, Dying, and Bereavement: Contemporary Perspectives, Institutions, and Practices*, edited by Judith M. Stillion and Thomas Attig, 233–242. New York: Springer Publishing, 2015.

Douglas, Mary. "Standard Social Uses of Food: Introduction." In *Food in the Social Order: Studies of Food and Festivities of Three American Communities*, edited by Mary Douglas, 1–39. 1973. Reprint, New York: Rutledge, 2003.

Flannery, Austin. "Church in the Modern World." In *Vatican Council II: The Conciliar and Post Conciliar Documents*, edited by Austin Flannery, revised edition, 903–1001. Boston: St. Paul Books & Media, 1992.

Hu, Woon. *The Dictionary of Buddhism.* Seoul: Dong Kook University Press, 2003.

Lupton, Deborah. *Food, the Body and the Self.* London: Sage Publications, 1996.

Pak, Won Ki. "The Aesthetic World of Young San Jae and the Meaning of the Chants." *Journal of Comparative Literature of East and West* 23 (December 2010): 129–156.

Powers, William K., and Marla M. N. Powers. "Metaphysical Aspects of an Oglala Food System." In *Food in the Social Order: Studies of Food and Festivities of Three American Communities*, edited by Mary Douglas, 40–96. 1973. Reprint, New York: Rutledge, 2003.

Sim, Sang Hyeon. *Young San Jae.* Seoul: National Research Institute of Cultural Properties, 2003.

"UNESCO & Heritages." www.unesco.or.kr/heritage/ich/korich_youngsan.asp, accessed January 15, 2015.

3

Sweetening Death
Shifting Landscapes of the Role of Food in Grief and Mourning

Candi K. Cann

Introduction

This chapter examines the ways in which people in the United States, Mexico, and China use foods involving sugar, starch, and wine in their remembrances for the dead; it investigates the different ways these foods reflect the relationship of the living with the deceased. The function of funeral foods in the United States is to remember the dead through the everyday act of eating, the primary function being to nourish the living and reintegrate the bereaved into the community in which the deceased no longer lives. In contrast, funeral feasts in Mexico and China do not simply remember the dead but also use foodstuffs of the living to care for and feed the dead in their newly altered state. I find the comparison of United States food memorialization practices with those in Mexico and China to be useful because it reveals the deep contrast in the way food is viewed and used. This chapter examines the roles of sugar, starches, and wine in funeral feasts and gravesite offerings, and the memorialization holidays of Halloween, Day of the Dead, and Qing Ming, arguing that throughout history, food has played a vital role either in relating to and caring for the dead, or in remembering the dead through communal food practices.

My focus in this chapter on sugar (and sugar's cousins, starch and wine) is not intended to exclude other foods, but is meant to be a way of allowing for a narrower focus that reveals different practices that use simi-

Texas Sheetcake

Serves 20–25, with a total preparation time of 1 hour and 10 minutes. The "Texas" appellation comes from both the size of the sheetcake ("everything is big in Texas") and the pecans on top, since the Texas state tree is the pecan tree.

Cake:
  2 sticks butter, softened
  1 cup water
  ¼ cup unsweetened cocoa powder
  2 cups flour
  2 cups sugar
  ½ tsp salt
  1 tsp baking soda
  ½ cup sour cream
  2 eggs, beaten
  ¼ cup milk

Frosting:
  1 stick butter, softened
  ¼ cup unsweetened cocoa powder
  6 tbsp milk
  4 cups powdered sugar
  1½ tsp vanilla
  1 cup chopped pecans

Preheat oven to 350° and combine first three ingredients in small saucepan over medium low heat. Heat until butter is melted and ingredients are mixed. Take the saucepan off the stove and let cool. Pour the saucepan ingredients into another bowl and add the remaining cake ingredients, beating until well combined. Pour into a large 10- by 15-inch cake pan and then bake 25 minutes, or until a toothpick inserted in the middle of the cake comes out clean. While the cake is cooking, melt the butter with the cocoa and milk on the stove in a large pot. Remove the pot from the stove, and stir in the sugar and vanilla. Spread the frosting over the cake after the cake has cooled, and top with the chopped pecans.

Texas Sheetcake, often served at funerals in Texas. (Shutterstock)

lar foods. By contrasting how sugar is conceptualized in different cultural contexts, I demonstrate how the dead are either excluded from the table or remembered through it. Funeral casseroles, American Halloween candy, Mexican sugar skulls, *pan de muerto,* Chinese wine offerings, and brown sugar funeral candy all symbolize an attempt to "sweeten" the sting of death through food. What is most fascinating is the ways in which food, in the form of sugary treats, has become interpreted and understood as a cultural signifier. Food is not an apolitical substance; rather, it is so common that we have overlooked it altogether. Food is the stuff that life is made of—in fact, the stuff that keeps us living—and an examination of the relationship between food and death allows us to look at the ways in which the living imagine, remember, and relate to the dead.

A Brief History of Sugar

Sugar has a rich history and until the seventeenth century, when slave labor reduced its manufacturing costs, was considered a luxury staple—one that connoted an upper-level status and earmarked sugar as a rare treat.[1] Until the last two centuries, serving sugar and sugary treats was a luxury only rarely afforded, one that indicated one's ability to purchase such foods.[2] Until the use by the British of sugar in their tea (and, later, Americans in their coffee), sugar was viewed largely as a spice, an occasional condiment that added sweetness or enhanced the flavor of foods—unlike the view of sugar today as a staple of both baking and cooking.[3] Sugar also marks a transition in the world economy from the Old World to the New—because of sugar's dependency on large amounts of labor, it became the privileged realm of colonial countries, with their access to large tracts of land and reliance on slave labor. Until the seventeenth and eighteenth centuries, honey had been the sweetener of choice, and the transition to a dependence on sugar marked an equally significant transition to a reliance on the New World. It is no small coincidence that sugar plays a far larger role in the bereavement and memorialization practices of Mexico (Día de los Muertos) and the United States (Halloween) than in China (though sugary foods such as *qing tuan,* or sweet rice cakes, and wine—which involves the fermenting of fruit sugars—also play an important role in memorialization practices for the dead in China). Sugar was an abundant food staple in addition to an economic marker of colonial identity.

Sugar's Place in the Meal and Its Biochemical Importance

Sugar and the foods that contain it are generally eaten at the end of a meal, as snacks in between meals, or in drinks and are viewed as optional, special, and additional. Perhaps it is in part because of the biochemical processes that occur in reaction to sugar that it has been charged with ending the meal—it creates a self-soothing response in the brain and body chemistry that releases endorphins of pleasure and relaxation—unlike many foods, with the exception of drugs and alcohol. One cannot write about sugar without noting its biochemical reactions in the brain. Unlike many other foodstuffs (except perhaps the caffeine stimulants found in coffee, chocolate, and tea), sugar creates a measurable chemical pleasure response in the body. It may be for these very basic reasons—the status-giving attributes of sugar and the biochemical reaction of pleasure in the body— that sugar initially became customary in celebrations associated with the dead. Shirley Lindenbaum notes in her work that sometimes hidden physiological reasons exist behind the cultural customs of food and food practices.[4] As we see in the traditional Irish wake and its association with alcohol, which takes advantage of alcohol's mind-numbing powers, sugar offers a soothing response in the body to stress and the difficult emotions of mourning.[5]

Sugar's Cousins: Starch and Wine

At first glance, one might not associate starchy foods with sugar, but it is the sugar in starchy foods that both makes them palatable and acts as a preservative. Starches are thus the main staple foods in nearly all cultures, and nearly every funeral feast features starch in some form. As Fernández-Armesto notes in his book *Food: A History:* "Starch is the source of energy that has supplied most people for most of recorded history, but it is inefficient until it is cooked. Heat disintegrates it, releasing the sugar which all starch contains. At the same time, dry heat turns dextrins in starch brown, imparting the comforting look we associate with cooked food."[6] Additionally, starches are generally considered to be staples because until they are cooked, they often last a long while and can be stored and preserved, which makes them ideal foods for travel or for storing in harsh climates. Fernández-Armesto also notes that "staples are almost always sacred, because people depend on them; they possess divine power."[7] The consumption of starch staples in funeral feasts and memorialization ceremonies is symbolic of their place in life—they are ubiquitous and universal; whether rice, wheat, or corn, these foods are literally the foods consumed to sustain life, and thus they are also the foods needed to sustain the dead in their afterlives.

Wine is a beverage heavily dependent on sugar, and, just as the yeast in bread metabolizes sugar, allowing the bread to rise, the yeast in alcohol breaks down the sugars in grapes and ferments them into wine. One of the oldest drinks in the history of humankind, wine has traditionally been associated in many cultures with a rich symbolism of water, milk, and blood.[8] It has also been (along with beer) one of the safest drinks to consume, as many places in the world have not had sufficient potable water supplies, and wine could be made, stored, and drunk when clean water was not readily available. Though it is not extensively explored in this chapter, since wine is not a food, I do want to mention its importance in the Chinese funeral and memorialization rituals, in contrast to those in the United States and Mexico.[9] In Texas, where the majority of my fieldwork has been conducted for the analysis of American funerals and memorializations, alcohol is usually *not* present in funeral feasts or memorializations, and the absence of alcohol (as noted in chapter 4) is one of the identity markers of a funeral feast's being decidedly Baptist or Methodist. (Methodist funerals generally permit alcohol, whereas Baptist ones most often do not.) In Mexican funerals and memorialization rituals, alcohol is present only if the deceased preferred it, and it is offered by the living on behalf of the deceased; however, the presence of alcohol, with the exception of the wine offered in Catholic Communion, is by no means standard. Thus, while it may be present in the feast or memorialization ritual, it is not discouraged, as it usually is in the Texan funeral feast or memorialization. In contrast, Chinese funeral feasts and the Qing Ming memorialization ritual both include wine as an essential element, and no feast is considered complete without the wine offering. This difference in the role of wine in funerals feasts and memorializations may ultimately reflect the differences in the view of the afterlife and the relationship of the living to the dead. First, however, I will turn to examine the role of food in American, and primarily Texan, funerals.

Funeral Food in the United States

Funeral food in the United States serves as a way to remember the dead by bringing together the community, using cherished recipes that have been handed down through generations, and asserting community and familial identity through food customs. Particularly in the southern United States, funeral dishes are usually casseroles or dishes meant to serve a large quantity of people, often are easily reheated and re-served, and are frequently able to be left out for long periods. Casseroles, crockpot dishes, and "one-pot" meals, meant to function as complete meals in and of themselves, provide sustenance for gatherings of people following a wake or a funeral and emphasize the communal nature of the funeral repast. Additionally, there tend to be many cakes and pies served at these meals, showcases of heritage recipes. They are not, however, generally intended to be shared with, and consumed by, the dead; they are served in the homes of the bereaved, rather than at the graves of the deceased.

Funeral food generally functions as a support service to those who are mourning, to minimize the labor and preparations for the daily necessity of eating. The funeral repasts are often copious, given to the bereaved families to help meet their dietary needs during the days following the death of a family member; they are meant to help lighten the family members' load so they can make funeral and burial arrangements for the deceased, and adjust to their shifting roles in light of the absence of their loved one. These meals, whether given on the day of the funeral or in the days or weeks following it, can be viewed as a way for the community to materially help the family of the deceased and as part of a gift-giving exchange in honor of the deceased. Generally, the more prominent the deceased or her family, the more food is delivered in her memory. The number of food gifts offered to the bereaved can be said then to mirror, to some extent, the status or class of those in mourning. Additionally, the gifts brought by the community serve to reinforce each individual's right to mourn with the rest of the community, while also revealing a person's relation to the dead, the family of the dead, or both. The funeral feast almost always occurs in the home of the deceased (though if the person who died was particularly prominent, then sometimes it will occur in a church or town hall), and this is another notable feature of the funeral food—that private space is temporarily appropriated and converted into public space.

In Texas, funeral food is traditionally viewed as belonging to the realm of women, as generations-old family recipes are brought to funeral repasts.[10] One woman I interviewed traditionally makes "Funeral Potatoes" from a recipe passed down from her grandmother, prepared and eaten specifically in, and only in, times of bereavement. In my research both online and in American cookbooks, I found the most popular and common recipes recommended for funeral food are "Funeral Potatoes," "Texas Sheetcake," and "Funeral Pie." Funeral Potatoes are a potato dish made from sliced or chopped potatoes, milk, cheese, and canned mushroom or cheddar cheese soup. Readily made from everyday ingredients on hand in most American kitchens, this dish reminds one of standard fare served in the 1950s, when dishes were supposed to be convenient and cooking time minimal. The casserole itself harks back to the postwar period, when women were expected to prepare the foods, but status was reflected in being able to take advantage of processed foods made in factories, readily available in urban areas, far from the plentiful produce of farms. In many ways, the casserole reflected the modern family—on the go, busy, urban; its ingredients were full of preservatives that gave them a long shelf life.

Texas Sheetcake is seen as an efficient and practical food (though it is not, like the potatoes, a staple). A sheetcake is a cake whose batter is spread out on a 10- by 15-inch baking sheet, and then frosted right in the pan. It can be moved from one kitchen to another with minimal fuss or worry. Because the pan is a large rectangle, the cake is easy to cut and serve, and because sugar is a well-known preservative, Texas Sheetcake can be left out for hours at a time without spoiling or becoming moldy. It is traditional in Texas funeral feasts for at least one family to bring a Texas Sheetcake, and its presence is seen as part of the traditional foodways of Texas culture. The fact that this sheetcake is generally served only at funeral feasts helps distinguish funeral feasts from other Texas rituals, such as tailgating picnics or eating black-eyed peas on New Year's.

One important aspect of these funeral feasts is the recognition of the participation of particular families in the funeral and mourning process through their food gifts. One woman I interviewed, the wife of a Baptist pastor of a large church, noted that her cake's presence at the funeral repast was symbolic and meaningful, as the larger faith community recognized her participation in the bereavement festivities through her cake's presence, her cake being an indirect symbol of her husband's pastoral function. In this way, the food offerings assert one's familial (clan) identity and reveal matrilineal ties to previous generations. Thus, while men are the bearers of the corpse (as pallbearers) in traditional American funerals, it is women who are generally in charge of the bereavement meals. With some exceptions, the women usually arrange the social affairs of the family, including the meals shared with other families in one's network, and are responsible for preparing and cooking the meal to be brought and shared with those who are grieving. Often the meals provided in the bereavement period extend beyond the initial funeral feast, and may sometimes be offered several weeks after the death. In fact, in several churches in Waco (a small college town in Texas between Dallas and Austin, mostly Protestant, heavily racially segregated, and where I currently live), it is common practice to generate an online calendar that is sent to other women in the parish, requesting them to pick a particular date and time to provide a meal for the family following a death. The calendar is almost always quickly filled, and meals are then dropped off at the family's house for a week or two following the funeral service itself. Participation in the online calendar is publicly shared and viewed, itself serving as a material reminder of each family's commitment to the shared social responsibility of caring for the bereaved. The dead linger in the living rooms through stories, memories, shared meals, and recipes, passively invoked but not necessarily active participants.

American Food Remembrances: Halloween

In addition to funeral potlucks, general remembrance customs are commonly practiced in the United States that mark the intersection of death and food. The first, of course, is Halloween, initially the celebration of the evening before All Saints' Day, or All Hallows' Eve, but which has turned into Halloween, a tradition focused on children and the collection of candy. Initially a holiday of remembrance for the dead, the modern institution of Halloween has inverted the original inception, focusing instead on the celebration of youth, while simultaneously commemorating the trickster aspect of the holiday. Candy is distributed to costumed children who wander from house to house (or now, in some cases, from car to car in parking lots) collecting candy, jokingly offering a threat of playing a "trick" if there is no "treat." Alan Dundes points out in his seminal work, *Interpreting Folklore,* that contemporary Americans have become youth-obsessed, and that perhaps this inversion of the Halloween tradition of remembering the dead is reflective of a greater tendency in American culture to value youth culture over that of our elders.[11] In any case, it is traditional to offer small, wrapped pieces of candy to children on this day, though this custom seems to bear little relation to the previous custom of honoring and remembering the dead.[12] It should also be noted here that candy, in general, is often marketed as a children's foodstuff—and it is frequently considered a reward or treat for children in the United States. This holds even deeper significance when seen in the light of the inversion of Halloween and Halloween customs; candy is now viewed as a temptation for adults and a special food for children. Perhaps sugar, in its initial association with death, has been relegated to the realm of children, whose youth will function as an efficient antidote to the dangers of death. That being said, however, with the rise in the Hispanic population in the United States and the increasing popularity of Día de los Muertos (particularly in the borderland states, such as Texas), perhaps the dead will once again find their place in this celebration.

In Waco (boasting a 30 percent Hispanic population, considerably higher than the nearly 18 percent overall population in the United States), for example, there is an annual Día de los Muertos festival held with an altar, traditional music, dances, and foods to honor the dead. More and more local Anglo Waco residents attend the festival, bringing pictures of their loved ones to leave at the altar, or, in some cases, they create small Día de los Muertos altars at home. Sugar skulls and sugar caskets are sold in cafés and craft shops in town, quickly selling out as people purchase them to become part of their home altars or to adorn their bookshelves in their offices at work. Anglo-Americans may in fact be adopting and co-opting these traditions as a way to recover traditions that honor the dead and keep them a part of their everyday lives. With the Hispanic population of the United States predicted to reach approximately one-third of the American population by 2060, it is little surprise that this holiday is melding with more traditional observations of Halloween. Both Halloween and Día de los Muertos are notable for their postcolonial exchange and consumption of sweets in response to death.

CALAVERA DE AZÚCAR (Sᴜɢᴀʀ Sᴋᴜʟʟs)

Makes 4 medium skulls; 4 hours prep time; skull molds can be purchased online or in specialty kitchen shops.

6 cups granulated sugar
¼ cup meringue powder
⅓ cup water
sugar skulls molds
royal icing (3 cups powdered sugar; ¼ tsp cream of tartar; 2 egg whites, beaten to stiff peaks
gel food color for icing decorations
pastry bags for icing

Mix sugar, meringue powder, and water together until completely wet and holding together. Firmly fill both cavities of the skull mold with the wet sugar, making sure the mold is well packed, and scrape off the excess with a straightedge. Flip skulls out of the molds and allow both fronts and backs to dry for about 24 hours. Make royal icing. Once the skulls are dry, spread royal icing on the straight backs of the skulls and press them together, then dry again until both halves of molded sugar are stuck together. Mix bowls or paper cups of royal icing with food coloring. Filling pastry bags with the royal icing, decorate the skulls. Colored foil is also often used in decoration. Let dry a few hours before using.

Mexican Graveyard Foods and Memorialization

At Mexican funerals,[13] food is generally served at the wake preceding the funeral service itself, and there are often opportunities for the extended community to gather together in remembrance of the deceased. The family usually sits with the deceased until the funeral Mass, and it is customary for wake feasts to be large community affairs with copious amounts of food, sometimes catered at the funeral home or church, sometimes assembled as potluck meals.[14] Frequently several rooms are used for the feasting, and the entire family network, including children, is invited; tables are set up for dominoes, cards, and other forms of family-friendly games, which take place during the feasting. The food served at these affairs tends to be regional, and it usually reflects the particular province of the family of the deceased, as well as his or her personal preferences. The most notable difference from American funeral feasts, however, is that it is almost always the favorite foods of the *deceased* that are served at both the Mexican wake and funeral feast. Thus, the food is not solely for the living, but also a meal that honors and respects the dead. Serving the favorite foods of the deceased acts to symbolically integrate the dead person into the wake and funeral. Consequently, there is no standard dish that is served at Mexican wakes and funerals (unlike the highly ritualized Chinese funerals), but the favorite dishes are generally common, everyday fare that the deceased might have regularly eaten, at the same time reflecting his or her local and regional identity.

Commonly served dishes are tamales, mole (pronounced "mo-lay"), and pozole, in addition to the standard fare of rice and beans. Tamales are cornmeal dough filled with various fillings, wrapped with cornhusks, and generally steamed. Like rice, potatoes, and other starchy foods, the corn masa used to make tamales is high in sugar and served in a way that is also very portable, making it an ideal food both to prepare and to serve at the wake and funeral feast. There are a variety of tamales one can make, ranging from bean and cheese to pork and chili pepper to pineapple and strawberry. Mole is a sauce made from many different spices, but features primarily both cocoa and chili pepper; every family has its own version of mole, which is served with meat, on enchiladas, or on other dishes. Many Mexican families pride themselves on their mole recipes (as southwestern Americans pride themselves on their chili recipes), and this dish tends to be a marker of family identity and status. Roasting and preparing the mole spices can take days, so the preparation and cooking of this dish reflect both leisure and time; a good mole is reputed to take at least three days, and some even a week. A "good" mole thus reflects the long labor required to develop it, and it can be seen as a marker of not only status, but also taste. Finally, pozole, like tamales, is also made from corn, and mixed with other vegetables, lemon, and bits of cubed pork. The ancient Aztec meal once supposedly contained the meat of human flesh, so it is no surprise that this meal has evolved into one of the more popular dishes served at the funeral feast. Eating the meat of the sacrificed dead, in ancient Aztec belief, was to eat the sacred itself (not so far from eating the flesh and drinking the blood that Christians reenact every Sunday to mark themselves as part of the body and blood of Jesus), but when the missionaries came to colonize Mexico, they banned cannibalism, and pork was substituted. The dual purpose of both nourishing the living and caring for the dead continues in other Mexican remembrance rituals at the grave sites of the deceased; this dual purpose is also seen in the annual festivities of Día de los Muertos.

In Mexico the graveyards are publicly owned, and because it is the community's responsibility to maintain the graveyard, church members and families come together to pull weeds and tend to the graves by leaving offerings of food and flowers. The graveyard, because of its proximity to the church, is often situated at the center of public space, thus making its maintenance doubly important. To replicate the sacred space of the cemetery, families construct a home altar where the deceased are honored with their pictures, and so the grave itself, the traditional nexus of the social sphere, is replicated in the more private sphere of the nuclear family home. The cemetery is both literally and figuratively the center of the world of the living and the dead, whereas the home altar represents the dead's return to his or her living relatives. The Mexican home altar invites the dead to return annually to the world of the living and consume their favorite foods and drinks in the comfort of their family home. Pictures, favorite memorabilia, religious iconography, flowers, candles, and food and drink offerings adorn the altar as a material recognition of the presence of the dead in the home. The geographical space of the dead in Mexico thus functions as a civic space in which Mexican identity is affirmed, recognized, and perpetuated through the visits of the living to the dead. Mexicans residing in the United States remap the realm of the dead onto the world of the living through the home altar, simultaneously reaffirming their ethnic, national, familial, and community ties through maintaining relationships with the deceased as though they were still alive.[15] In Mexico, on Día de los Muertos, the family takes chairs, tables, food, drink, flowers, candles, and pictures to the cemetery, feasting with extended family members both alive and dead, spending the day with the present family, telling stories about the dead family members, saying prayers for their souls, and giving offerings of both food and drink. The purposes are to remind those who are alive that life is short and to connect the living, through the stories, to the dead, situating the place of the dead in this world through narrative and the fixed location of the tomb.[16]

Día de los Muertos—Mexico's Remembrance of the Dead

The Mexican Day of the Dead ceremony emerged from the popular Catholic practice of memorializing the dead on the Catholic feast of All Souls' Day, which originated in Catholic beliefs in purgatory and the need to intercede in behalf of the dead. Saint Cluny is credited with first establishing the practice of observing All Souls' Day on November 2, 998. The practice of praying for the dead soon spread to the rest of the Cluniac order before traveling to southern Europe, and finally reaching Rome in the fourteenth century. Historians, however, argue that Cluny merely instituted what was already a widely adopted popular practice. Originally one day of intercession for the dead, the November 2 observance soon spread to cover the entire month of November; names of the deceased were prayed over in Masses for the dead held on All Saints' Eve on October 31, All Saints' Day on November 1, and All Souls' Day on November 2, and continuing throughout the rest of the month.[17] When the Spanish colonists settled in Mexico in 1519, the Roman Catholic tradition was fused with an indigenous Aztec tradition of remembering the dead through reverence of the goddess Mictecacihuatl, known today as the Lady of the Dead. The images of the Lady of the Dead are not that different from those of the Grim Reaper popular in Europe in the sixteenth century, both having a similar emphasis on the macabre as everyday. The reminder in both images is that of death made commonplace. The indigenous summer holiday of the Lady of the Dead was moved to coincide with the later church date, and thus a new and indigenous interpretation of All Souls' Day was begun. The Aztec practice of remembering the dead included placing the skull of the deceased on the altar with his or her name written on it, to honor the place of the dead in the afterworld; the modern practice is similar, though the human skulls have been replaced with sugar skulls. It is important to note the fusing here of both material body relics and food—the Day of the Dead has essentially transformed the unpalatable body of the deceased into a skull made of sugar.[18]

It is believed that the sugar skulls characterizing the celebration of the remembrance for the dead in Mexico emerged from the sociopolitical landscape at the time. Mexicans, who had abundant sugar but little capital, wanted to adorn their churches with decorations similar to those so popular with their colonial conquerors, so they turned to sugar's malleable

A traditional Day of the Dead altar. Note the sugar skulls, marigolds, and *pan de muerto*. (Shutterstock)

properties to make colorful and edible decorations for the church and home altars. The sugar skulls are made from sugar, meringue powder, and food coloring, and they are molded into sweet representations of Lady Death, also known as Saint Death. The popularity of Day of the Dead images flooding the American market are indicative not only of the increase in the Hispanic American population, but also of the increase in the popularity of Santa Muerte, Saint Death, the macabre skeleton and patron saint of marginalized communities, whom the official Catholic Church has barred from receiving official recognition. Believed to be the patron saint of drug dealers and more violently inclined people, Santa Muerte has also found appeal among the marginal immigrant communities in the United States, and her image adorns much Day of the Dead regalia across the United States.[19] The shaping of sugar into skulls (and caskets), however, is a unique cultural phenomenon from Mexico; it indicates that though we all must face the reality of death, there are still aspects of life that are *sweet* and should be savored.

In addition to sugar skulls, marigold flowers often adorn the graves, altars, and churches in remembrance of the dead. It is believed that the colors of the flowers—earth tones—help guide the dead home and return their souls safely to their homes and altars. Unlike American Protestant notions of salvation as final and resolute, Mexican Catholic beliefs in purgatory allow for the intercession of souls and the gradual admission into heaven, which are dependent on the prayers, offerings, vigils, rosaries, and so on of the living to help ensure the place of the dead. This means that food offerings of the living for and to the dead are interwoven with theological understandings of salvation and the afterlife. These understandings imbue the food gifts at the graves with a personal, familial, and religious significance. It is also common to bake pan de muerto, or Day of the Dead bread, made with flour, butter, sugar, eggs, orange peel, anise, and yeast. The bread is kneaded and shaped into little buns and decorated with skulls and crossbones. The pan de muerto, sugar skulls, and oranges are offered at the family altars, which are decorated with pictures of the deceased, candles, and flowers. The pan de muerto strongly resembles hot cross buns, buns made with a sweet yeast dough, currants or raisins (or both), and icing crosses piped along the tops of the buns. Hot cross buns were traditionally eaten on Good Friday because they symbolized the end of the Lenten fasting period (when leavened products were often given up), and because the icing cross on the top symbolized the cross of the Crucifixion and the promise of salvation through the death of Jesus. Stanley Brandes notes that the pan de muerto was made for the dead to consume (reminiscent of the Middle Ages' corpse cake), whereas sugar skulls are made for the living.[20]

The yeast found in bread is symbolic of life's ultimate ability to overcome death; the rising of the bread is a symbolic reenactment of the resurrection of the souls in the afterlife. The yeast must feed on sugar in order to change its chemical properties and allow the dough to rise, in much the same way the Christian understanding inverts the inevitable decay of death on mortal bodies through the concept of the resurrection of the dead. Angel Méndez Montoya writes in his book, *The Theology of Food: Eating and the Eucharist,* that "food is envisioned as a life that overcomes death, and simultaneously as a symbol of deification."[21] The offering of yeasty bread in ceremonies celebrating death thus ultimately becomes a testament of life in response to death. Sergei Bulgakov writes that differences between the living and the dead are erased through food: "The boundary between living and nonliving is actually removed in food. Food is natural communion—partaking of the flesh of the world. When I take

QING TUAN (SWEET GREEN RICE CAKES OR QING MING RICE CAKES)

Qing tuan is traditionally made with juice from the Chinese mugwort plant, but the recipe here substitutes juice made from spinach leaves, which are similar to the deep green color and taste of mugworts. The spinach juice is meant to lend a somewhat herbal flavor to the rice cake, which might otherwise be cloyingly sweet. Another option, if desired, is to substitute 1 tsp matcha or green tea powder, though this is not authentically Chinese.

1 handful spinach, washed
⅛ tsp salt
2 cups water (only ¾ cup will be used after boiling)
1 cup Mochiko sweet rice flour*
¼ cup sugar
8 oz. red bean paste, refrigerated until ready to use (can be found in Asian grocery stores or in specialty food stores)
cornstarch for dusting

Boil the spinach leaves and salt in the water for five minutes, until the water has turned green. Drain spinach, conserving the water, and throw away spinach (or use it for another meal). Mix ¾ cup of spinach water, sugar, and Mochiko rice flour together in a glass bowl, adding more of the spinach water if the mixture is too dry. Transfer the bowl to a steamer and steam for twenty minutes. Remove the rice mixture from the steamer, and while it is still hot, roll pieces of it into small balls, making an indentation in the center of each. Fill the indentation with the cold red bean paste (keeping it cold should allow for easier handling), and then roll the rice cake around the bean paste filling. Shape into round balls of about 1 inch diameter each; dust each cake with cornstarch so they don't stick together.

---

*The recipe offered here uses rice cake flour; rice cakes are traditionally made from pounding rice for a half hour or so with a wooden mallet, whereby the starches break down and the rice becomes glutinous. Most modern kitchens take the shortcut of using premade sweet rice flour.

food, I am eating world matter in general, and in so doing, I truly and in reality find the world within me and myself in the world, I become a part of it."[22] Food then—and bread in particular—connects the living and the dead. Perhaps it is no small irony that yeast needs sugar to thrive, fermenting rotting food to transform into something better, like wine or bread. The notion of the heavenly afterlife transforming rotting bones and decaying flesh mirrors the action of yeast converting raw materials into rich yeast breads.

Chinese Graveyard Foods and Rituals

In China food plays a prominent role in both the funeral ceremonies for the deceased and again afterward in remembrances of the dead.[23] When a person dies, a wake is often held before interment, and the family and friends sit with the body for the days between death and burial in order to deter any evil spirits and to help guide the deceased in his or her journey to the afterlife. Until the burial, the family is expected to maintain a vegetarian diet to honor the deceased, in addition to keeping a simple lifestyle in dress and activity. In China meat was traditionally considered a luxury item that connoted status, and even today it is generally expected that the family and close relatives of the deceased refrain from eating meat following a death. In more ancient times, this practice also allowed the family to put its money toward the expenses of purchasing meat for the funeral. This is not so much an issue today, but refraining from eating meat until the funeral itself is still commonly observed, and some believe that eating meat can be seen by the gods as impure because it contains blood. Abstaining from meat until the funeral ceremony also provided an opportunity to demonstrate one's filial piety through the offerings of luxury items to the deceased, which revealed both the importance of the deceased and the social status of the mourners within the community.

Key among the offerings made at the grave site are raw rice and wine, though in many areas of China—particularly in ancient China—millet (and now noodles) was more frequently offered, as rice was considered a luxury crop because of its heavy dependence (like sugar's) on labor. Fernández-Armesto writes that "rice became a symbol of abundance and a mainstay of the menu in a process inseparable from the making of China—a process of expansion and acculturation which fused two contrasting environments."[24] Today, though, rice is common, and it is traditional to offer a bowl of raw rice at the grave site. The offering of raw rice indicates the transition of the deceased into the realm of the dead; since the dead are no longer living, they no longer need the same preparations of food as do the living, and they can consume food in its raw state. This is also done for pragmatic reasons, as the rice is cooked and consumed by the living after it has been offered to the dead. Here the dead are shown preference over the living by being given the first meal of the rice before it is cooked or eaten. The serving of raw rice, in many ways, thus reveals the importance and role of the dead in the realm of the living. Other dishes, however, are either prepared twice (such as the twice-cooked pork dish described in chapter 1) or are prepared in such a way that they will not spoil while being offered to the dead. Qing Ming rice cakes (above) are one such foodstuff, since the starches of the rice are broken down through both cooking and additional preparation. The addition of sugar acts as a preservative for the sweet rice cakes, which are portable and will last about a week without spoiling.

Tea and wine are generally beverages that reflect hospitality exchanges between host and guest, and they are used to reflect the continuing relationship between the deceased and the living. The offering of food and drinks to the deceased allows the living to demonstrate their transactional relationship with the deceased by promising, through carefully prepared food offerings, that the living will continue to care for the dead. In return, it is believed that the dead will also look after the living, interceding with the gods in their living relatives' behalf. This hospitality exchange fits perhaps most closely with the Catholic view of purgatory, in which the living need to take care of the dead during their liminal state, and, in return, the dead offer protection (and sometimes patronage) to the living. The hospitality exchange is not meant to include, but to limit, define, and exclude— clearly delineating, through the exchange, who is part of the group and who is not. Participating in these exchanges affirms these familial and clan identities and allows the living to reaffirm their own social ties and kinship networks.

All the food offerings and incense are presented on a table set up next to the grave site, and both the table and its placement symbolize the ongoing presence of the dead in the world of the living. The table is where the living are nourished, but it is also where the dead are now nourished alongside them. Besides the foodstuffs, offerings of money and cardboard representations of necessities (such as an elaborate cardboard home, car, iPhone, iPad, etc.) are burned at the graveside to aid the deceased in his or her journey to the afterlife. Finally, those who have attended the funeral will be given a candy of brown rock sugar upon their departure, as a gesture meant to "sweeten the sting of death." This rock candy plays a role similar to that of Halloween candy in the United States and the sugar skulls in Mexico. The candy is meant to be consumed before going home to prevent negative thoughts or sad spirits to follow one home from the funeral. A belief in ghosts remains highly prevalent in modern China, and many practices surrounding death reflect these beliefs.[25] (One example is the placing of a mirror on one's front door to prevent a ghost from entering one's home when a death has occurred nearby; apparently, the ghost will be frightened by its reflection and flee.) Sugar, through candy, helps guard against the pollution generated by a funeral while acting as a deterrent to the negative effects of ghosts.

Qing Ming and Chinese Remembrance of the Dead

Following the funeral, families continue to make food offerings at the grave (or to the ancestral tablet located in the home—or both) on the anniversary of the death of the deceased, at the Chinese New Year, and again in the annual Qing Ming festival, a sort of Chinese memorial day that closely resembles the American Thanksgiving and Memorial Day all wrapped up in one. For all these, food and wine offerings are made at the site of the grave, the grave is swept clean and tended, wine is poured into cups and left on the tombstones, and food is offered and then consumed by the family on behalf of, for, and "with" the dead. The individual grave site thus becomes transformed into a social space though the act of eating. When the living enact traditional hospitality rituals at the grave, the dead are able once again to partake in the realm of the living, and their graves become woven into the social fabric of the Chinese community.

The practice of leaving food during informal graveside visits is more intimate than the observance at formal Chinese holidays and often reflects the personal preferences of the dead. At the Chinese American cemetery in Honolulu, Hawaii, for example, hamburgers, Spam musubi, French fries, soda, and sweets are often left on the graves for the deceased, along with the more usual offerings of flowers and balloons. Here food is meant as a way to maintain the relationship with the deceased and to reintegrate them into the world, and the food gifts left at these graves are markedly personal rather than ritualistic in nature.

In contrast to grave-site food gifts left throughout the year, the Qing Ming offerings follow specific precepts that mark time through ritualistic foods and reflect a more religious motive. Fernández-Armesto writes, "Dishes to celebrate the completion of the harvest and tempt the souls of the dead to earth . . . [are] elaborately prepared and of uncompromising purity."[26] Like the Thanksgiving meal in American culture, the food gifts offered at the grave during Qing Ming reflect the first gifts of the spring harvest; these ritually recognized foods affirm the role and importance of the Chinese ancestors. The foods are not merely for the ancestors to consume, but are a symbolic acknowledgment by the living of the dependence of the living on the dead for their welfare; these prescribed foods, drinks, and rituals also reenact the interchange between the living and the dead. In the United States the Thanksgiving meal is not merely an opportunity to gather family and friends and eat a commonly prescribed meal of turkey, stuffing, and traditional side dishes; it is also a cultural reenactment of the (largely invented) story of the American colonists' first harvest celebration.[27] Participating in the Thanksgiving meal allows family members and friends to reaffirm and partake in civic rituals of national identity, while also confirming family identity through shared food rituals. Qing Ming functions similarly. Qing Ming involves a prescribed set of foods that are displayed, organized, and symbolically offered by the living to the deceased at the tombstone, after which the deceased eats first, and then is joined in consumption by the family. In this way, the meal's traditions reassert clan and familial identity, while also inviting the dead to participate. The family members are expected to physically return to the ancestral tomb from wherever they are living to celebrate Qing Ming.[28]

Only cold foods are eaten on Qing Ming, a tradition stemming from the pragmatic necessity of having to take foods to the ancestral graves that were often not close to home, which required that foods be both portable and unlikely to spoil. Ritual foods of rice cakes, *zhongzi* (a savory dish made with beans, lotus roots, and rice, then wrapped in banana leaves for mobility), and wine are the distinguishing foods of the Qing Ming festival, though there are local specialties also served in different locales.

Conclusion: Dying to Eat or Dying to Decay

The dead map their place on the world through the material presence of food. Just as food nourishes the living, it sustains the dead, either through the memories of the living as they continue as participants in their social world (as in the United States), or by providing a material conduit to nourish the dead in their afterlife (as in Mexico and China). The living also map their place in the world through sustaining their relations to the dead. By tending the graves of the dead and making food offerings to the dead, the living assure themselves that they are in fact not dead, and they place themselves firmly in a family lineage through treasured recipes and their accompanying narratives. Food reminds the living of their place in history through materiality and kinship. In this brief comparison a core difference between the relationships between food and death is highlighted. In Mexico and China, food serves as a bridge to the afterlife—because of purgatory in Mexican Catholicism and the bureaucratic necessities of the Chinese afterlife, food serves as a way for the living to continue to interact with the dead. In both Mexico and China, the dead depend on the living to help them navigate their afterlives, compelling the living to remember the dead and tend to them. The relationship between the dead and the living is a reciprocal one, in which food and wine serve as intercessory materials between the two realms. To forget to feed the dead equates to forgetting the dead. The dead, through food, are able to assert their place in the world, no longer lingering in the liminal state occupied by ghosts, forgotten ancestors, and spirits. This differs greatly from the function of food in the American example, in which food is used to sustain the living while they remember the dead. Characteristic American funeral food, such as casseroles and sheetcakes, reorients the bereaved into the community after the departure of the deceased and reassures the bereaved that they will be able to renegotiate their lives without the dead playing a part in them.

Hospitality food exchanges in funerals and memorialization rituals in all three cases serve to underscore the roles of both the deceased and the bereaved in society. The quantity and quality of foods in all three cases reveal the status of the deceased, while reinforcing the roles of the community in relationship to both the deceased and the bereaved. Preparation and consumption are nearly as important as the hospitality exchange that occurs between the living and the dead. In the act of preparing the food, one must first secure the ingredients, prepare them for cooking, and then transform the food into the dish that will be offered to be eaten. Cooking is a transformative act that changes the very nature of the food, altering it through fire and heat. It is also a ritualistic act that recalls previous preparations and takes note of small adjustments necessary to improve the product (the oven should be turned down twenty-five degrees, ham should be substituted for bacon, and the like). Richard Wrangham argues that cooking not only transforms food into biological energy, but also transforms ritual space, time, and divisions of labor.[29]

Space and place are another key difference found in the funeral feasts and memorialization acts of these three cultures. In the United States, the funeral feast is generally located in the home of the deceased and is seen as the first step to reintegrating the bereaved into a world that no longer contains the deceased. It is a restructuring of the social network of the bereaved without the deceased. Holding the funeral feast in the home of the deceased reinforces this function. In Mexican funeral feasts and Chinese rites for the dead, the dead are included in the feasting through a symbolic invitation for the dead to continue to participate in the act of eating. Many times, a small table is even brought to the graveyard to accommodate the dead's place at the table, and to give them a place at which to eat. More generally, the dead are present because they are specifically accommodated in the funeral and memorialization rituals as though they are active participants. In the Mexican funeral, the deceased is fed all his favorite foods and drinks, along with cigarettes or any other special treats. And the same holds true for the Chinese case. The decedent is present at her funeral and expects to be fed (clothed, given money, and so on); for the living, not to do so will result in a tenuous relationship between the living and the dead.

Consumption plays a pivotal role in all these situations: food and the body (through either its presence or its absence) are central actors. The preparing of food ties one to one's past—to the dead themselves and to the foods they liked when they were living—but it is in the act of consuming food that the living are able to assert their difference from the dead and thus reaffirm life. The very act of eating reminds me that I am not dead yet. Preparing, cooking, and eating food are all acts of the living, though the dead are often remembered in, and embodied through, these acts.

Food becomes the ultimate *Dasein,* the ultimate affirmation of life. It is little wonder, then, that food becomes a central actor of religious ceremonies regarding afterlives. The dead who need to be nourished can still be viewed as alive, even in their altered states. To eat is to live. It is in the area of consumption that the three cases most strongly differ. In the American example (really, Protestant Texas), families and friends gather to recount stories of the dead and place them firmly in their shared histories and social networks, while sharing a meal that is communal, portable, and convenient. The intent of the meal is to remember the dead, but not to feed them. In the Mexican Catholic and traditional Chinese examples, family and friends prepare food to be fed to the deceased during their wake and funeral, and afterward at regular memorialization rituals that mark time and shared social space between the living and the dead. Food not only nourishes the dead, but helps sustain and reinforce their relationships with the living. The dead eat and live, just like the living. Sugar, whether in raw form (as sugar skulls or brown rock candy), or transformed into yeast in bread (pan de muerto) or alcohol (served at the graves in both Mexico and China), plays an active role in sustaining the connection between this world and the next. One could argue, however, that sugar in its raw form is intended primarily for the world of the living, while it is the transformation of sugar (through fermentation) that sustains the dead. Transformation remains deeply linked to consumption in both the Mexican and Chinese contexts.

Notes

1. Beyond the scope of this chapter, but absolutely vital to the understanding of the role of sugar in a study of death, is Vincent Brown's work "Eating the Dead: Consumption and Regeneration in the History of Sugar," in *Food and Foodways: History and Culture of Human Nourishment* 16, no. 2 (2008): 117–126. In this work Brown discusses the intersection between sugar and death by examining the slave trade. What is important here is to note the underlying association of status with sugar: that it was expensive and therefore bestowed status on anyone consuming it.

2. Sidney Wilfred Mintz, *Sweetness and Power: The Place of Sugar in Modern History* (New York: Viking, 1985), 124.

3. Fernández-Armesto writes, "Sugar was the only Atlantic product which could compete as a high value condiment with the spices of the east." Before that time, "sugar was an exotic condiment, properly classifiable with pepper, cin-

namon, nutmeg, cloves, and mace." Felipe Fernández-Armesto, *Food: A History* (London: Macmillan, 2001), 177, 206.

4. For more on this, see Shirley Lindenbaum, "The 'Last Course': Nutrition and Anthropology in Asia," in *Nutrition and Anthropology in Action,* ed. Thomas K. Fitzgerald (Assen: Van Gorcum, 1977), 141–155.

5. It is important here that one also remember the connection between sugar as a commodity and its consumption as it pertains to class connotations. William Roseberry writes, "Coffee and sugar belong to a small subset of commodities that can illuminate capitalist transformations in other ways in that they link consumption zones (and the rise of working and middle classes that consumed the particular products in ever increasing numbers) and productions zones in Latin America, the Caribbean, Africa, and Asia (and the peasants, slaves, and other rural toilers who grew, cut, or picked the products)." Roseberry, "The Rise of Yuppie Coffees and the Reimagination of Class in the United States," in *The Cultural Politics of Food and Eating,* ed. James L. Watson and Melissa L. Caldwell (Malden, Mass.: Blackwell, 2005), 135. For the commodities once inadequately termed "dessert foods" and now increasingly called "drug foods," Sidney Mintz offers a more arresting phrase—coffee, sugar, tea, and chocolate were "proletarian hunger killers." See Sidney W. Mintz, "Time, Sugar, and Sweetness," *Marxist Perspectives* 2, no. 4 (1978): 56–73.

6. Fernández-Armesto, *Food: A History,* 11.

7. Ibid., 34.

8. Elvin M. Jellinek, "The Symbolism of Drinking: A Culture-Historical Approach," *Journal of Studies on Alcohol* 38, no. 5 (1977): 852–866.

9. For an in-depth examination of alcohol and its association with death in the United States, Mexico, and China, see my article "Mothers and Spirits: Religious Identity, Alcohol, and Death," *Religions* 7, no. 7 (2016): 94.

10. I would argue that part of the reason for this cultural legacy (rather than a legacy of inheritance) lies in the fact that American women were traditionally not allowed to own property in their own names until 1839 (starting with the state of Mississippi). Thus, a women's inheritance was often cultural and of little economic consequence. Recipes became one way in which women could reassert their matrilineal ties and identity in a way that was not threatening to men.

11. Dundes writes: "For example, in the celebration of All Souls Day in Europe, respect is paid to the dead, that is, to the ancestors, to the *past.* (The same is true of All Saints Day inasmuch as saints are part of the past.) In the United States, the Halloween festival has been converted to a celebration for *children,* not parents. Though remains of departed spirits survive in the forms of ghosts and other creatures, memorial visits to the graves of ancestors have been replaced by parents giving treats to children who threaten to play pranks on them. . . . The emphasis is upon the child, the future, rather than upon the deceased ancestors, the past." Alan Dundes, *Interpreting Folklore* (Bloomington: Indiana University Press, 1980), 80; emphasis in original.

12. My graduate assistant Tim Orr rightly points out the use of costumes to "play" with the subject of death. He writes, "Costumes vary drastically but the vast majority seem, in some way, to see the children impersonating either dead "monsters" (zombies, mummies, vampires, etc.) or creatures associated with the dead (witches and demons)."

13. To highlight notable differences from a broader perspective, it is important to note that the comparison of the American, Mexican, and Chinese examples favors generalizations over details. A comprehensive analysis of Mexican funeral and memorialization practices, for example, reveals distinct regional differences, contrasts between urban and rural communities as well as mestizo and indigenous communities, varying practices among different classes, and so on. For more in-depth analyses of bereavement and memorialization practices in Mexico, the reader can start with Rosario Esteinou's "Death and Grief in Mexican Families," in *The World of Bereavement Cultural Perspectives on Death,* ed. Joanne Cacciatore and John DeFrain (New York: Springer, 2015), 131–145; Beth A. Conklin's *Consuming Grief: Compassionate Cannibalism in an Amazonian Society* (Austin: University of Texas Press, 2001); and Anne C. Woodrick's "A Lifetime of Mourning: Grief Work among Yucatec Maya Women," *Ethos* 23, no. 4 (1995): 401–423. These offer excellent ethnographic analyses of indigenous grief traditions. For the purposes of this chapter, however, I have offered a brief overview and introduction to nearly universal practices, focusing on contemporary Mexican and Mexican Catholic traditions.

14. Hispanic funeral homes in the United States have been quick to capitalize on this trend, and most funeral homes geared toward the Hispanic market now offer catering services in addition to the other services of embalming and body disposal.

15. The exception to this may be the rise of material memorials, which extend to ghost tales and folklore, in which the dead are remapped onto the imaginations of the living. For a more detailed causative analysis of the rise of material memorials, see my book, *Virtual Afterlives: Grieving the Dead in the Twenty-first Century* (Lexington: University Press of Kentucky, 2014).

16. See Stanley Brandes's article "The Day of the Dead, Halloween, and the Quest for Mexican National Identity," *Journal of American Folklore* (1998): 359–380, for more on this.

17. See Jacques Le Goff, *The Birth of Purgatory,* trans. Arthur Goldhammer (Chicago: University of Chicago Press, 1986), who argues that purgatory and the practices associated with it did not fully emerge until the twelfth century.

18. For an in-depth history of Mexico's Day of the Dead, see Stanley Brandes, "Iconography in Mexico's Day of the Dead: Origins and Meaning," *Ethnohistory* 45, no. 2 (1998): 181–218.

19. For more on this, see Andrew R. Chesnut. *Devoted to Death: Santa Muerte, the Skeleton Saint* (New York: Oxford University Press, 2011).

20. Stanley Brandes. *Skulls to the Living, Bread to the Dead: the Day of the Dead in Mexico and Beyond* (Malden, Mass.: John Wiley & Sons, 2006).

21. Angel F. Méndez Montoya, *The Theology of Food: Eating and the Eucharist* (Malden, Mass.: Wiley-Blackwell, 2009), 85.

22. Sergei Bulgakov, *Philosophy of Economy: The World as Household,* trans. and ed. Catherine Evtuhov (New Haven: Yale University Press, 2000),103.

23. As in the Mexican example, there are more specific ethnographies discussing mourning and memorialization rituals in China, which vary according to region, ethnicity, and along urban-rural divides. For in-depth studies, see Kaming Wu's "Monuments of Grief: Village Politics and Memory in Post-Socialist Rural China," *Ethnology* 46, no. 1 (2007): 41, and Erik Mueggler's "The Poetics of Grief and the Price of Hemp in Southwest China," *Journal of Asian Studies* 57, no. 4 (1998): 979–1008. Also of interest is Erik Mueggler's book *The Age of Wild Ghosts: Memory, Violence, and Place in Southwest China* (Berkeley: University of California Press, 2001).

24. Fernández-Armesto, *Food: A History,* 106.

25. Keping Wu writes that the belief in ghosts remains highly prevalent in urban Chinese culture, and perhaps this belief persists because it reflects modern urban anxieties. For more on this, see Keping Wu, "Ghost City: Religion, Urbanization and Spatial Anxieties in Contemporary China," *Geoforum* 65 (2015): 243–245. Also see Mueggler, *The Age of Wild Ghosts.*

26. Fernández-Armesto. *Food: A History,* 127.

27. Jon D. Holtzman, "Food and Memory," *Annual Review of Anthropology* 35 (2006): 369.

28. In recent years, the People's Republic of China has had issues with the massive influx of travel traffic at Qing Ming, and it now promotes "virtual Qing Ming ceremonies" as part of its impetus to decrease Qing Ming travel. State-run cemeteries offer "green" incentives to encourage people to move their Qing Ming practices online, where they can offer virtual cups of wine or cigarettes, sing prayers or songs, and order "Real Life" flowers or request the burning of paper money and other objects at the grave site itself. Liu Lu, "Virtual Memorial," *China Daily USA,* April 1, 2011, *http://usa.chinadaily.com.cn/life/2011-04/01/content_12262543.htm*, accessed December 25, 2016.

29. See Richard W. Wrangham, *Catching Fire: How Cooking Made Us Human* (New York: Basic Books, 2009).

Bibliography

Alkon, Alison Hope, and Julia Agyeman, eds. *Cultivating Food Justice: Race, Class, and Sustainability.* Cambridge: MIT Press, 2011.
Anderson, Eugene. *The Food of China.* New Haven: Yale University Press, 1988.

Arnold, Philip P., ed. "Religious Dimensions of Food." Special Issue of *Journal of Ritual Studies* 14, no. 1 (2000): 4–22.

Atkins, Peter, and Ian Bowler. *Food in Society: Economy, Culture, Geography.* London: Hodder Education, 2001.

Avieli, Nir. "Feasting with the Living and the Dead: Food and Eating in Ancestor Worship Rituals in Hôi An." In *Modernity and Re-Enchantment: Religion in Post-revolutionary Vietnam,* edited by Philip Taylor, 121–160. Singapore: Institute of Southeast Asian Studies, 2007.

Bourdieu, Pierre. *Distinction: A Social Critique of the Judgment of Taste.* Cambridge: Harvard University Press, 1984.

Brandes, Stanley. "The Day of the Dead, Halloween, and the Quest for Mexican National Identity." *Journal of American Folklore* (1998): 359–380.

———. "Iconography in Mexico's Day of the Dead: Origins and Meaning." *Ethnohistory* 45, no. 2 (1998): 181–218.

———. *Skulls to the Living, Bread to the Dead: The Day of the Dead in Mexico and Beyond.* Malden, Mass.: John Wiley & Sons, 2006.

———. "Sugar, Colonialism, and Death: On the Origins of Mexico's Day of the Dead." *Comparative Studies in Society and History* 39, no. 2 (1997): 270–299.

Brown, Vincent. "Eating the Dead: Consumption and Regeneration in the History of Sugar." *Food and Foodways: History and Culture of Human Nourishment* 16, no. 2 (2008): 117–126.

Bulgakov, Sergei. *Philosophy of Economy: The World as Household,* translated and edited by Catherine Evtuhov. New Haven: Yale University Press, 2000.

Bynum, Caroline Walker. *Holy Feast, Holy Fast: The Religious Significance of Food to Medieval Women.* Berkeley: University of California Press, 1987.

Cann, Candi K. *Virtual Afterlives: Grieving the Dead in the Twenty-first Century.* Lexington: University Press of Kentucky, 2014.

Carrasco, David. "Cosmic Jaws: We Eat the Gods and the Gods Eat Us." *Journal of the American Academy of Religion* 63, no. 3 (1995): 429–463.

Catto, Rebecca. "Graham Harvey, Food, Sex and Strangers: Understanding Religion as Everyday Life." *Theology* 117, no. 4 (2014): 294–295.

Chang, Kwang-chih, ed. *Food in Chinese Culture: Anthropological and Historical Perspectives.* New Haven: Yale University Press, 1977.

Chesnut, R. Andrew. *Devoted to Death: Santa Muerte, the Skeleton Saint.* New York: Oxford University Press, 2011.

Conklin, Beth A. *Consuming Grief: Compassionate Cannibalism in an Amazonian Society.* Austin: University of Texas Press, 2001.

Coveney, John. *Food, Morals and Meaning: The Pleasure and Anxiety of Eating.* 2nd edition. New York: Routledge, 2006.

Counihan, Carole, and Penny Van Esterik, eds. *Food and Culture: A Reader.* New York: Routledge, 2013.

Dodson, Jualynne E., and Cheryl Townsend Gilkes. "'There's Nothing Like Church Food': Food and the U.S. Afro-Christian Tradition: Re-Membering

Community and Feeding the Embodied S/spirit(s)." *Journal of the American Academy of Religion* 63, no. 3 (1995): 519–538.

Dundes, Alan. *Interpreting Folklore.* Bloomington: Indiana University Press, 1980.

Dwyer, Graham. "Krishna Prasadam: The Transformative Power of Sanctified Food in the Krishna Consciousness Movement." *Religions of South Asia* 4, no. 1 (2010): 89–104.

Esteinou, Rosario. "Death and Grief in Mexican Families." In *The World of Bereavement: Cultural Perspectives on Death,* edited by Joanne Cacciatore and John DeFrain, 131–145. New York: Springer, 2015.

Feeley-Harnik, Gillian. "Religion and Food: An Anthropological Perspective." *Journal of the American Academy of Religion* 63, no. 3 (1995): 565–582.

Fernández-Armesto, Felipe. *Food: A History.* London: Macmillan, 2001.

———. *Near a Thousand Tables: A History of Food.* New York: Simon and Schuster, 2002.

Fuller, Robert C. "Wine, Symbolic Boundary Setting, and American Religious Communities." *Journal of the American Academy of Religion* 63, no. 3 (1995): 497–517.

Greenspoon, Leonard J., et al., eds. *Food and Judaism.* Omaha: Creighton University Press, 2005.

Griffith, R. Marie. *Born Again Bodies: Flesh and Spirit in American Christianity.* Berkeley: University of California Press, 2004.

Gutiérrez, Jorge R. *The Book of Life,* 2014. Animated film. www.bookoflifemovie.com/, accessed May 15, 2015.

Holtzman, Jon D. "Food and Memory." *Annual Review of Anthropology* 35 (2006): 361–378.

Houghton, Azula A., and Frederic J. Boersma. "The Loss-Grief Connection in Susto." *Ethnology* 27, no. 2 (1988): 145–154.

Ingham, John M. *Mary, Michael, and Lucifer: Folk Catholicism in Central Mexico.* Austin: University of Texas Press, 1986.

Jellinek, Elvin M. "The Symbolism of Drinking: A Culture-Historical Approach." *Journal of Studies on Alcohol* 38, no. 5 (1977): 852–866.

Khare, Ravindra S. "Anna." In *The Hindu World,* edited by Sushil Mittal and Gene Thursby, 407–428. New York: Routledge, 2004.

———, ed. *The Eternal Food: Gastronomic Ideas and Experiences of Hindus and Buddhists.* Albany: State University of New York Press, 1992.

Khare, Ravindra S., and M. S. A. Rao, eds. *Food, Society, and Culture: Aspects in South Asian Food Systems.* Durham, N.C.: Carolina Academic Press, 1986.

Koepping, Elizabeth. *Food, Friends and Funerals: On Lived Religion.* Berlin: Lit Verlag, 2008.

Korsmeyer, Carolyn, ed. *The Taste Culture Reader: Experiencing Food and Drink.* New York: Berg, 2005.

Kraemer, David. *Jewish Eating and Identity through the Ages.* New York: Routledge, 2007.

Lalande, Kathleen M., and George A. Bonanno. "Culture and Continuing Bonds: A Prospective Comparison of Bereavement in the United States and the People's Republic of China." *Death Studies* 30, no. 4 (2006): 303–324.

Le Goff, Jacques. *The Birth of Purgatory.* Translated by Arthur Goldhammer. Chicago: University of Chicago Press, 1986.

Leland, John. "It's My Funeral and I'll Serve Ice Cream If I Want To." *New York Times,* July 20, 2006.

Lepine, David. "'High Solemn Ceremonies': The Funerary Practice of the Late Medieval English Higher Clergy." *Journal of Ecclesiastical History* 61, no. 1 (2010): 18–39.

Lindenbaum, Shirley. "The 'Last Course': Nutrition and Anthropology in Asia." In *Nutrition and Anthropology in Action,* edited by Thomas K. Fitzgerald, 141–155. Assen: Van Gorcum, 1977.

Liu Lu, "Virtual Memorial," *China Daily USA,* April 1, 2011. *http://usa.chinadaily.com.cn/life/2011-04/01/content_12262543.htm,* accessed December 25, 2016.

Long, Lucy M. "Learning to Listen to the Food Voice: Recipes as Expressions of Identity and Carriers of Memory." *Food Culture and Society* 7, no. 1 (2004): 118–122.

López-García, Julian. "Estética y lógica social en las mesas para las almas maya-chortís." *Bulletin de la Société Suisse des Américanistes* 64–65 (2000): 125–30.

Manalansan, Martin, Anita Manmur, and Robert Ku, eds. *Eating Asian America: A Food Studies Reader.* New York: New York University Press, 2013.

McGowan, Andrew Brian. *Ascetic Eucharists: Food and Drink in Early Christian Ritual Meals.* Oxford: Clarendon Press, 1999.

———. "Food, Ritual, and Power." In *A People's History of Christianity: Late Ancient Christianity,* edited by Virginia Burrus, 145–164. Minneapolis: Augsburg Fortress, 2005.

McLaren, Anne Elizabeth. *Performing Grief: Bridal Laments in Rural China.* Honolulu: University of Hawai'i Press, 2008.

Méndez Montoya, Angel F. *The Theology of Food: Eating and the Eucharist.* Malden, Mass.: Wiley-Blackwell, 2009.

Miles, Margaret R., ed. "Food and Religion." Special Issue of *Journal of the American Academy of Religion* 63, no. 3 (1995).

Mintz, Sidney Wilfred. *Sweetness and Power: The Place of Sugar in Modern History.* New York: Viking, 1985.

———. "Time, Sugar and Sweetness." *Marxist Perspectives* 2, no. 4 (1978): 56–73.

Morán, Elizabeth. "Feasts for the Gods: Food and Consumption in Aztec Veintena Rituals." *Latin American Indian Literatures Journal* 26, no. 2 (2010): 116–139.

Mueggler, Erik. *The Age of Wild Ghosts: Memory, Violence, and Place in Southwest China.* Berkeley: University of California Press, 2001.

———. "The Poetics of Grief and the Price of Hemp in Southwest China." *Journal of Asian Studies* 57, no. 4 (1998): 979–1008.

Norman, Corrie E. "Food and Religion." In *The Oxford Handbook of Food History,* edited by Jeffrey M. Pilcher, 409–427. New York: Oxford University Press, 2012.

———. "Religion and Food." In *The New Encyclopedia of Southern Culture,* vol. 7, *Foodways,* edited by John T. Edge, 95–100 (Chapel Hill: University of North Carolina Press, 2007).

Pearson, Anne Mackenzie. *Because It Gives Me Peace of Mind: Ritual Fasts in the Religious Lives of Hindu Women.* Albany: State University of New York Press, 1996.

Robbins, Kathleen. "The Hostess Project." *Journal of Visual Culture* 7, no. 3 (2008): 335–348.

Roseberry, William. "The Rise of Yuppie Coffees and the Reimagination of Class in the United States." In *The Cultural Politics of Food and Eating,* edited by James L. Watson and Melissa L. Caldwell, 122–143. Malden, Mass.: Blackwell, 2005.

Rosenthal, Stephen F. "Food for Thought: Kosher Fraud Laws and the Religion Clauses of the First Amendment." *George Washington Law Review* 65 (1997): 951.

Sack, Daniel. *Whitebread Protestants: Food and Religion in American Culture.* New York: St. Martin's, 2000.

Seraïdari, Katerina. "Mourier et renaître en Grèce: Quand les femmes cuisinent les *Kolliva.*" *Terrain* 45 (2005): 153–166.

Smith, Dennis E. *From Symposium to Eucharist: The Banquet in the Early Christian World.* Minneapolis: Augsburg Fortress, 2003.

Sterckx, Roel, ed. *Of Tripod and Palate: Food, Politics, and Religion in Traditional China.* New York: Palgrave Macmillan, 2004.

Sutton, David E. "Food and the Senses." *Annual Review of Anthropology* 39 (October 2010): 209–223.

Tomkins, Kyla Wazana. *Racial Indigestion: Eating Bodies in the 19th Century.* New York: New York University Press, 2012.

Watson, James L., and Melissa L. Caldwell, eds. *The Cultural Politics of Food and Eating.* Malden, Mass.: Blackwell, 2005.

Woodrick, Anne C. "A Lifetime of Mourning: Grief Work among Yucatec Maya Women." *Ethos* 23, no. 4 (1995): 401–423.

Wrangham, Richard W. *Catching Fire: How Cooking Made Us Human.* New York: Basic Books, 2009.

Wu, Ka-ming. "Monuments of Grief: Village Politics and Memory in Post-Socialist Rural China." *Ethnology* 46, no. 1 (2007): 41–55.

Wu, Keping. "'Ghost City': Religion, Urbanization and Spatial Anxieties in Contemporary China." *Geoforum* 65 (2015): 243–245.

Zeller, Benjamin E. Review of *Eat and Be Satisfied: A Social History of Jewish Food* by John Cooper. *Food, Culture and Society: An International Journal of Multidisciplinary Research* 12, no. 1 (2009): 114–117.

Zeller, Benjamin, Marie Dallam, Reid Neilson, and Nora Rubel, eds. *Religion, Food, and Eating in North America.* New York: Columbia University Press, 2014.

Part 2

Eating After

Food and Drink in Bereavement and Remembrance

4

Funeral Food as Resurrection in the American South

Joshua Graham

Introduction

The funeral period in the American South is marked by gifts of food from members of the extended family and the community at large. Certain dishes are traditionally served as funeral food and often have a fuller name, usually a possessive matronymic (e.g., Maw Maw's Chess Pie), a highly gendered phenomenon, which has not been addressed in the funeral context by the scholarly community.[1] The attachment of the deceased's name to an iconic dish is most readily explained by the continuing bonds theory, in which the bereaved actively seek to maintain or reclaim connections with the deceased.[2]

In addition, in the American South funerals themselves keep the long-departed socially alive through the use of their recipes; thus, traditions marking one person's recent death have the net effect of resurrecting the social influence of the long-dead. There is a collapsing of meaning here: the recently dead provide a conversational gateway to the long-dead and sometimes stand in for them. The handing down and sharing of funeral food recipes, lore, and memories both help maintain strong family and community bonds and stave off individual social death—an anthropological concept that these funeral food traditions force us to reevaluate and expand the definition for. Material-semiotic methods and theories such as actor-network theory and the theory of material-semiotic actors describe ways in which objects, up to and including food and the dead, exert agency over and with the living. But when a memorial dish is not prepared on a regular basis, the individual being memorialized is at risk of

Maw Maw Wallace's Chess Pie*

2–4 tbsp flour (depending on humidity)
⅛ tsp salt
1½ cups white sugar
¼ lb butter (1 stick)
3 eggs
1 tbsp vanilla
4 tbsp buttermilk
1 unbaked pie shell

Preheat oven to 300°F. Mix flour, salt, and sugar. Melt butter and add to sugar mixture. Mix well. Beat eggs and add to sugar mixture, along with vanilla and buttermilk. Pour into unbaked pie shell. Bake 40–50 minutes.

---

*This was basically my family recipe, which I received when I moved out of my childhood home for university.

Women of a community in north Georgia laying out food after a bereavement in the late 1970s.

social death—that is, not only being forgotten by individuals, but also ceasing to exert influence and exercise agency within a particular social group—if other continuing bonds are not in place. Therefore, a broader conceptual understanding of social death is needed.[3] To determine this understanding, I conducted two periods of observational fieldwork and conducted a series of interviews. The study's subjects were twenty-one adult, white-identifying, middle- to working-class members of an extended north Georgia community. The interviews consisted of long narrative conversations, directed mainly by the participants, about the topic of funeral food and their personal experiences thereof.

Funeral food gifts in the South also act as an extension of a region's dominant Protestant identity, and in certain cases the particular dishes offered "perform" a specific denomination—that is, in the South, the acts of preparing, serving, and consuming particular dishes at particular significant moments help create and renew the identity of Baptists, Episcopalians, or other denominations. Furthermore, these acts must be observed by the community and those on the fringes of and outside the community to create and renew this identity effectively; the acts of performing for observation and observing are critical to the creation of identity through funeral food traditions. But though these dishes may be understood in denominational terms (e.g., a typically Episcopalian dish), class has long been tied to denominational membership in the American South and may be the actual metric under discussion.[4] Thus, in the South funeral food mediates a broad range of social relationships, from family to faith community to the community at large, and calls on a larger than usual range of actors, including the living and the dead.

Southern Funeral Foods: An Overview

Certain dishes are traditionally served as funeral food, sometimes achieving their apotheosis in the funeral context. Hearty, homemade dishes with long shelf lives, such as desserts, biscuits, fried chicken, baked ham, and a multitude of casseroles, typify funeral food offerings in the region, and chess pie, a very sweet dessert of indeterminate origin, in particular is served throughout the region known as the Deep South.[5] When writing about the close association between death and southern cookbooks, Donna Lee Brien, an Australian academic, describes chess pie as a lemon tart, although in my personal experience chess pie does not usually have lemon among its ingredients, and Sidney Saylor Farr describes chess pie as "a very rich, thin pie," a fair, if not very illuminating, assessment.[6] John Lachs's description may capture the dish best: "Chess pie can be flawed in a variety of ways. The crust may be too soft; the taste, not sweet enough; the consistency of the filling, too loose."[7] Chess pie is a particular specialty of my own family, and while I may not agree entirely with the definitions of chess pie uncovered in the academic literature, Brien's other observations ring true. Drawing on ancillary writings in cookbooks, Brien notes that chess pie was referred to by the person contributing the recipe as funeral pie.[8] This fits with funeral traditions in the region, where with death comes hunger—not existential hunger, or a hunger for answers, comfort, or connection: rather, death in the American South is marked by an abundance of food. As I have observed both from my fieldwork and in personal, autoethnographic experience, from the moment that the wider community is informed of a death, community members and extended family produce copious amounts of food and take it to the bereaved, with whom they share stories of death and the dead, talk about the funeral, and eat. But in the midst of all this, they talk about the food. This is most apparent in the meal directly following the interment ceremony. In their fictionalized book of humor and recipes, *Being Dead Is No Excuse: The Official Southern Ladies Guide to Hosting the Perfect Funeral,* Geyden Metcalfe and Charlotte Hays describe the situation thus: "During the reception, we gossip, tell stories about the deceased, and maybe indulge in a toddy or two. . . . You can't bury a self-respecting Deltan without certain foods. Chief amongst these is tomato aspic with homemade mayonnaise . . . closely followed by Aunt Hebe's Coconut Cake, and Virginia's Butterbeans."[9] And here I return to chess pie, because like Aunt Hebe's Coconut Cake, it too takes on a fuller name and the status of a proper noun, and with them a new function. At any other event the chess pie may remain unremarked upon; someone might comment on the taste, but the pie itself is not a point of discussion. When chess pie is transformed into funeral pie, however, the full name is used: in my family, Maw Maw Wallace's Chess Pie.[10] I never got to know Maw Maw Wallace in person, but I have learned about her at every funeral through the recipes she bequeathed to my family. This is not peculiar to my family, nor is it a regional trend. Scholars have remarked on the tendency to keep the dead active through living traditions elsewhere across the South, but the connection with food has been examined more often in pop culture publications than in academic literature. Joyce and Les Brown note that the tradition of naming dishes after their originators is a highly gendered recognition of artistry and a demand for acknowledgment of unique talents, but how that phenomenon relates to funeral food remains unexplored in the academic literature.[11] Thus, we must turn to pop culture and social media outlets to examine how people conceptualize funeral food.

Women as Guardians of Community

It does not take long, when one looks into this topic, to realize that women's voices still predominate in discussions of funeral food. One blogger, in a post about making a Coca-Cola cake for the meal following the burial of her husband's friend's grandmother, writes of her brother's confusion over the details of southern funeral food traditions.[12] A commenter on the blog writes that she contributes "to the funeral dinners at [her] (Methodist) church . . . whether I know the family or not. It's just the way I was raised."[13] Likewise, in an online column, Terri Evans discusses the fond memories and continued tradition of "Aunt Melba's butterscotch pie, or some of Granddaddy H'Earl's chess pie. If Granddaddy H'Earl were here today, I would still be unable to get the recipe for his chess pie. He always said, 'it was 'jes pie."[14] While this is a rare example of a man's memorialization in cookery, the memorial dish still centers on an individual who was key to the food's original production. Even while giving this masculine example, Evans addresses the strongly gendered aspects of this funeral tradition:

> When the crowds come to show their respect, they descend upon the grieving household, their favorite recipe prepared—in a dish of course, that need not be returned. A designated friend whose grief, while real, is not as great as that of the primary bereaved would meet the donators at the door. She (even now this is clearly a role for the women folk) accepts the comfort food, voices the appropriate clucking sounds of approval, makes note of who brought what, lest there be some confusion at the time of thank you notes, then heads off to find a place of honor for the contribution.[15]

A third blogger discusses the honor of being asked to join the small group of women from the local church that provides the bulk of the food for an unknown number of guests after a funeral.[16] Funeral food in the Deep South plays an active part in the social lives of both the living and the dead. As another blogger claims, "Food personifies a Southern funeral."[17]

Redefining Social Death in Light of Continuing Bonds

Academically, the attachment of a deceased person's name to an iconic dish is most easily explained by the continuing bonds theory, in which the bereaved actively seek to maintain or reclaim connections with the deceased in order to continue the relationship that existed before death.[18] This attempt is not exclusive to funerals, but to judge from the way food is discussed in southern cookbooks, cooking blogs, and other forms of social media, it seems most prominent at funerals. Even when dishes for other occasions have lost their matronymics, the matronymics for funeral foods linger on. Because continuing bonds is a well-researched area, insofar as anything in death and grief studies is, food is not an unfamiliar outlet for expression in the research.[19] Christine Valentine offers examples of similar eating habits acting as an aspect of continuing bonds narratives in England, and there is a strong body of literature about food that allows for continuing bonds when the living offer it to the dead for the deceased to enjoy.[20] More conceptually, food has been shown as both a primary point of loss and a point of continuing bonds to one's former culture in immigrant populations; this is important because, beyond merely providing a link to the departed, funeral food in the South creates and renews an identity both through this connection with the dead and by performing cultural identity in a way similar to immigrant populations' use of food to continue, discontinue, or mourn the cultural identity they left behind.[21] When the tradition of taking specific food items associated with the memory of specific people to funeral gatherings is interrupted or stopped, the physically dead but socially active members of the family and community are at risk of social death, a process not unlike the damage to immigrants' cultural identity that results from the loss of culturally significant dishes.

The current understanding of social death is overly limited. Stefan Timmermans and David Sudnow describe social death as the treatment

of a still-living person as a dead corpse.[22] This is fair as a functional assessment of the heroic resuscitation incidents Timmermans and Sudnow
discuss in their work, but as an overall description of social death, it is
deeply problematic. First of all, the valuation uncritically links physical
death with lack of agency. Likewise, there is also a claim that social
death is preferable to physical death in institutional settings. Michael
Mulkay and John Ernst attempt to insert more flexibility into the definition, but their focus remains on the social death of the still-living or
those nearing the transition to physical death, rather than the long-
dead.[23] I suggest that these definitions be broadened to include the notion that for the physically dead, who are remembered most frequently
through memorials, social death is the ultimate outcome when the process of continuing bonds ceases and the physically dead finally lose all
agency in the living world. This acknowledgment of objects such as
food, dead bodies, and the dead themselves as actors fits with material-
semiotic methods and theories presented by scholars such as Madeleine
Akrich and Bruno Latour in their work with actor-network theory, John
Law in his contributions to the same concept, and Donna Haraway in
her theory of material-semiotic actors.[24] Akrich, Latour, Law, and Haraway all describe ways in which objects, up to and including food and
the dead, have agency and exert that agency over the living, thus effectively broadening the concept of social death extensively enough to effectively change it. As long as the dead are still able to influence the
living, as Ross Jamieson's discussion of social death shows, they maintain agency and avoid social death, achieving something like Robert Lif-
ton's notion of symbolic immortality.[25] This process, however, is not
always smooth. In the American South, the serving of funeral dishes
named after the long-departed is a primary means of keeping that person socially active. When a memorial dish is not prepared on a regular
basis, the individual being memorialized can be forgotten if other continuing bonds are not in place; when this happens, the individual formerly memorialized and active becomes functionally socially dead. The
individual loses any agency or power to influence the social world. If the
dish is rediscovered, however, the individual has a chance of regaining
agency. This reclaiming of agency after social death is the social resurrection outlined by John Mason and pioneered by Orlando Patterson
and Ran Greenstein.[26]

Community Building and Christianity

The performance of individual identities and relationships is not the sole observable identity performance. As previously mentioned, women, often as members of local church congregations, provide the bulk of food gifts. This leads to social interactions involving funeral gifts in which both personal identity and church affiliation are performed. Metcalfe and Hays observe, "We [Southerners] take the food not because we regard death as the chance to throw a wingding—at least not officially—but because we want to express our sympathy, comfort the afflicted, and lessen the burden of having to feed out-of-town mourners who have descended upon the family to pay their last respects."[27] In interviews this sentiment was often summed up as "just the Christian thing to do." This particular notion of Christianity is both universally applied and not reflected on. While all informants in the sample had been raised in Protestant families and communities, those who still identified as Christian (more than 75 percent of the sample, which reflects general Christian religiosity trends in the greater community) assumed that the southern food gift tradition associated with funerals was common to all Christian mourning. This opinion was presented with no point of doctrine or belief to support it, but as a way to emphasize the interconnectedness of community. As Christian individuals living in a culturally Christian community, respondents noted a perception of interconnectedness with others that was displayed through such cultural traditions as this. Only those not participating in an ongoing Christian faith acknowledged an option for difference in funeral food traditions.

This perception of Christian universality may exist because women connected to church groups tend to perpetuate the traditions. One informant, a teacher named Karen, observed that when a teaching assistant with whom she worked had a death in the family, she and her coworkers coordinated to pool money to take a deli cold-cut platter and bread to the bereaved family. Karen went on to note, however, that if her relationship to the bereaved had been personal instead of professional, or if the bereaved had been part of her church community, her reaction would have been different. Karen explained that, in those more intimate cases, a women's Bible study group or a woman of the church group would have stepped in to coordinate the food gifts for the time surrounding the funeral. This planning would ensure both that enough food would be present for the extended event and that the food present would be, in the words of my informants, "appropriate" to the family and the funeral environment— that is, traditional to the occasion and matched to the family's size, tastes, or religious beliefs. A new dish, for instance, may not be appropriate if it does not conform to community standards for funerals. Karen also said that she assumed that this was happening in the teaching assistant's case, but as outsiders to the family's inner circle, she and her colleagues would have been unaware of it. For Karen, this lack of a more personal relationship and lack of knowledge of specific religious background made the "generic" gift of a deli tray more appropriate. But although this kind of intimacy stops at the bounds of the church community, in the context of funeral food, the church community itself becomes more inclusive. In separate interviews, two sisters, Bev and Denise, noted that the involvement of churchwomen extended to members of the congregation who had not been active participants in the church community for many years before they died. Another informant, Lee, reiterated this point, adding that in her church, several different women's groups rotated the responsibility for funeral food gifts and preparation so as not to unduly burden a single member or group in their community. Becky, an informant who no longer identifies with a specific denomination, noted that although she has been outside a specific church community for over twenty years, "The little old church ladies from the communities I grew up in still come if we have a death near them." She added that it is always the "church ladies" who bring the most food and try to manage the event, even if that management is unwanted. Funeral food gifts are thus a Maussian *prestation totale*, magically re-creating the social fabric to include the long-departed and create a bridge between the living and the dead for the recently departed to cross over.[28]

Denominational, Congregational, and Class Differences

Likewise, the informants all agreed that the food gifts that the church ladies provided were, as one informant described them, "normal foods but nice foods." This typically meant foods that would not be unusual to have as a part of a normal weekday meal, but were still considered "nice" because of either the cost of the ingredients or the time needed to make the dish. The specifics of what was meant by this concept of "normal but nice" varied by informant, however. Southern staples such as homemade biscuits and fried chicken were so abundant in descriptions that one informant asked rhetorically, "How can anyone die without fried chicken?" But the specifics of most dishes, from which casseroles were served to the types of cakes and side dishes, were attributed to denominational differences. Metcalfe and Hays dedicate an entire chapter, "The Methodists Ladies vs. the Episcopal Ladies," to discussing the differences between denominational funeral food gift patterns. In it they discuss how the more hidebound Episcopalians prefer aspic, small rolls, cheese straws, and fudge cake, all laid out and presented on recently polished silver, whereas the Methodists are summed up with the line "You can always tell when a Methodist dies—there are lots of casseroles."[29] Metcalfe and Hays go on to describe how popular and enjoyable, even to Episcopalians, the Methodists' "funeral goo" is. The term *funeral goo* categorizes portable communal dishes made with canned soups or Velveeta, a processed cheese used in dips and casseroles. The inclusion of these goos at funeral events offers a variety of functional options. The dishes themselves are reported in Metcalfe and Hays, on internet blogs and forums, and in interviews as both filling and comforting; they make it possible to feed a large crowd efficiently while providing a familiar dish conceptually connected to ideas of home. Because goos typically contain a variety of highly processed foods, they have a longer shelf life and are useful for longer events, where food temperature might otherwise be an issue. But it is important to keep in mind that, while Metcalfe and Hays discuss these dishes as denominational in character, class may actually be the important factor. Metcalfe and Hays refer to polished silver dishes at one event, strong markers of class but not actually defining Episcopalian symbols. Sean McCloud shows how class has long been tied to denominational membership in the American South and how that membership can substitute for class in vernacular conversations.[30] Socioeconomic class and the affordability and availability of particular serving dishes, utensils, ingredients, and foods— rather than denomination—form part of the greater narrative here.[31]

Metcalfe and Hays may admit that the subjects of their book partake in a toddy or two after the funeral, but their focus tends to be a humorous take on the social differences and rivalries between Methodists and Episcopalians in their area of the Mississippi Delta.[32] In interviews, however, the public consumption of or abstention from alcohol at funerals emerges as one of the most important markers for group membership and an important aspect of displaying that group's religious denomination. One informant, Ellen, whom I was able to interview as she was performing her flower-arranging duties for the altar guild of a local Episcopal church, mentioned that the best-received funeral food gift she provides is a plastic cooler filled with Coca-Colas, wine, and beer. Ellen was quick to mention, however, that this practice works well only when she knows that the deceased and members of his or her immediate family are also Episcopalian; if they are Baptists, she feels compelled to replace the beer with bottled water.[33] Ellen observed that the gift of alcohol would not be appreciated by any Baptist families she might give it to—even if they did drink alcohol in the normal course of their lives—and that it might also both offend them and mark her as an outsider. This is why Ellen relegates her gifts of wine and beer to her fellow Episcopalian congregation members—not for financial reasons, but because they are the only members of the community she can give them to without committing a faux pas or creating a social rift. Most informants agree that the food gifts across Christian denominations in the area have the same social norms, but alcohol emerges as a strong dividing line. "People drink coffee during funerals for some reason. We have a lot of sweet tea. There's no beer, you know, because we're Baptist," commented another informant, Bev.

This complex relationship between class and denomination is brought into sharp focus within the north Georgia site of my observations and interviews. Class in the American South is particularly stratified and complicated, linked to family ties, location, denomination, congregation, education, accent, employment, and economic well-being. While class is often coded as denomination in the American South, this multivalent coding is not always straightforward or universal.[34] In any given locale, one denomination may have several churches, and each one may be of a different class: there may, for instance, be the "nice" Baptist church, the mill workers' Baptist church, and the country Baptist church, each with its particular culture linked to the socioeconomic class of its members. Junior Leaguers, not mill workers, eat aspic and mayonnaise in the South, and the socioeconomic character of the congregation with Junior League members (or mill workers) will be marked by their particular dishes. A large portion of the local population at my field site identify as members of the Baptist Church, where locally there is a wider division of social and economic power within the community. Both poor and wealthy citizens occupy the same denominational category here, and locally, specific congregations rather than entire congregations serve as class markers. This field site is not unique in congregations' serving as more specific indicators of socioeconomic class; across the South, denomination is used as a rough marker of class, but within any particular region, congregational specifics make the congregation a more precise and useful indicator. In interviews that inform this project, naming specific congregations allows for a more nuanced discussion of religion to emerge, even though categories based on congregation rather than denomination still carry implicit references to both class and race. For instance, a casserole that is considered fancy—perhaps asparagus casserole, as one informant suggested—may mark the giver as a member of the Main Street Baptist Church, whereas a humbler offering, such as the ubiquitous hash-brown casserole, might signal that the bearer is part of a more rural congregation. These systematic differences, however, do not attach themselves to the titles of the dish. As such, while they may influence the type of foodstuff chosen, the specific dish and the overt memorialization are still connected to the matronymic title and thus a specific individual.

Conclusion

The funeral period in the American South, marked by gifts of food from both family and community, mediates a broad range of social relationships with a larger than usual range of actors, including the living and the dead. Because members of local church congregations provide the bulk of food gifts, church affiliation is performed in these particular social interactions, extending funeral food's influence beyond the realm of the family and into the broader realms of the religious community and the community at large. Certain kinds of funeral food, such as beer and goo, or certain ways of presenting that food, such as the typically Episcopalian practice of using silver dishes, may signal particular denominations, although we need to account for the local community context before making that conclusion, as other metrics, such as class or the particular congregation, may be more accurate identifiers. The handing down and sharing of dishes traditionally served as funeral food, although a highly gendered phenomenon, reinforces relationships among family members regardless of gender, both living and dead. Continuing bonds theory, material-semiotic methods, actor-network theory, and the theory of material-semiotic actors are theoretical tools that help explain the ongoing network relationships that exist between funeral food offerings and the individuals who create and consume them.[35] This forces us to reevaluate and expand our understanding of social death theory. As long as the dead are still able to influence the living, they maintain agency, but they are at risk of social death. That threat of social death does not necessarily mean that the cessation of a particular dish's creation, giving, and consumption results in social annihilation. Instead, because participants exist in a network with physical items, including photographs, serving dishes, and objects such as recipe cards, objects can remind and influence participants to re-create lost dishes in a manner that allows formally socially dead members of the extended community to be remembered once again.[36]

Notes

Many thanks to Kerry Higgins Wendt for her early advice and editing on this chapter. All mistakes are mine and should in no way reflect on her.

1. Joyce Compton Brown and Les Brown, "The Discourse of Food as Cultural Translation and Empowering Voice in Appalachian Women during the Out-migration Process," *Journal of Appalachian Studies* 7, no. 2 (2001): 325.

2. Dennis Klass, "Continuing Conversation about Continuing Bonds," *Death Studies* 30, no. 9 (2006): 843–858.

3. Madeleine Akrich and Bruno Latour, "A Summary of a Convenient Vocabulary for the Semiotics of Human and Nonhuman Assemblies," in *Shaping Technology/Building Society: Studies in Sociotechnical Change,* ed. Wiebe E. Bijker and John Law (Cambridge: MIT Press, 1992), 259–264; Donna J. Haraway, *Simians, Cyborgs, and Women: The Reinvention of Nature* (New York: Routledge, 1991), and Haraway, "The Promises of Monsters: A Regenerative Politics for Inappropriate/d Others," in *Cultural Studies,* ed. Lawrence Grossberg, Cary Nelson, and Paula A. Treichler (New York: Routledge, 1992), 295–337.

4. Sean McCloud, *Divine Hierarchies: Class in American Religion and Religious Studies* (Chapel Hill: University of North Carolina Press, 2007), 1, 159, 171.

5. "Taste of the South: Chess Pie," *Southern Living,* www.southernliving.com/food/kitchen-assistant/chess-pie-recipes, accessed April 23, 2014.

6. Donna Lee Brien, "'Concern and Sympathy in a Pyrex Bowl': Cookbooks and Funeral Foods," *M/C Journal* 16, no. 3 (2013), http://journal.media-culture.org.au/index.php/mcjournal/article/viewArticle/655, accessed October 5, 2016;

Sidney Saylor Farr, "Fried Pies, Chess Pie and Egg Custard Pie," *Appalachian Heritage* 34, no. 4 (2006): 76.

7. John Lachs, "Good Enough." *Journal of Speculative Philosophy* 23, no. 1 (2009): 2.

8. Brien, "'Concern and Sympathy in a Pyrex Bowl.'"

9. Gayden Metcalfe and Charlotte Hays, *Being Dead Is No Excuse: The Official Southern Ladies Guide to Hosting the Perfect Funeral* (New York: Miramax, 2005), 2.

10. Maw Maw is a nickname used in the South for grandmother. In this case, Maw Maw Wallace was my mother's paternal grandmother.

11. Brown and Brown, "The Discourse of Food as Cultural Translation," 325.

12. "Coca Cola Cake—The Perfect Funeral Food," *Sinful Southern Sweets,* June 11, 2010, http://sinfulsouthernsweets.blogspot.co.uk/2010/06/coca-cola-cake-perfect-funeral-food.html, accessed March 31, 2017.

13. Ibid. Parentheses and ellipses are in the original.

14. Terri Evans, "Good Grief: Southern Funeral Food," *Like the Dew: A Journal of Southern Culture and Politics,* April 4, 2009, http://likethedew.com/2009/04/04/good-grief-southern-funeral-food/, accessed March 31, 2017.

15. Ibid.

16. Beverly, "Southern Funeral Food," *Beverly's Back Porch,* Last modified January 20, 2010, http://beverlysbackporch.blogspot.co.uk/2010/01/southern-funeral-food.html.

17. Katie Coakley, "Anatomy of a Southern Funeral," *Katie on the Map,* September 18, 2013, http://katieonthemap.com/2013/09/18/anatomy-of-a-southern-funeral/.

18. Klass, "Continuing Conversation about Continuing Bonds."

19. Margaret S. Stroebe, Georgios Abakoumkin, Wolfgang Stroebe, and Henk Schut, "Continuing Bonds in Adjustment to Bereavement: Impact of Abrupt versus Gradual Separation," *Personal Relationships* 19, no. 2 (2012): 255–266; Clare C. O'Callaghan, Fiona McDermott, Peter Hudson, and John R. Zalcberg, "Sound Continuing Bonds with the Deceased: The Relevance of Music, Including Preloss Music Therapy, for Eight Bereaved Caregivers," *Death Studies* 37, no. 2 (2013): 101–125; Briana L. Root and Julie Juola Exline, "The Role of Continuing Bonds in Coping with Grief: Overview and Future Directions," *Death Studies* 38, no. 1 (2014): 1–8.

20. Christine Valentine, *Bereavement Narratives: Continuing Bonds in the Twenty-first Century* (London: Routledge, 2008), 24; Jeanne W. Rothaupt and Kent Becker, "A Literature Review of Western Bereavement Theory: From Decathecting to Continuing Bonds," *Family Journal* 15, no. 1 (2007): 12; Dennis Klass, "Grief in an Eastern Culture: Japanese Ancestor Worship," in *Continuing Bonds: New Understandings of Grief,* ed. Dennis Klass, Phyllis R. Silverman, and Steven Nickman (Washington, D.C.: Taylor & Francis, 1996), 59–70, and Klass, "Continuing Bonds in the Resolution of Grief in Japan and North America," *American Behavioral Scientist* 44, no. 5 (2001): 742–763.

21. Salman Akhtar, *Immigration and Identity: Turmoil, Treatment, and Transformation* (New York: Jason Aronson, 1999); Hani M. Henry, William B. Stiles, Mia W. Biran, James K. Mosher, Meredith G. Brinegar, and Prashant Banerjee, "Immigrants' Continuing Bonds with Their Native Culture: Assimilation Analysis of Three Interviews," *Transcultural Psychiatry* 46, no. 2 (2009): 257–284.

22. Stefan Timmermans and David Sudnow, "Social Death as Self-Fulfilling Prophecy: David Sudnow's *Passing On* Revisited," *Sociological Quarterly* 39, no. 3 (1998): 454.

23. Michael Mulkay and John Ernst, "The Changing Profile of Social Death," *European Journal of Sociology* 32, no. 1 (1991): 172–196.

24. Akrich and Latour, "A Summary of a Convenient Vocabulary for the Semiotics of Human and Nonhuman Assemblies"; John Law, "Actor Network Theory and Material Semiotics," in *The New Blackwell Companion to Social Theory*, ed. Bryan Tuner (Malden. Mass.: Wiley-Blackwell, 2009), 141–158; Haraway, *Simians, Cyborgs, and Women* and "The Promises of Monsters."

25. Ross W. Jamieson, "Material Culture and Social Death: African-American Burial Practices," *Historical Archaeology* 29, no. 4 (1995): 39–58.

26. John Edwin Mason, *Social Death and Resurrection: Slavery and Emancipation in South Africa* (Charlottesville: University of Virginia Press, 2003); Orlando Patterson, *Slavery and Social Death: A Comparative Study* (Cambridge: Harvard University Press, 1982); Ran Greenstein, "The Study of South African Society: Towards a New Agenda for Comparative Historical Inquiry," *Journal of Southern African Studies* 20, no. 4 (1994): 641–661.

27. Metcalfe and Hays, *Being Dead Is No Excuse*, 102.

28. This community-based food gift exchange creates a reciprocal system of giving, as explored by Marcel Mauss and E. E. Evans-Pritchard in *The Gift: Forms and Functions of Exchange in Archaic Societies* (New York: Norton, 1967). For a greater exploration of this concept, see Robert T. Green and Dana L. Alden, "Functional Equivalence in Cross-Cultural Consumer Behavior: Gift Giving in Japan and the United States," *Psychology & Marketing* 5, no. 2 (1988): 155–168.

29. Metcalfe and Hays, *Being Dead Is No Excuse*, 34.

30. McCloud, *Divine Hierarchies*, 1, 159, 171.

31. See Sam Bowers Hilliard, *Hog Meat and Hoecake: Food Supply in the Old South, 1840–1860* (Carbondale: Southern Illinois University Press, 1972), and Jennifer Jensen Wallach, "New Introduction," in *Deep South: A Social Anthropological Study of Caste and Class*, by Allison Davis, Burleigh B. Gardner, and Mary R. Gardner (1941; repr., Columbia: University of South Carolina Press, 2009), xiii–xxix.

32. Metcalfe and Hays, *Being Dead Is No Excuse*, 27.

33. Southern Baptists, by long tradition, do not drink alcohol. For a modern statement on alcohol use by the Southern Baptist Convention, see the 2006 Southern Baptist Convention Resolution, "On Alcohol Use in America," www.sbc.net/resolutions/1156, accessed September 14, 2015.

34. See Elizabeth S. D. Engelhardt, *A Mess of Greens: Southern Gender and Southern Food* (Athens: University of Georgia Press, 2011); Lucy M. Long, *Regional American Food Culture* (Santa Barbara, Calif.: Greenwood, 2009), 19–28; Beth A. Latshaw, "Food for Thought: Race, Region, Identity, and Foodways in the American South," *Southern Cultures* 15, no. 4 (2009): 106–128; and Mary Rizzo, "The Café Hon: Working-Class White Femininity and Commodified Nostalgia in Postindustrial Baltimore," in *Dixie Emporium: Tourism, Foodways, and Consumer Culture in the American South,* ed. Anthony J. Stanonis (Athens: University of Georgia Press, 2008), 264–286.

35. Klass, "Continuing Conversation about Continuing Bonds"; Akrich and Latour, "A Summary of a Convenient Vocabulary for the Semiotics of Human and Nonhuman Assemblies"; Law, "Actor Network Theory and Material Semiotics"; Haraway, *Simians, Cyborgs, and Women* and "The Promises of Monsters."

36. Mason, *Social Death and Resurrection;* Patterson *Slavery and Social Death;* Greenstein, "The Study of South African Society."

Bibliography

Akhtar, Salman. *Immigration and Identity: Turmoil, Treatment, and Transformation.* New York: Jason Aronson, 1999.

Akrich, Madeleine, and Bruno Latour. "A Summary of a Convenient Vocabulary for the Semiotics of Human and Nonhuman Assemblies." In *Shaping Technology/Building Society: Studies in Sociotechnical Change,* edited by Wiebe E. Bijker and John Law, 259–264. Cambridge: MIT Press, 1992.

Beverly. "Southern Funeral Food." *Beverly's Back Porch,* January 20, 2010. http://beverlysbackporch.blogspot.co.uk/2010/01/southern-funeral-food.html.

Brien, Donna Lee. "'Concern and Sympathy in a Pyrex Bowl': Cookbooks and Funeral Foods." *M/C Journal* 16, no. 3 (2013). http://journal.media-culture.org.au/index.php/mcjournal/article/viewArticle/655.

Brown, Joyce Compton, and Les Brown. "The Discourse of Food as Cultural Translation and Empowering Voice in Appalachian Women during the Out-migration Process." *Journal of Appalachian Studies* 7, no. 2 (2001): 315–329.

Coakley, Katie. "Anatomy of a Southern Funeral." *Katie on the Map,* September 18, 2013. http://katieonthemap.com/2013/09/18/anatomy-of-a-southern-funeral/.

"Coca Cola Cake—The Perfect Funeral Food." *Sinful Southern Sweets,* June 11, 2010. http://sinfulsouthernsweets.blogspot.co.uk/2010/06/coca-cola-cake-perfect-funeral-food.html.

Engelhardt, Elizabeth S. D. *A Mess of Greens: Southern Gender and Southern Food.* Athens: University of Georgia Press, 2011.

Evans, Terri. "Good Grief: Southern Funeral Food." *Like the Dew: A Journal of Southern Culture and Politics,* April 4, 2009. http://likethedew.com/2009/04/04/good-grief-southern-funeral-food/.

Farr, Sidney Saylor. "Fried Pies, Chess Pie and Egg Custard Pie." *Appalachian Heritage* 34, no. 4 (2006): 75–77.

Green, Robert T., and Dana L. Alden. "Functional Equivalence in Cross-Cultural Consumer Behavior: Gift Giving in Japan and the United States." *Psychology & Marketing* 5, no. 2 (1988): 155–168.

Greenstein, Ran. "The Study of South African Society: Towards a New Agenda for Comparative Historical Inquiry." *Journal of Southern African Studies* 20, no. 4 (1994): 641–661.

Haraway, Donna J. "The Promises of Monsters: A Regenerative Politics for Inappropriate/d Others." In *Cultural Studies,* ed. Lawrence Grossberg, Cary Nelson, and Paula A. Treichler, 295–337. New York: Routledge, 1992.

———. *Simians, Cyborgs, and Women: The Reinvention of Nature.* New York: Routledge, 1991.

Henry, Hani M., William B. Stiles, Mia W. Biran, James K. Mosher, Meredith G. Brinegar, and Prashant Banerjee. "Immigrants' Continuing Bonds with Their Native Culture: Assimilation Analysis of Three Interviews." *Transcultural Psychiatry* 46, no. 2 (2009): 257–284.

Hilliard, Sam Bowers. *Hog Meat and Hoecake: Food Supply in the Old South, 1840–1860.* Carbondale: Southern Illinois University Press, 1972.

Jamieson, Ross W. "Material Culture and Social Death: African-American Burial Practices." *Historical Archaeology* 29, no. 4 (1995): 39–58.

Klass, Dennis. "Continuing Bonds in the Resolution of Grief in Japan and North America." *American Behavioral Scientist* 44, no. 5 (2001): 742–763.

———. "Continuing Conversation about Continuing Bonds." *Death Studies* 30, no. 9 (2006): 843–858.

———. "Grief in an Eastern Culture: Japanese Ancestor Worship." In *Continuing Bonds: New Understandings of Grief,* edited by Dennis Klass, Phyllis R. Silverman, and Steven Nickman, 59–70. Washington, D.C.: Taylor & Francis, 1996.

Lachs, John. "Good Enough." *Journal of Speculative Philosophy* 23, no. 1 (2009): 1–7.

Latshaw, Beth A. "Food for Thought: Race, Region, Identity, and Foodways in the American South." *Southern Cultures* 15, no. 4 (2009): 106–128.

Law, John. "Actor Network Theory and Material Semiotics." In *The New Blackwell Companion to Social Theory,* ed. Bryan Tuner, 141–158. Malden. Mass.: Wiley-Blackwell, 2009.

Long, Lucy M. *Regional American Food Culture.* Santa Barbara, Calif.: Greenwood, 2009).

Mason, John Edwin. *Social Death and Resurrection: Slavery and Emancipation in South Africa.* Charlottesville: University of Virginia Press, 2003.

Mauss, Marcel, and E. E. Evans-Pritchard. *The Gift: Forms and Functions of Exchange in Archaic Societies.* New York: Norton, 1967.

McCloud, Sean. *Divine Hierarchies: Class in American Religion and Religious Studies.* Chapel Hill: University of North Carolina Press, 2007.

Metcalfe, Gayden, and Charlotte Hays. *Being Dead Is No Excuse: The Official Southern Ladies Guide to Hosting the Perfect Funeral.* New York: Miramax, 2005.

Mulkay, Michael, and John Ernst. "The Changing Profile of Social Death." *European Journal of Sociology* 32, no. 1 (1991): 172–196.

O'Callaghan, Clare C., Fiona McDermott, Peter Hudson, and John R. Zalcberg. "Sound Continuing Bonds with the Deceased: The Relevance of Music, Including Preloss Music Therapy, for Eight Bereaved Caregivers." *Death Studies* 37, no. 2 (2013): 101–125.

Patterson, Orlando. *Slavery and Social Death: A Comparative Study.* Cambridge: Harvard University Press, 1982.

Rizzo, Mary. "The Café Hon: Working-Class White Femininity and Commodified Nostalgia in Postindustrial Baltimore." In *Dixie Emporium: Tourism, Foodways, and Consumer Culture in the American South,* ed. Anthony J. Stanonis, 264–286. Athens: University of Georgia Press, 2008).

Root, Briana L., and Julie Juola Exline. "The Role of Continuing Bonds in Coping with Grief: Overview and Future Directions." *Death Studies* 38, no. 1 (2014): 1–8.

Rothaupt, Jeanne W., and Kent Becker. "A Literature Review of Western Bereavement Theory: From Decathecting to Continuing Bonds." *Family Journal* 15, no. 1 (2007): 6–15.

Stroebe, Margaret S., Georgios Abakoumkin, Wolfgang Stroebe, and Henk Schut. "Continuing Bonds in Adjustment to Bereavement: Impact of Abrupt versus Gradual Separation." *Personal Relationships* 19, no. 2 (2012): 255–266.

"Taste of the South: Chess Pie." *Southern Living.* www.southernliving.com/food/kitchen-assistant/chess-pie-recipes.

Timmermans, Stefan, and David Sudnow. "Social Death as Self-Fulfilling Prophecy: David Sudnow's *Passing On* Revisited." *Sociological Quarterly* 39, no. 3 (1998): 453–472.

Valentine, Christine. *Bereavement Narratives: Continuing Bonds in the Twenty-first Century.* London: Routledge, 2008.

Wallach, Jennifer Jensen. "New Introduction." In *Deep South: A Social Anthropological Study of Caste and Class,* by Allison Davis, Burleigh B. Gardner, and Mary R. Gardner, xiii–xxix. 1941. Reprint, Columbia: University of South Carolina Press, 2009.

5

The Circle of Life
Memorializing and Sustaining Faith

Lacy K. Crocker and Gordon Fuller

Introduction

Food symbolizes life and future. It also, however, plays a role in how Jews memorialize and participate in the faith of their ancestors, and it thereby connects modern Jews to the past, the dead, and death. At times this connection occurs through kosher food preparation and consumption, whereas at other times, such as Yom Kippur, Jews fast and perform rituals that serve as a rehearsal for death.[1] Traditionally, women mediate the link between the faith of deceased ancestors and the current generation of Jews through the preparation of food.[2] The grieving process in Judaism does not make extensive use of food. Typical foods include lentils and hard-boiled eggs because their rounded shapes symbolize the cycle of life and represent the continuity between birth and death.[3]

Jews and Food

Jews and food are intimately connected. The old joke that almost any Jewish holiday can be summarized as "they tried to kill us, we won, let's eat!" reflects this connection. Perhaps one of Judaism's unique contributions is the combination of religious law and eating, called *kashrut*, or "keeping kosher." Kosher is a word that translates as acceptable; therefore, food that is acceptable is kosher food, whereas food that is not acceptable is *treyf*, a Yiddish word meaning "not kosher," from the Hebrew *treyfah*, meaning "torn." The laws of *kashrut* come from two basic sources: the Torah (five

---

BAGELS

1½ cups warm water
1½ tsp yeast
1 tbsp oil
1 tbsp sugar
2 tsp black molasses
4½–5½ cups bread flour
2 tsp kosher salt

Toppings (choose as many as you like, or none):
poppy seeds
sesame seeds
soaked onion flakes
garlic salt

Boiling pot:
At least 6 quarts water
2 tbsp molasses
1 tsp kosher salt

additional flour for dusting
two baking sheets
clean kitchen towel
parchment paper
cornmeal (optional)

Whisk water, yeast, oil, sugar, and molasses. Stir in 1 cup of flour, add salt, then remaining flour. Turn dough onto a floured surface and knead 10 to 13 minutes, until it is very stiff. Fold into a smooth ball, place on a board, and cover with a cloth. Let the dough rest on the board about 12 minutes. Fill pot about three-quarters full with water. Add the molasses and salt and bring the water to a rolling boil. Preheat the oven to 450°F. Separate the dough into about 12 sections or balls and roll each into a 9- to10-inch long roll or strip. Press the ends together to seal them and make a ring. Lay rings on a lightly floured pan or board near the stove and let them rest again 15

---

books of Moses that make up the first part of the Hebrew Bible) and the Talmud (a legal compilation that was finally written down in about the seventh century C.E.). The Torah is referred to as the written law, while the Talmud is considered rabbinic or oral law.

Bagels, the circle of life. (Photo by Harvey Hartenstein)

to 20 minutes. They should be "half proof," which means they should rise slightly or be puffy. Place two baking sheets side by side. Place a kitchen towel on one and parchment paper on the other; sprinkle the parchment paper with cornmeal if using. Reduce the boiling water to a simmer and add three or four bagels at a time. They will sink and then come to the surface; let them simmer there for about 55 seconds. Flip them over and cook the other side for about 45 seconds. Remove them from water and place them on the towel-lined baking sheet to drain slightly, then put them on the parchment-lined baking sheet. Do not overhandle. Sprinkle with toppings, if using. Put them in the oven, reduce heat to 425°F and bake until crispy on top (about 18–22 minutes), turning them once.*

---

*Recipe courtesy of Dan Hartenstein. Dan writes that if you want to make cinnamon raisin bagels, it is best to use golden raisins, and not to soak the raisins before adding them to the dough, as they will make it mushy. Rather, let the dough itself add moistness to the raisins.

There are a number of different theories about the reasons for these dietary laws. One popular theory has to do with health—that mixing dairy products with greasy meats (such as the "cooking a kid in its mother's milk" in Exodus 23:19; 34:26; and Deuteronomy 14:21) made for difficult digestion, or that declaring a pig unfit (because it is a mammal that does not meet the two qualifications of having a split cloven hoof *and* chewing its cud) was the result of fears of trichinosis (a disease caused by undercooked pork).[4] Theories such as these are just that, however—theories. As Julius Preuss writes, "The Biblical dietary laws are included in the chapter on 'Hygiene' solely because it is difficult to conceive of a reason other than sanitation and health for their ordination. Ultimately, it must be emphasized that the Torah gives no reason at all for these laws, and the later sources do so only rarely."[5]

Also clearly prohibited is eating the blood of a living thing, for "the life is in the blood."[6] This led to the rabbinic law requiring that any meat be both salted and soaked to remove any blood before it is cooked for consumption. An interesting note is that kosher salt, which is available in virtually every grocery store, is not kosher because of anything in its content, for all salt is kosher. It is simply that the coarser grind of kosher salt was more efficient for removing the blood and easier to rinse off before cooking the meat.

The rabbis of the Talmud also came up with seven laws that they considered binding on *all* human beings, not just Jews. These laws are called the Noahide Laws.[7] It is interesting to note that one of those laws has to do with eating. Even for gentiles, eating the meat of an animal that was not slaughtered for that purpose, or eating any piece taken from a live animal, is prohibited. This law reflects respect for animals: they should not suffer needlessly. The dietary laws not only govern Jews' daily approach to food but also provide a connection to their ancestors and continuity with the faith of the deceased.

Women, Death, and Food

Traditionally, women mediate the memorialization of the faith of the dead through careful food preparation rituals, observing the dietary laws. The dietary laws relate to daily food preparation, and some Jews observe these laws more rigidly during certain holy days. Women historically have prepared and overseen the holiday meals. The food preparation consists of a practical task that is also highly theological. Susan Starr Sered examined the connection between food and holiness in the lives of elderly Middle Eastern Jewish women in Jerusalem.[8] Her study demonstrates that these women saw it as their duty to imbue the food with the holiness of the ancestors by preparing the meals according to the kosher traditions passed down from mother to daughter. At times rabbis corrected these women's *kashrut* observance, either critiquing them for over-adequately or inadequately performing the *kashrut* customs, but the women dismissed this male intervention usually with a smile or shrug. The women did not disregard the importance of the *kashrut* laws; rather, they found any traditions their female ancestors performed sacred. These women used the traditional foods and preparation rituals to strengthen their children's bond to the faith of their deceased ancestors. Many of these women believed that these traditional foods and how they prepared them formed the primary link between their children and the faith of their deceased ancestors, since their descendants were not highly religious. For these women, observing the *kashrut* customs created the holiday because it memorialized the faith of their ancestors and strengthened their descendants' bond to Judaism.[9]

The Value of Life, Impending Death, and Food

Judaism gives priority to life because the very breath of God resides in every person. In the Creation story in the book of Genesis, the first human being, Adam, comes to life when God breathes into his nostrils after forming him from the dust of the earth (Hebrew: *Adamah,* from the color red, called *adom,* which is the color of the earthen clay in the Israeli Middle East). It is written, "The Lord God formed man from the dust of the earth. He blew into his nostrils the breath of life, and man became a living being" (Genesis 2:7). Earlier, it is also written, "And God created man in His image, in the image of God He created him, male and female he created them" (Genesis 1:27). In Jewish values, these verses teach that every single human being (regardless of race, color, creed, sexual orientation, social class, and so on) is created in the image of God, and therefore has a spark of divinity in her. And since God breathes into humans to give life, it is as if the soul (Hebrew *n'shamah*) is the breath (also *n'shamah,* from the infinitive *linshom,* "to breathe") of God in each and every person. Jews are therefore taught to respect every single human being just as they are supposed to respect God.

At times, preserving life conflicts with the observance of a God-given commandment. Jews are commanded to keep the dietary laws, but they should not starve because of them. This was, unfortunately, thoroughly tested during the Holocaust, when many observant Jews chose to eat whatever was available in order to survive, even if it was not kosher. Esther Farbstein writes: "Moreover, even when things were permitted on the grounds of coercion, they made a point of doing them in a way that minimized the violation. For instance, Rabbi Yehoshua Moshe Aronson told those around him in Auschwitz to eat chametz [leavening] on Pesach [Passover] and non-kosher meat all year round in small quantities and with pauses, so as to lessen the severity of violating a Torah prohibition, even though it was undeniably a case of *pikuach nefesh* [saving a life]."[10]

This emphasis on life is so important that the Jewish tradition actually teaches that Jews are *required* to break *any* of the 613 commandments in order to save a life, except for three. Those three are the commandments against idolatry, sexually immoral practices (mostly cultic prostitution practices related to idolatry), and murder. Though Jewish law forbids Jews to kill innocent people, they may do whatever is needed to stop the perpetrators of violence, including killing them, to save their own lives or the lives of others.

Jews give priority to life and seek to preserve life, but Judaism does not promote delaying impending death. Accepting impending death also relates to the use of food for the nearly deceased. The Hebrew term *gosess* translates as "flickering candle." This term is applied when a person's life force is compared to the flame of a flickering candle, about to be extinguished at any moment. In general, accepted rabbinic regulations understand this term to be used when a person is given seventy-two hours or less to live. When a person is deemed to be a *gosess,* there is no question that he or she should be allowed to die, with as much dignity and comfort as possible. Judaism attempts to discern between "prolonging life" and "delaying death." Where life can, indeed, be prolonged so that there is a reasonable expectation of continued time on this Earth that is characterized by a good quality of life, every possible intervention should be considered to continue that life. If, however, medical interventions are only delaying death, and there is no realistic hope of any true recovery, then no heroic measures should be taken—heroic measures include the use of forced feedings or feeding tubes. Jews, in fact, are encouraged to have living wills, or advance directives, so that these decisions can be made in concert with Jewish law and family wishes, well before a time of crisis.

A second category requires a bit more moral and ethical judgment. This category is called *terefah*, which translates as "an imperiled life." In these cases, the ability to prolong life may be available, but the circumstances raise questions about whether this should be applied or done. Such cases include terminal illness as well as incurable suffering. From a Jewish perspective, people in this *terefah* category should be offered normal treatments, but no heroic measures should be taken to save them. Care providers may offer those in the *terefah* category normal food and liquid nourishment, but they would not force-feed them. Additionally, all reasonable measures should be taken to alleviate their pain and suffering, and they should continue to be visited by friends and family. Judaism preserves and values life to a high degree, but at the same time, Judaism recognizes death as part of the cycle of life. Jews, therefore, accept impending death and do not go to extreme measures, including forced feeding, to delay death.

Judaism and Death

In Judaism death is fully accepted as part of the normal cycle of life. The holiday Yom Kippur functions as rehearsal for death and illustrates Judaism's acceptance and preparation for death. On this holiday Jews abstain from food, sex, and personal beautification, such as wearing leather or jewelry. These acts reflect a retreat from life and symbolize one's own death.[11] When Jews abstain from food and other activities that represent life on Yom Kippur, they symbolically acknowledge the difference between life and death. Some background regarding how Jews conceive of the afterlife will better aid the discussion pertaining to Judaism's rehearsal of death, that is, Yom Kippur. This overview will also provide deeper insight into how the Hebrew Bible at times portrays death with a voracious appetite that swallows the dead while also depicting the God of Israel as swallowing death and transforming the mourning caused by the ills of this world into joy.

In the Hebrew Bible, whenever male leaders of note die (except Joseph), the phrase used is almost the same, "*Va'yei'asef el amav*—and [name] was gathered unto his people."[12] Some have interpreted this oft-repeated phrase to mean that though bodies die when someone dies, the souls go on to "be gathered unto our people"—a sort of heavenly gathering with all those loved ones who have passed on before them. Jews do not believe in either a heaven or a hell in the way Christians do. Jews learn from Genesis 3:19: "for dust you are, and to dust you shall return." This fairly clear statement indicates that, at the very least, the physical self ends, and the body goes back to the earth, whence it was created. Science seems to bear this concept out as well: "Water covers about 70 percent of the earth's surface. Also, water makes up about 70 percent of the human body. . . . Six elements make up almost 99 percent of the human body's mass: oxygen, carbon, hydrogen, nitrogen, calcium and phosphorus. All of these elements—and several others—make up the earth as well."[13]

For Jews, *shamayim,* which is usually translated as "heaven," is the realm of God, whereas *aretz,* mostly translated as "earth" or "land," is the realm of human beings. More recently (second century B.C.E. and forward), a concept of *olam haba*—"the world to come," crept into Judaism, probably from contact with Greek and Roman polytheists, and later Christians and their version of heaven. The Jewish concept of such a world to come was most likely (as evidenced in many places in the Talmud) an apologetic view of the suffering that righteous Jews had to endure in this world under the persecution of Greeks, then Romans, and then Christians. It also became the name given to the future messianic era, when such persecution, it was hoped, would cease.

Neither is there a concept of a punitive hell in Judaism. There are three words that may be translated as hell that come from the Jewish tradition. The first is *Sheol,* which appears many times in the Hebrew Bible. In early iterations, such as Genesis 37:35, Jacob declares he will "go down mourning to my son in *Sheol,*" meaning his grief over his perceived loss of his son, Joseph, will lead him to his own death. There is no specific description there of what the place is like. Later, however, *Sheol* gains different descriptors, such as in Isaiah, Ezekiel, and Job, where it is pictured as a dark and gloomy place. In the Hebrew Bible, some texts indicate *Sheol* receives the dead through the act of swallowing.[14] In fact, Nicholas Tromp claims that the Hebrew Bible favors the verb "to swallow" in order to characterize how *Sheol* receives the dead.[15] Death swallows figuratively in some passages, and this characteristic appears familiar since it serves as a metaphor for describing greed, arrogance, and violence (cf. Prov. 1:12;

Hab. 2:5). Other times the earth opens up and swallows people, and this act serves as God's judgment and punishment against those who have violated his commands (Exod. 15:12; Num. 16:30, 32; Deut. 11:6; 2 Sam. 17:6; Ps. 106:17). Hence, the Hebrew Bible portrays *Sheol* as consuming the dead with a voracious appetite (e.g., Isa. 5:14).[16] Death makes an appearance at a victory feast intended to celebrate the kingship of Israel's God (Isa. 25), creating the possibility of transforming the celebratory feast into a funerary feast.[17] Instead, the text indicates that the God of Israel will "swallow death into perpetuity" (Isa. 25:8), and in doing so, God turns mourning into joy (Isa. 25:8–9). In this text, death represents the source of suffering in life, including political and military powers that harm God's people.[18] Though Judaism accepts death as part of the cycle of life, this text illustrates the fear and mourning caused by death. The text also communicates God's comfort and salvation because of his power and reign over death.

A second hellish place, known to some as Gehenna, actually comes from the Hebrew *Gei Ben Hinnom*. This translates as the valley of the person named Ben (son of) Hinnom. A place just outside and to the southwest of the old city of Jerusalem carries that name today. It is a very steep, small valley, which is believed to be the place where Canaanite tribes sacrificed children to the god Molech. Only a parent who has lost a child can understand the true hellishness of such a place, though any parent can imagine it. Finally, *Azazel* is the name given to the place where the high priest sends the scapegoat on Yom Kippur, the Jewish Day of Atonement. In Leviticus 16:6–10 this ritual is described in detail. The high priest takes two goats; one is to be sacrificed to God for atonement, the other has the sins of the people of Israel placed on its head and is led off to *Azazel*. Again, the place is never described, but it does seem to be a collecting place for sins. Indeed, in modern-day Israel, if someone tells you "*lech l'azazel*," you are being told to go to hell, just as in the English vernacular.

Perhaps one of the biggest differences between Judaism and other religions is that it is focused on behavior, not on beliefs. Whether there is a heaven or hell is really of very little consequence to Jews. It is not just a religion, but also a peoplehood—a way of life. Jews believe that they are put on this Earth to be a moral light to the other nations. Their primary way of achieving this is by what is called *tikun olam*—"fixing the world."

This is what they believe those 613 commandments mentioned earlier were to guide. So they focus on this world, this life, and do their best to make it better for everyone. There is relatively little concern for the afterlife in comparison to religions like Christianity.

When Jews die, according to the Talmud, they will face God and be asked the following questions:

1. *Nasata v'natata be-emunah?*—Were you honest in your business dealings?
2. *Kavata itim la-Torah?*—Did you fix time for study?
3. *Asakta bifria ur'viah?*—Did you engage in procreation?
4. *Tzipita lishuah?*—Did you hope for salvation?
5. *Pilpalta b'chochmah?*—Were your arguments for the sake of heaven (i.e., as opposed to ego-driven)?
6. *Havanta davar mitoch davar?*—Did you seek deeper meaning in life?[19]

It is interesting to note that none of these questions is of a religious ritual nature—nothing about keeping the Sabbath or the dietary laws, for example. Yet on the basis of their answers to these, theoretically, Jews will either merit entrance into the world to come—or not. Of course, Judaism also has a "judgment day" scenario, too, which is particularly prominent in the liturgy of the fall High Holiday season (Rosh Hashanah and Yom Kippur), whereby God sits on a throne and judges all past deeds. If the good outweigh the bad, a person is granted another year of life (or if not another year, then admitted into the "heavenly gathering"); otherwise, there is no punishment—just the end.

Jews' acceptance of death as part of the cycle of life means they also prepare for death in many ways. As mentioned, Yom Kippur serves as a time for Jews to prepare for death. Jews prepare for their deaths by recounting their deeds and misdeeds and making restitution to God and humans. The rituals associated with Yom Kippur serve to remind Jews of the ultimate point of atonement. On Yom Kippur, a Jew has the opportunity to be the dead person and mourner simultaneously. On Yom Kippur, Jews rehearse death by abstaining from life, including eating, having sex, and wearing jewelry or leather. Jews also wear white on Yom Kippur, and these clothes represent burial shrouds. Jews also memorialize the dead on Yom Kippur and mourn the deaths of loved ones and martyrs.[20]

Jewish Funerals and Mourning

According to Jewish tradition, a person should be buried as soon as possible after dying.[21] In ancient times, when family members lived near each other, this was no obstacle, and funerals were generally performed the very next day (unless it was a Sabbath or holiday). This was also important from a health perspective, since there were no coolers to prevent the decaying process from beginning. It is still contrary to Jewish law to use any sort of preservative chemicals or embalming, as Jews do not want to interfere with the natural processes and keep the body from being returned to God. Today, however, because family members often live as many as thousands of miles apart, and coolers are available to prevent the decay of the body, funerals can be delayed for a number of days until family gathers; still, the sooner the better.

The initial preparation of the body for being returned to God is called *taharah,* which translates as "purification." A *chevre kadishah* (holy society) is convened to do the purification rituals, as well as to recite Psalms to aid in the soul's ascent to heaven. These groups are usually only four or five people of the same sex as the deceased. It is considered a great deed of loving kindness to be on a *chevre kadishah,* for there is no expectation that the deceased will ever pay one back. It is a holy task that requires great sensitivity and humility. In fact, the final act of the *chevre kadishah* is to speak to the deceased and to ask for forgiveness, just in case any insensitivity or injustice was done to the deceased.

The ritual first involves removing all jewelry, makeup, and any other sort of adornment if this has not already been done. Out of sensitivity, the body is covered at all times, except for the specific area being cleansed. The body is cleansed by rinsing with clear, lukewarm water, one area at a time, starting with the head, and the limbs are then straightened. The body is then raised onto its feet, and twenty-four quarts of water are poured over the head in a continuous stream. The body is then dressed in pure white, a simple shroud with no pockets (in which to put worldly goods) or permanent fasteners (including buttons—only ties are allowed) and laid in the casket. It is then closed and watched by *shomrim* (volunteer guards) until the funeral. In Judaism there is traditionally no open casket or viewing of the body. In addition to watching the body of the deceased, the *shomrim* may choose to recite from Psalms as a way to help elevate the soul of the deceased. The casket itself, according to Jewish tradition, is to be a plain pine box, the simpler the better. (In modern-day Israel, caskets are not even used at all; rather, bodies are placed in body bags and put directly into graves.) In addition, traditional Jews will have holes drilled in the bottom of the casket to promote the natural decaying process and the return of the body to God.

Jewish law requires one to mourn for seven relations: father, mother, sister, brother, son, daughter, and spouse. In ancient times, the tradition was to tear one's garment immediately upon hearing of the death of one of these relatives. Today, this is observed by either tearing a piece of clothing or putting a torn ribbon on one's clothing at the funeral itself. In traditional Judaism, a procession is made from the hearse to the grave site. The leader of the funeral procession (who does not have to be clergy) recites a Psalm but stops the procession briefly a number of times, which shows a reluctance to fulfill the commandment to accompany the dead to their final rest. When the procession arrives at the grave site, the casket is placed on the lowering mechanism.

The Jewish funeral ceremony is fairly brief. It generally opens with some Psalms or readings, which are followed by one or more eulogies. A prayer called *tziduk hadin* ("the righteous judgment") is recited, and the casket is lowered. As part of that commandment to accompany the dead to their final rest, first family and then others are invited to put spadefuls of earth onto the casket. Again, however, to show reluctance to do this, traditional Jews follow two rules: first, use the back of the shovel for at least one scoopful; and second, place the shovel on the ground rather than handing it to another person. Generally, Jews put in enough earth to cover the casket. In more Orthodox circles, the attending family and friends stay until the entire grave is filled in by hand shovels. Once the body is interred, the focus shifts from the commandment to accompany the dead to their final rest (*levayat hameitim*) to the commandment to comfort mourners (*nichum aveilim*). It is at this point that the family first recites the traditional *kaddish* (sanctification, i.e., of God) prayer. Interestingly, there is nothing in this prayer about death, or life, or life after death. Rather, it is simply a declaration of our faith in God and in fact appears in every religious service.

Food and Mourning in the Jewish Tradition

The family now begins the period of mourning called *shiva,* from the Hebrew word for seven because this initial period lasts seven days. The mourning relatives generally observe this together in one home of their choosing. The community comes to them to hold the daily prayer services and recitation of the *kaddish* prayer. The community also supports them by bringing food and tending to other needs, so that the family members can focus on their mourning. So that the mourners can focus on their grief, they are not to go to work, look in mirrors, wear jewelry, or worry in any way about how they look. In fact, they are not even supposed to launder their clothes, cut their hair or nails, or shave during this period. Additionally, by tradition they sit on low stools or chairs without cushions, and some will even sleep on the floor. Though the commandment to comfort mourners includes many things to help the family achieve this focus, an interesting part of the ritual is that visitors are not supposed to speak to mourners until spoken to. Instead, they are simply supposed to be present and to support. Though the tradition prescribes following this for a full seven days (counting the day of the funeral as the first day), today in America many families will observe fewer days of this intense mourning.

Long before modern theories about the process of grieving had been written, the rabbis of the Talmud had ritualized those various stages in the Jewish way of mourning. It is hard to deny the death of a loved one after hearing the thud of hard earth on a wooden casket containing the body. Then, the *shiva* period with its focus on mourning begins, and even within that, the first three days are generally more intense than the later days. During the *shiva* period the community supports the family by bringing food so they do not have to worry about their sustenance in their grief. On the evening of the sixth day of mourning, it is traditional to have a *se'udah mafseket*—a concluding meal. Though these foods can be eaten throughout the seven-day mourning period, the traditional foods for the concluding meal include hard-boiled eggs and lentils. These are chosen because both are round and so symbolize the cycle of life, but the egg also symbolizes rebirth. Though mourning the loss of a loved one, those who survive need to eat so that they can continue to sustain their lives and go on to do more of God's work. Other foods are certainly permissible, but these are the symbolic ones. On the seventh day, the mourning period concludes with the morning service. Breakfast is usually provided afterward, but this is after the *shiva* has ended.

Once the mourners conclude their seven-day period, a less intense twenty-three-day period of mourning commences. The mourners can return to work and their normal routines and resume most of their usual activities, but some restrictions remain: no parties, no music, and no shaving or cutting hair. The ribbon or torn clothing is no longer worn, and the *kaddish* prayer is recited at the synagogue rather than at the home. At the end of *shloshim* (Hebrew for thirty days), the mourning period concludes. The only exception is that for one's parents; one continues an even less intense mourning for ten more months, for a total of eleven months. At that point, the recitation of the *kaddish* ceases, but it is resumed on the anniversary of the funeral every year (called the *yahrzeit,* a Yiddish word for "that annual time"). Once the thirty-day period has passed, but before the first anniversary of the funeral, it is customary to have an unveiling of the gravestone. Many families observe the tradition by waiting specifically for the first anniversary to do so, but this observance is not a requirement.

When one goes to a Jewish cemetery, one often sees stones placed on the top of the gravestones. This tradition goes back to the time of Jacob, when his beloved Rachel died on the road to Bethlehem. Genesis 35:20 reads, "Over her grave, Jacob set up a pillar; it is a pillar at Rachel's grave to this day." Jacob was so distraught over Rachel's death that he could not wait to get to the family burial spot at the cave of Machpelah, but buried her on the side of the road and erected the pillar of stones to mark the place. Because weather and travelers would make the pillar of stones fall down, loved ones would reerect the stone pillar when they came to visit the place. As a reminder of that act of loving kindness, it became a tradition for Jews to place a stone on the graves of those they visited to show that they cared. The actual pillar, of course, is replaced today by the granite stones that memorialize the dead.

Conclusion

Judaism contains rich traditions that enable humans to embrace the cycle of life, including death. These traditions, such as Yom Kippur, prepare Jews for death and remind them how to live as moral lights. The *kashrut* customs, generally carried out by women as they traditionally oversee meal preparations, connect current generations with the faith of their deceased ancestors. The traditional meals served on holidays memorialize and sustain the faith of past generations for modern-day Jews.

Just as this chapter begins with a bagel, it ends with a story about a bagel and about how humans grapple with the circle of life. This abridged version of the original story, written by Mara Altman, narrates her grandmother's last days in a nursing home before she died, and is titled "All Choked Up." Unable to eat solid foods in her last days, Altman's grandmother had a last request that her family eagerly sought to meet:

My brother says, "Grandma, are you hungry?"

There is a long pause during which all we hear is the pump of the oxygen machine.

"Bagel," she finally says. "I need bagel with cream cheese."

My dad and brother run out like medics dispatched to a building collapse. She hasn't wanted anything—had any desire whatsoever—for so long that supplying her with what she craves feels like a code-blue emergency.

Besides, eating is an action reserved for the living. It implies a future. You are repowering your batteries—consuming nutrients—because you plan to go on longer. So even though she was on hospice, a clear marker of the impending end, we can't help experiencing the restless tingling of newfound hope. . . .

While we wait for the bagel, I ask if she wants to listen to some Frank Sinatra, a musician she's always enjoyed. "No," she says, "I'm concentrating on the bagel."

My cousin asks if there is anything else we can get her.

"Tell me a story about bagels," she says.

I hold her hand and think for a moment. No great dramatic bagel narratives come to mind. I take a deep breath and tell her how each time we have a family gathering with a big bagel spread, she constructs the most magnificent structures with the right ratio of capers. "And despite your tiny mouth," I say, "you are somehow always able to cram the whole thing right down your throat." . . .

As the caregiver brings the bagel toward Grandma's mouth, my aunt steps forward, concerned. "She can't swallow solid food," she warns. "She'll choke." . . .

Someone suggests that maybe she could hold the bagel and smell the bagel and that those sensory experiences might be just as satisfying as actually eating the delicacy she has loved since her childhood in Brooklyn.

We all agree.

Her caregiver lets the bagel hover near her nose and places it into her hands, but Grams doesn't look pleased. She is trying to lift it toward her mouth, but doesn't have enough strength. "I want to bite into it myself," she says. . . .

Before she even swallows, she opens her mouth wide—dentist-office-teeth-cleaning wide—in preparation for the next bite. Her caregiver is looking to us for validation or for a sign to shut this experiment down, but nobody is certain. Grams has lived nearly 92 years and if she says she wants a bagel right now at the very end of her life, shouldn't she get a bagel?

Her eyes are still shut as she goes in for another big mouthful, unaware that we are both thrilled and horrified. She seems O.K., but we watch cautiously. We fear a choke might show up tardy and be dead set on taking her.

Within three minutes, the bagel is gone and she is sound asleep.[22]

Bagels, for Jews, are an enduring symbol of the endless cycle of life, even in the midst of death.

Notes

1. Rebecca T. Alpert, "Grief and Rituals Surrounding Death: A Jewish Approach," in *Religion, Death, and Dying,* ed. Lucy Bregman, 3 vols. (Santa Barbara: ABC-CLIO, 2010), 3:26.

2. Susan Starr Sered, "Food and Holiness: Cooking as a Sacred Act among Middle-Eastern Jewish Women," *Anthropological Quarterly* 61, no. 3 (1988): 133.

3. Alpert, "Grief and Rituals Surrounding Death," 35.

4. For more see Lisë Stern, *How to Keep Kosher: A Comprehensive Guide to Understanding Jewish Dietary Laws* (New York: William Morrow, 2004).

5. Julius Preuss, *Biblical and Talmudic Medicine,* trans. Fred Rosner (1978; repr., Northvale, N.J.: Jason Aronson, 2004), 501.

6. Leviticus 17:10–14

7. Babylonian Talmud, Tractate *Berakot* 56a&b.

8. Sered, "Food and Holiness."

9. Ibid., 132–133.

10. Esther Farbstein, *Hidden in Thunder: Perspectives on Faith, Halachah and Leadership during the Holocaust,* trans. Deborah Stern (Jerusalem: Mossad Harav Kook, 2007), 161.

11. Alpert, "Grief and Rituals Surrounding Death," 26–27.

12. This is the case with Abraham in Genesis 25:8, Ishmael in Genesis 25:17, Isaac in Genesis 35:29, Jacob in Genesis 49:33, and Aaron in Deuteronomy

35:20. The failure to use this phrase for the death of notable women in the Hebrew Bible is upsetting.

13. "Similarities between the Human Body and the Earth," *IU Health,* April 22, 2015, http://iuhealth.org/blog/detail/similarities-between-the-human-body-and-the-earth/, accessed October 4, 2015.

14. Paul Kang-Kul Cho and Janling Fu, "Death and Feasting in the Isaiah Apocalypse (Isaiah 25:6–8)," in *Formation and Intertextuality in Isaiah 24–27,* ed. James Todd Hibbard and Hyun Chul Paul Kim (Atlanta: Society of Biblical Literature, 2013), 120–123.

15. Nicholas J. Tromp, *Primitive Conceptions of Death and the Nether World in the Old Testament* (Rome: Pontifical Biblical Institute, 1969), 172.

16. Cho and Fu, "Death and Feasting in the Isaiah Apocalypse," 123.

17. Ibid., 124.

18. Ibid., 132.

19. Babylonian Talmud, Tractate *Berakot* 31b.

20. Alpert, "Grief and Rituals Surrounding Death, " 26–27.

21. For a more complete and detailed description of Jewish practices, see Maurice Lamm, *The Jewish Way in Death and Mourning,* rev. ed. (Middle Village, N.Y.: Jonathan David, 2012).

22. This is condensed from the original story. See Mara Altman's "All Choked Up," *New York Times,* September 9, 2015, *http://opinionator.blogs.nytimes.com/2015/09/09/all-choked-up/?_r=0,* accessed October 7, 2015.

Bibliography

Alpert, Rebecca T. "Grief and Rituals Surrounding Death: A Jewish Approach." In *Religion, Death, and Dying,* edited by Lucy Bregman, 3 vols., 3:25–40. Santa Barbara: ABC-CLIO, 2010.

Altman, Mara. "All Choked Up," *New York Times,* September 9, 2015, http://opinionator.blogs.nytimes.com/2015/09/09/all-choked-up/?_r=0, accessed October 7, 2015.

Berger, Dr. Natalia, ed. *Jews and Medicine: Religion, Culture, Science.* Philadelphia: Jewish Publication Society, 1997.

Cho, Paul Kang-Kul, and Janling Fu. "Death and Feasting in the Isaiah Apocalypse (Isaiah 25:6–8)." In *Formation and Intertextuality in Isaiah 24–27,* edited by James Todd Hibbard and Hyun Chul Paul Kim, 117–142. Atlanta: Society of Biblical Literature, 2013.

Deutsch, Jonathan, and Rachel D. Saks. *Jewish American Food Culture.* Westport, Conn: Greenwood, 2008.

Dorff, Elliot N. *Matters of Life and Death.* Philadelphia: Jewish Publication Society of America, 1998.

Farbstein, Esther. *Hidden in Thunder: Perspectives on Faith, Halachah and Leader-*

ship during the Holocaust. Translated by Deborah Stern. Jerusalem: Mossad Harav Kook, 2007.

Greenspoon, Leonard J., Ronald A. Simkins, and Gerald Shapiro, eds. *Food and Judaism.* Omaha: Creighton University Press, 2004.

Kraemer, David C. *Jewish Eating and Identity through the Ages.* New York: Routledge, 2008.

Lamm, Maurice. *The Jewish Way in Death and Mourning.* Revised edition. Middle Village, N.Y.: Jonathan David, 2012.

Preuss, Julius. *Biblical and Talmudic Medicine.* Translated by Fred Rosner. 1978. Reprint, Northvale, N.J.: Jason Aronson, 2004.

Roffman, Joel A., and Gordon A. Fuller. *Coping with Adversity: Judaism's Response to Illness and Other Life Struggles.* Dallas: Brown Books, 2008.

Sered, Susan Starr. "Food and Holiness: Cooking as a Sacred Act among Middle-Eastern Jewish Women." *Anthropological Quarterly* 61, no. 3 (1988): 129–139.

Stern, Lisë. *How to Keep Kosher: A Comprehensive Guide to Understanding Jewish Dietary Laws* (New York: William Morrow, 2004).

Tromp, Nicholas J. *Primitive Conceptions of Death and the Nether World in the Old Testament.* Rome: Pontifical Biblical Institute, 1969.

Zeller, Benjamin E. Review of *Eat and Be Satisfied: A Social History of Jewish Food,* by John Cooper. *Food, Culture and Society: An International Journal of Multidisciplinary Research* 12, no. 1 (2009): 114.

6

Moroccan Funeral Feasts

David Oualaalou

Introduction

While funeral customs in the Muslim world share some similarities, funeral rituals differ not only from one region to another, but also from one
country to another. For instance, though Morocco observes the same
number of mourning days as other Muslim countries, it is customary in
Morocco to serve a traditional dish called couscous after a family member
passes away. Before delving deeper into the funeral rituals themselves, it is
important to highlight why one of the main parts of this ritual is serving
Morocco's most traditional dish, couscous. What is couscous, and why is
it a funeral food that most, if not all, Moroccan society serves?

Couscous consists of granulated semolina grains, usually topped with
mutton, veal, chicken, or beef, and various vegetables, including tomatoes,
pumpkins, onion, and cabbage, among others. Besides being associated with
funerals, this traditional dish is served for lunch on Fridays in most Moroccan
households. The various vegetables used in this dish neither have spiritual significance nor reflect any special meaning for the deceased while alive. Rather,
when served during funeral ceremonies, couscous represents unity with and
support of the grieving family. When members of the community share a
meal like couscous in a communal bowl from which everyone eats, a powerful
image is created. Gathering over couscous reflects our common mortality, reminding us that no matter how long a person lives, he or she will one day die.

An Islamic Perspective: The Meaning of Repasts during Funerals

This chapter addresses the meaning of repasts served during funerals within the Islamic tradition, mainly in Morocco. Before doing so, however, I

MOROCCAN COUSCOUS

Before cutting, wash all the vegetables and herbs thoroughly and pat them dry.

½ cup (or more depending on number guests) raw chicken, well washed, or your favorite meat: veal, lamb, or beef
¾ tsp salt
½ tsp white or black pepper
¾ tsp turmeric
¾ tsp ground ginger
¼ tsp ground red pepper
oil
1 bunch parsley or cilantro, chopped
3 cups canned chickpeas, rinsed
2 carrots, sliced
handful of green beans, tips removed and cut into bite-size pieces
1 sweet potato, peeled and thinly sliced
1 red or yellow bell pepper, sliced
½ small squash (pumpkin), sliced
1 white zucchini, sliced
1 green zucchini, sliced
¼ cabbage, sliced into bite-size strips
1 onion, diced
1 tomato, chopped
3 cups couscous
3 cups water

Traditionally, Moroccan couscous is prepared in special cookware called a couscousier. The couscousier consists of two parts: (1) the lower, bigger part, where one places the meat with vegetables and spices; and (2) the top part, the steamer. Combine the chicken or other meat, salt, black or white pepper, turmeric, ginger, red pepper, oil, parley or cilantro; add water to cover. Place the pot on the stove, and bring to a boil. Lower the tempera-

want to situate this discussion within the context of the ongoing debate among world religions and academic institutions about the meaning of death. Muslim scholars agree that death represents a transition from the physical world to the eternal hereafter. Similarly, Western scholars such as Christine Schirrmacher support this assertion. She writes:

Moroccan couscous: traditional funeral repast. (Shutterstock)

ture to medium or medium-low, depending on the type of stove. Let it cook for about 40 minutes; be sure not to let it overcook.

Once the chicken is cooked, remove it from the pot, and place it on a dish while keeping the broth in the pot. Add the chickpeas to the broth and let cook for about 20 minutes. Add the vegetables to the pot and cook for about 10 minutes. Remove the vegetables and chickpeas, and place them in a bowl.

Prepare the couscous. Pour three cups of couscous into a bowl and gently add 3 cups very hot water; stir the mix. Cover the bowl and let it sit for about 10 minutes. Gently fluff the couscous to separate the grains. Place the couscous on a serving plate that will be the base for the dish. Once the plate is covered with couscous, add the cooked chicken or meat atop the couscous, and layer the vegetables and chickpeas atop the meat. Be creative in laying out the vegetables. Place the leftover broth in a pitcher, and pour over the couscous, moistening the couscous according to taste.

From the viewpoint of the Koran and Islamic theology, this life has its basic meaning in being preparation for the hereafter. Mankind is a creation of God and limited in his knowledge. Mankind is reliant upon the guidance of God, the eternal and almighty One, who is to be basically distinguished from mankind and is alien to man in his

essence. The task of mankind is to recognize God as Creator and
Judge, to submit to him and be devoted, that is to say, to be "Muslim,"
to keep to his commands and to sculpt life here in view of the
hereafter.[1]

Yet many religious traditions in the world differ in explaining the meaning of repasts served during funerals. Those meanings differ not only
within the tradition itself, but also within families of the same culture.
Some traditions fade as generations change when it comes to the meaning
of repasts during funerals, but serving meals during this difficult time
provides an opportunity for comfort in which the family of the deceased
can find refuge. In Islam, however, the meaning of repasts differs *from
within* the tradition; practices depend on whether the grieving family follows the Sunni or Shi'ite tradition. Those differences are strong in some
areas while minor in others.

For instance, consider prayers. Sunni tradition has different rituals
from the Shi'ite. Shia Muslims pray three times a day, as they join the last
two prayers of the day, *Maghrib* and *Isha,* whereas Sunni Muslims pray
five times a day. Both Shia and Sunni are allowed to combine prayers
when traveling, for instance. The Shia justification for combining prayers
even when one is not traveling is simply that Islam allows it. (This is a matter of some contention among non-Shia religious schools.) Yet the two
sects of Islam do not differ widely regarding funeral arrangements, especially in contemporary Islam. Muslims in Great Britain, for example,
whether Sunnis or Shi'ites, see the dead body as sacred; thus, religious
customs surrounding death, such as washing the body and making burial
arrangements, are similar in Shi'ite and Sunni communities.[2]

In this chapter I present Morocco as a "test case" for two reasons.
First, Morocco highlights how the country approaches funeral rituals
shared within the Muslim world. The Moroccan example stresses how
food—especially couscous—offers a deeper meaning that goes beyond
sharing a meal where attendees pay their respects and give condolences to
the family of the deceased. Second, the story of Moroccan funeral practices makes readers aware of a funeral practice distinct from those of other
Muslim countries, which take different approaches to food and funerals.
In Morocco, major differences exist between the north and south concerning funeral traditions. The same can be said for variances between

rural and urban areas. Despite those dissimilarities, most of the Muslim world shares the common practice of burying the deceased within twenty-four hours of his or her death.

Muslims firmly believe that human beings have one life to live, enjoy, and worship the creator, God (Allah), before transitioning to the hereafter. Muslims also perceive death as a bridge to the final destination. The final destination is Judgment Day, when, on the basis of one's deeds on Earth, one is led to either *Jannah* (paradise or heaven) or *Jahannam* (hell). Funeral food served following the burial of a Muslim represents respect, honor, and relief as the deceased moves from the physical world to a spiritual one. In the spiritual world, he or she faces judgment that is based on deeds rather than wealth, social status, and ownership of property or other earthly goods. Thus, the food served after burial holds special meaning because it reflects human mortality and divine judgment rather than worldly successes. Within this context, each Muslim country follows its own traditions and rituals related to the food it serves following a burial.

In Morocco, the funeral meal traditionally consists of honey, butter, and bread. Though honey is naturally sweet, it does not represent any particular aspect when it comes to either the funeral procedure or the deceased; in China, in contrast, mourners offer candies in a symbolic effort to "sweeten" the event (see chapter 3). Equally important, funeral rituals in Morocco—or the Muslim world, for that matter—reflect the status of the deceased. Regardless of whether the deceased was wealthy, poor, well educated, or a common person, however, she or he is given the same burial administered to all Muslims regardless of their social status. I believe this approach is different from that in other cultures. In Chinese funeral traditions for the elderly, funeral rituals reflect and befit a person's age and status in the community, which sometimes compels the family of the deceased to go into debt in support of that funeral rite.[3]

Moroccan views of honey differ. Offering sweets does not change the outcome for the deceased on Judgment Day. His or her good deeds matter more than what food gifts the family has to offer. Muslim views indicate that one is only borrowing items on Earth and has to leave them behind when one's time comes. Funeral feasts remind the bereaved that no matter what and how much one eats and accumulates while alive, the day will come when one leaves behind the physical world. Funeral feasts serve not only a religious function, but a social one as well; particular traditions in-

fluence what the gathered community is served. The older generation traditionally associates honey and butter with the funeral meal
commemorating the passing of a family member, because honey, butter,
and bread reflect simplicity, modesty, and mortality.

A Moroccan adage states, *"La tadkar al-ma'ida ma akalat ila wajbat
ba'd al-dafn,"* which translates, "The stomach does not remember what it
eats except for the meal served after one's burial." Honey, butter, and bread
are believed to be the foods of the common people. Serving honey, butter,
and bread after a burial creates a communal occasion that allows the family members of the deceased, their friends and neighbors, and sometimes
even strangers to gather around a table to honor the departed. In other
words, mourners do not have to worry that they may feel out of place by
being served lavish meals on which the wealthy or successful dine. Indeed,
the meal may not even satisfy hunger, nor is that its meaning or purpose.
Simple food serves to remind gatherers of the deeds of the departed, rather
than of his or her wealth, social status, or religious position. After the funeral has taken place, the attendees (the family members of the deceased,
relatives, friends, and others) gather at the deceased's home to recite the
Qur'an and share a meal. The meal serves the religious function of bringing merit to those who have gathered to share in the communal feast.

When I lived in Morocco, tradition held that families and their guests
ate the funeral repast from a communal bowl, usually without utensils,
while seated on the floor. That tradition still exists, mostly in rural parts
of the country. As Moroccan society changes demographically and socially, however, most postfuneral repasts in urban areas are served on a table
and utensils are used. A few years ago, I visited my native country of Morocco after a twenty-six-year absence. Before arriving, I was informed by
my family of the passing of one of my relatives. When I arrived in Morocco, my family said that the mourners served fruits and desserts as
though it were a celebration. That news upset others in my family because
they believed that the practice strayed from social norms and traditions.
Serving different kinds of fruits and the like departed from the traditional
funeral foods of honey, butter, bread, and couscous, and suggested that
the gathering had become more about catching up with family members
than remembering and reflecting on the life of the deceased.

If the experience in my own family is typical, then Moroccan society
may no longer have the traditional view of death that it had when I lived

there. Indeed, when I conversed with different family members during my visit to Morocco, I learned that, in the urban areas, serving fruits at funeral repasts had become the norm. This changing practice suggests a new attitude, and possibly even a new thinking, about death. Moroccan perceptions of death seem to be transitioning from a reflection on grief and sorrow to a celebration of the decedent's life (not unlike the American change from the funeral to the "celebration of life"). As a result, repasts provided during funerals are also changing. As stated earlier, funeral traditions in rural areas differ greatly from those in the urban areas within Morocco for a host of reasons. Chief among those reasons are education, availability of funds, and the role of technology. Each of these will be detailed separately.

Moroccan urban areas tend to be populated by better-educated people and to be more demographically diverse than rural areas. This phenomenon arises from new opportunities created by economic and social changes that are more prevalent in urban areas than in rural ones. The kind of education one chooses is usually thought to be based on economic factors; the pressure for schooling is a response to new opportunities created by economic and social change.[4] As a result, death, as a concept, is placed within the context of how education is perceived in rural areas versus urban ones. Rural areas tend to see traditional education, mainly Qur'anic schools, as part of the cultural traditions and a hallmark of village communities' identity. Jarmo Houtsonen argues, "One modern school teacher explained that people in Bounaamane see modern schools as alien; they can see their children's future only in terms of their own village. Modern schools represent 'city culture' because most teachers there come from cities and cannot speak the local language; instruction in the modern school is in French and Arabic. Qur'anic schools represent local cultural traditions; they have been integral parts of village communities for hundreds of years."[5] Since education positively affects one's thinking in many ways, the perception or concept of death in urban areas differs not only in style (in the matter of funeral arrangements) but also in substance (in the perception and meaning of death). For this reason, one notices that, during urban funeral events, there is less wailing when a family member dies, more focus on serving food (fruit platters) other than couscous, and an urgency to regain some normalcy in the daily routine. These practices differ from those in rural areas, where people tend to be conservative, are less financially well off, and have limited educational levels.

Equally important, urban families have far greater monetary resources than those in rural areas. In urban communities, families have more access to higher-paying jobs, which allows them to afford more expensive funeral services than rural families can afford. In rural areas, where many families base their livelihood on farming and other lower-income occupations, families cannot afford expensive funerals. Income from extracting oil from olive trees, for instance, generates the equivalent of about ten U.S. dollars per month.[6] In the urban areas, on the other hand, income tends to be higher both in public and private sectors. Even within the public sector, as Hassan Al-Ashraf argues, "Morocco is known amongst African countries for the wide gap between the income of top officials and that of average civil servants. For example, a minister in Morocco gets a monthly salary of 75,000 Moroccan dirhams ($9,385) while an employee at a government institution gets no more than 2,000 dirhams ($250)."[7] This income disparity defines the kind of funeral arrangements a family can afford. The downside to having a high income is that urban families tend to compete with each other in their abilities to offer the best funeral service. That situation contrasts with that of rural families, which, given their modest incomes, mark their funeral services with simplicity by providing only the basics in order to honor the deceased.

As Moroccan society changes, access to technology fundamentally alters the approach to funerals. In particular, the enormous growth of mobile phones facilitates more rapid and regular communication: "Morocco has 20,029 million mobile subscribers, up from 16,005 million at the end of 2006 and 2,550 million in 2000. Mobile penetration has reached 65.66 percent of the population, and only about 4 percent use postpaid services, while the rest are prepaid."[8] Technology, mainly cell phones, now allows people to communicate news of family events such as deaths, weddings, and graduations to family members who reside in different cities or abroad. Yet the availability of mobile phones is not as widespread in rural areas as it is in urban ones. Rural areas have more limited access to technology—cell phones, the Internet, and so forth—given the lack of technological infrastructure. Thus, when a family member passes away, it may take days before news reaches relatives who reside in a faraway city within the country or abroad.

Technology helps expedite funeral arrangements. When my aunt passed away, for instance, her grown-up children, my cousins, were residing abroad. My cousins' access to advanced technologies like cell phones, instant messaging, fax, and e-mail made it easier for them to make arrangements to return to Morocco to attend the funeral service, less than forty-eight hours after being notified of their mother's death. Technology played a role not only in enabling my cousins to communicate with family members, but also in hastening the completion of funeral arrangements. Moroccan families depend heavily on technology, despite the expense, to inform other members not only of emergencies such as the deaths of loved ones but also of celebrations like weddings. Hsain Ilahiane and John Sherry write, "One of the most significant changes in the telecommunication deals in Morocco is known as 'the new culture of the market.' As one Moroccan telecommunications official put it, 'by catering to the diverse needs of consumers, the new Telecom operators have been successful in fostering not only a culture of "consumer is king," but also managed to smooth the transition to getting consumers used to the idea of new technological features and types of mobile technologies.'"[9] Technology is contributing to social change in Morocco, and it is contributing to changing customs in the areas of death and mourning.

Differences from within Moroccan Society

We cannot address these different approaches to funeral rites between rural and urban families without noting the historical and cultural contexts in which each group operates. Culturally speaking, rural families in Morocco tend to be more conservative, religiously oriented, economically disadvantaged, and educationally underprivileged than families living in urban areas. These various differences thus contribute to a disparity in funeral practices. I believe that some of these differences are direct leftovers from the colonial era. When France and Spain colonized Morocco, France established a colonial school system in urban areas to introduce a more modernized form of education than the religiously based Moroccan religious education system. Thus, the gap became more evident as Moroccan residents in urban areas started to educate themselves and engage socially.[10]

In Morocco the degree to which different groups accepted French colonialism contributed fundamentally to the difference between rural and urban approaches to social customs and culture. Urban centers were more likely to embrace France's lifestyle; however, rural traditionalists resisted the French influence, particularly in the nineteenth century. Consider, for example, the academic efforts of Ahmad al-Wansharisi (1431–1508), who defied Morocco's colonial-inspired changes. The interference of European powers, and particularly of France, was evident in the differences between rural and urban Moroccan families. The funeral rituals clearly exhibit that influence.[11] Urban families who embraced the French education system pursued education at French universities, which resulted in less conservative thinking about funeral arrangements; rural families rejected French influence and retained the old traditions.

That said, most urban families have held on to some Moroccan religious customs. For example, though washing and preparing the deceased's body happens at home, the deceased has to face Mecca, and the burial is usually performed within twenty-four hours of the death. The belief in these customs, argue Hend Esmael-Yasien and Simon S. Rubin, allows the bereaved to better understand and accept that death awaits us all. They write:

> Presumably these beliefs influence the way the bereaved understand, accept, and respond emotionally to the death. One can see how such ritual serves to structure the response of the bereaved and the community in such a way as to reduce anxiety and confusion. Some of the ritual and the things that are said to the deceased are designed for the benefit of those who view the service. The goal is to remind those present of the fate that awaits all persons. As a result, it is prudent to plan for the future end of a person's life. The rituals are a sharp reminder to rethink and to strengthen one's relationship to religion and one's connection to God.[12]

The colonialist cultural and social dynamics lead one to observe that thinking about how death is perceived today has changed over the past twenty or thirty years. Despite the generational changes within the country, new perceptions regarding death are not embraced by the society as a whole, especially not by people in rural areas.

Similarly, approaches to food and dying also suggest that the younger generation views death through cultural and social lenses that are different from those through which the more traditional, older ones view it. Supplied with social media platforms, Morocco's younger generation communicates its thoughts, feelings, and grievances through Facebook, LinkedIn, and other social media outlets. Social media platforms become important, effective tools that allow communication to flow freely. In 2011 social media outlets played a pivotal role during the Arab Spring demonstrations. Julian York writes: "On the Moroccan Internet, otherwise verboten topics are discussed routinely. Trilingual and multicultural, the country's blogosphere thrives and expands as Moroccans communicate via Facebook and Twitter. As they do, the topic of conversation changes, leaning more toward the political. Individuals' blogs fill in perceived gaps in local mainstream reporting while group blogs like *Mamfakinch* publish information about ongoing protests sparked by the February 20th movement. Using Twitter and Facebook, people share videos of demonstrations, debate the movement's relevance, and analyze the mainstream media's depiction of what's happening in the streets and in the halls of power."[13] Interestingly, social media's contribution to shaping views and facilitating communication among people allows for the emergence of a new way of thinking. As a result, the increased conversation over social media about death allows many to perceive death as not only a natural phenomenon, but also an everyday part of our existence. Thus, the grieving of a younger Moroccan generation may not necessarily adhere to the tradition of grieving for forty days, as is the norm, but rather a shorter period of a few days, for instance.

Social media's role, however, is linked not only to how fast the news about the death of a loved one can travel, but also to how families start to perceive death when it happens. In other words, social media outlets give families the opportunity to mobilize, prepare, and attend the funeral service quickly. Social media underscore the differences between rural and urban families when it comes to conceptualizing the meaning of death and sharing grief. As a result, cultural changes and emerging differences of opinion manifest themselves in the funeral repast served in rural areas versus that served in urban regions. From these dynamics, a debate emerges about the true meaning of the link between food and death. In this regard, traditionalists suggest that presenting nontraditional food during funerals emphasizes the family's status in society. Thus, the funeral service becomes a platform for the family of the departed to display its wealth and creativity, which reinforces the notion that social division exists. The counterargument is, however, that families in rural and conservative areas have always focused their grieving on seeking forgiveness for their deceased loved one through serving a communal meal like couscous. It is a Moroccan tradition to serve couscous at funerals, and its meaning, at least from the conservative viewpoint found in rural areas, is that feeding others will eventually erase or lessen the misdeeds the deceased committed while alive.

This belief is widely held in certain Sunni circles of the Islamic tradition. When people share a meal together, God (Allah) sends down his blessings. If there were little food and too many people, everyone would be satisfied and no one would go hungry, metaphorically speaking. Thus, the type of food that is served holds no importance; rather, it is the blessing offered through sharing a communal repast that is significant. One should note, however, that traditions differ between the West and Islamic peoples in regard to funeral practices. In the West, funerals are usually about honoring the wishes of the deceased. For example, when there is a viewing, the deceased usually lies in his or her casket, dressed in the clothes he or she enjoyed wearing while living. Funerals can become extensions of the deceased's preferences, ranging from the ways the deceased sought to be buried to the serving of foods the deceased enjoyed in life at the postfuneral feast. By contrast, in Muslim custom, the central aim of the funeral is *not* honoring the wishes of the dead, but rather respecting the preferences of the living. Food served after the funeral allows the family of the deceased to mourn and grieve in the comfort of the family's home while surrounded by relatives and friends. This is why, in the Moroccan tradition, couscous is served in a communal bowl using hands rather than utensils. The hope is that God grants his blessings on the deceased's family, and the communal sharing of the meal reveals the emphasis of community over and above the deceased. When the family of the deceased serves food following the burial—couscous, in this case—the belief is that feeding others serves two objectives: First, God blesses the food the family provides during this difficult time; and second, in the act of feeding others during a funeral, God forgives some of the deceased's misdeeds. As to what types of misdeeds are forgiven, only God can decide.

Another point that merits emphasis has to do with whether funeral repasts are eaten with bare hands or utensils. There is a debate on what is appropriate in such a setting. The argument most conservatives in Morocco make is that the funeral repast gives guests the opportunity to follow in the customs set forth by the Prophet Muhammad when he used his bare hands while eating food. There are those who argue that Islam has evolved, and modern life, as we know it today, renders impossible embracing the ascetic lifestyle of the Prophet Muhammad's era. I suggest that when Islam was established some 1,400 years ago, individuals used their bare hands when eating because there were no utensils available. The argument was and is, mainly in most conservative regions of the Muslim world, that when one eats with one's hands, God blesses the food that is about to be eaten. Because of this interpretation, some argue that when it comes to funeral rituals, whether in Morocco or in other Muslim countries, both rural and urban families hold on to the notion that in difficult times, such as the burial of a loved one, the focus and hope are always on ensuring that the deceased's misdeeds are forgiven. That said, I can understand that some families in Morocco might not want to follow the tradition of eating couscous during funerals—or any other time—using bare hands. Rather, the family of the deceased focuses on honoring the loss of its loved one while hoping that his or her misdeeds are forgiven. To illustrate, in her article "Mind Your Manners: Eat with Your Hands," Sarah Digregorio argues, "Eating with the hands evokes great emotion."[14] Digregorio's assertion stresses the different assumptions about the significance and meaning of eating without utensils. Our focus remains on whether using bare hands triggers some sort of link between death and food.

Religious beliefs in Morocco center on the fact that food serves functions other than satisfying hunger. Chief among its functions is its use as a conduit to seek God's blessings and forgiveness. In funeral rituals, the family of the deceased hopes that having members of the community and relatives gather after the burial to eat couscous served in a communal bowl provides an opportunity to have the misdeeds of the departed forgiven. Forgiveness through this meal seems to be attributed more to popular religious belief than to scriptural interpretation. There is no basis in the Qur'an or in the Sunnah, the record of the saying and deeds of the Prophet Muhammad, and Muslims believe that only God can make the final decision to grant forgiveness to the dead. Yet mourners believe that serving food to family members and strangers in this way offers merit to the dead (rather than the living), since the intention has never been to receive a reward for serving the repast: "We feed you only for the countenance of Allah. We wish not from you reward or gratitude."[15] Thus, the food served in no way signifies that the wishes *of the dead* are honored. The family serves the repast to pay its respects following the loss of a member of their community. Yet honoring the dead is considered a cornerstone of the funeral procedure, because the relatives of the deceased pay their respects to the dead and even comfort themselves in the mourning process by honoring various wishes of the deceased.[16]

The Funeral Tradition across Cultural Boundaries

Serving the meal is an important part of the hospitality customs of the funeral, and it communicates to the funeral attendees a sense of how much the deceased's family loves and appreciates them. It also demonstrates the importance of the role of food in emphasizing community. Equally important is the fact that food traditions differ from one country to the next, from one culture to the next, and from one region to the next. These differences are evident even within one particular culture or country. For instance, residents in northern Morocco may enjoy food like brouchettes, or steak or swordfish kebabs, which residents in the south may dislike, while those in southern Morocco are known for their love of spicy food. Yet, when it comes to national dishes such as couscous or tajin (tagine)— also known as "Moroccan crockpot" because it is used to slow-cook meat—both regions share an appreciation for national dishes.

The common link, however, is that all Muslim culture associates food with a welcoming hospitality and friendship. Because of this significance, food possesses great meaning in Muslim culture. As stated earlier, food served at a funeral is intended to do more than just satisfy hunger. Food serves as a means of spiritual communication: in serving the repast after the burial, the family of the deceased hopes to ease the transition of its loved one as he or she faces questions in the grave. Seyyed Hossein Nasr argues: "In death, man finds nothing but his own attributes, no longer veiled by the corporeal body but revealing themselves to him in forms appropriate to his new abode. . . . Man awakens to the realities of his own words, acts, and moral qualities; his moral substance, whether good or evil, assumes corporeal shape. Everything that had been hidden in the lower world becomes outwardly manifest."[17]

In short, food reflects the hospitality of the Arab culture, even during difficult times such as funerals, when families are grieving. Despite the agony and sadness that a family suffers in the aftermath of losing a loved one, some mourners are relieved when, for instance, their loved one who suffered from a long, untreatable health condition has finally passed away. Some mourners prefer not to see their loved one suffer, and death provides an end to that suffering.

Offering postfuneral repasts is considered part of the bereavement rituals in the Moroccan tradition but is not necessarily incorporated into other branches of Islamic culture. In the Moroccan tradition, the funeral feasts symbolize the emotional support given by the family to the deceased. For this reason, in Morocco, when mourners return home to share honey, butter, and bread after the burial, the family of the deceased does not question strangers attending the funeral feast even when it is clear that they are not part of the family. One concludes that the communal meal following the burial serves as a means of expressing emotions and the need for allowing others to share in the grief of the family of the deceased. This communal meal is a ritual that has been in practice for generations, and it is commonly understood that this meal functions as a communally binding practice. On the other hand, Muslim culture often rejects other practices of Moroccan culture, such as wailing when a family member dies.

In Western culture, family members of the deceased may seek professional help from a therapist to resolve the emotional turmoil of losing a loved one. In Morocco and in Islam, however, offering the postburial repast *itself* serves to heal. The healing mechanism depends heavily on human contact rather than a set of psychological strategies. Once again, using Morocco as a guide and illustration, the ritual accompanying the repast, in this case couscous offered to the guests, involves almost everybody eating with his right hand rather than utensils. There is, however, etiquette one needs to follow when it comes to using one's hand. For instance, it is considered ill-mannered to eat with the left hand or to use all the fingers of the right hand. Rather, one should use the right hand and only the thumb, index finger, and middle finger. The enactment of this ritual does not suggest the transition of the departed from a physical life, as we know it, to a spiritual one. Rather, it is a belief that Muslims ought to emulate the prophet Mohammed in all his actions and deeds, including the use of one's right hand when eating. Since Muslims are advised to take the prophet as an example, most if not all funeral guests follow this tradition. Equally important is a widely held belief that eating with the right

hand demonstrates one's respect for the deceased and the profound personal, social, and spiritual significance of death.

Another important custom can be found in the role of visitation. In
the United States, for example, visitation allows mourners to display grief,
but neither Moroccans nor the entire Muslim world, for that matter, views
visitation as having that purpose. Displaying the body or allowing a viewing reflects an appreciation of, and an expression of love for, the body as it
decays.[18] Viewings of important community members or leaders illustrate
the contrasting beliefs. In the Catholic tradition, for instance, the viewing
of Pope John Paul II was understood within the context of how people remembered his life; they demonstrated their love for him and expressed, as
members of the community, their conclusions about the existence, or non-
existence, of an afterlife. Yet displaying his body in a public building also
gave mourners the opportunity to remember the significance of the deceased *as historical.* Thomas Quartier et al. write, "The deceased is still
part of the narrative reconstruction of people in the social networks of
which he or she was a part. The members of this network need to relate to
the past and future of the deceased. We seek to establish continuity in
time when we remember the past of the deceased and our past with that
person; and we give that person a future in some form. For example, we
may name a street or public building after the deceased, or remember the
person when we come together."[19] Thus, the function of the viewing is
both to situate the dead in time, in the past, and to allow his or her legacy
to live on.

In the Moroccan tradition, however, offering repasts not only allows
the display of family grief, but also expresses the importance of the relationship the deceased had in life with the community. A viewing is not
considered necessary because the funeral feast offers a chance for mourners to gather together to remember the deceased. That is also why the family welcomes strangers attending funerals. These strangers are considered
part of the community and might have heard about the deceased during
his or her life. Their attendance during and after the burial is their way not
only of paying respects, but also of expressing their sympathies to the family. In the Moroccan tradition, attendees also proclaim certain axioms following the repast. Those include expressions such as *"Allah yarzuqoka
al-kathir,"* which translates to "May God grant you plenty more"; this
phrase reflects simultaneously the generosity of the family of the deceased

and the appreciation of the guests, especially if the family is not well-off financially. It is interesting to note how beliefs about food and death in general vary in different cultures. Regardless of place or time, when considering the experience of another's death, food represents a sacred aspect that is valued and shared among cultures of the world. The link between food and death represents something eternal, like a spiritual existence that could live on forever.

Consider what food came to represent, for example, among ethnic groups such as Native Americans. I do not suggest a literal comparison of funeral traditions and customs in Morocco to those of Native Americans. Undeniably, more differences exist than do similarities. Rather, my objective is to illustrate how, despite the cultural and historical differences between the two traditions, Moroccans and Native Americans alike appreciate the meaning of celebrating a loved one's death through funeral feasting. In both traditions, funeral rituals, including repasts, reinforce and confirm the reality of death. Equally important, when family members of the deceased, guests, and members of the community get together for a meal after the burial, the act itself acknowledges the wide range of feelings they all share. Yet each community expresses those feelings in its own way. Paul Giblin and Andrea Hug write: "The nature of ritual is that it provides a sense of structure, order, and role for participants. It helps set a smaller grieving family into the context of an extended family, church, and community. Survivors do not grieve alone. Funerals confirm and reinforce the reality of death. They assist in the acknowledgment and expression of a wide range of often conflicting feelings."[20] Giblin and Hug express the common denominator that I argue exists in both Moroccan and Native American experiences of grief.

The other significant contribution made by the Moroccan funeral repast is one of emotional support and an enhancement of social relations among family members of the deceased in terms of their comfort level at the time of death. "Funeral rituals appeared to enhance mourners' comfort at the time of death, both by facilitating social support and by connecting the griever with deeper levels of meaning with which to understand and frame their loss experience," Louis Gamino et al. write.[21] The repast offers the opportunity for the community not only to get together to pay its respects, but also to celebrate as one cohesive entity; thus, funeral ritual is considered a communal process.[22] The takeaway is that despite being on opposite ends of the spectrum in their bereavement customs, both Moroccans and Native Americans share a commonality: the meaning of repasts and the role of food in celebrating the dead. Funeral rituals are the platform on which family members of the deceased can write not only the narrative of their loss, but also the story of their departed loved one.

In the bereavement rituals of Creek Indian culture, it was customary to place food, along with few personal items, in the casket.[23] The practice suggests that, according to Creek tradition, as in modern Muslim culture, food has always been a symbol of hospitality—personal, cultural, or spiritual—between two worlds. The difference between the Creek traditions and those of Muslim culture lies in one question: For whom was the food significant? In Creek culture only the deceased's favorite food was served or placed in the casket. In Muslim culture, however, the repast does not feature the deceased's favorite food—the focus is not on remembering and marking the desires of *the deceased*. Rather, within the culture and its traditions, this is a ritual that most, if not all, families who experience death are expected to perform for the benefit of *the community*. As stated earlier, the food served following the burial is a way for the family to reflect on the good deeds its deceased loved one did during his or her life. It expresses the family's wish that by their serving the food, the deceased's sins will be forgiven. Yet the most important factor in many societies, including the Muslim world, is religion, which plays one of the most influential roles in food choice.[24]

Yet many ask whether there is a link or a relationship between bereavement rituals and culture. To what degree does one influence the other? If there is some evidence in support of such a relationship, could it suggest why, despite a new perspective on death in Morocco, families still hold, to some degree, to cultural norms and traditions when they honor the dead? For instance, most Moroccan families in both rural and urban areas still observe the forty days' grieving period. Though the perception about death might have changed, the fact that families still follow certain traditions speaks volumes about the value of those rituals.

In other religions, traditions, and cultures, changes in bereavement rituals have been noted. In a recent book, *Dead but Not Lost,* the authors argue that cultures and traditions play a pivotal role in imposing certain conditions and rules to maintain specific traditions (like the forty days of grieving in Moroccan rituals), thus suggesting the importance of culture when it comes to interpreting what bereavement entails.[25] As the literature indicates, bereavement rituals not only in the Islamic faith but also in the Creek, Indian, Baha'i, and Hindu faiths (among others) have changed over time. But it is cultural constraints that play a major role in how a family, a society, or a culture interprets the meaning of death, bereavement rituals, and grief. Andrea Walker and David Balk state, "All cultures impose rules either promoting or forbidding continuing bonds with the dead; further, sociologists . . . have argued forcefully that an individual interpretation of bereavement, grief, and mourning misses the fundamental role of culture."[26]

These changes in rituals reflect new understandings, particularly those challenging the perception of death. Do younger generations continue to see death the way their parents saw it? Or do they adjust their perception in light of new realities and thinking imposed on them through social media, technology, and new ways of thinking about death? To relate the latter question to ways that thinking about death has evolved in Morocco, I argue that this change reflects the younger generation more than it does the older one. Access to technology and unlimited sources of global information have influenced the thinking of the new generation in regard to its perception of death. I am not suggesting that the new Moroccan generation is *detached* from understanding the meaning of death; rather, it sees death as a natural phenomenon that all humans experience at some point in their existence on Earth. What distinguishes the younger generation from the older one is that the grieving period is much shorter than it was twenty or thirty years ago. The argument that the influence of other cultures or the effect of globalization might have something to do with the shift in perception about death, however, can't be proven. When visiting Muslim countries such as Egypt, Lebanon, and Jordan, among others, one realizes that this shift in thinking is pervasive among the younger generation. Equally important, scholars, including Gabeba Baderoon, argue that, within the context of Muslim tradition, food has a meaning different from what one might expect. "Making what I knew as 'Muslim' food gave me a creative rather than nostalgic relationship with South Africa."[27] What this suggests is that the meaning of food differs from one area to another, and even among individuals; thus, one sees various explanations and meanings regarding the relationship between food and death.

Despite geographical differences within Morocco when it comes to funeral repasts, there is a common Muslim understanding regarding the reason behind our presence on Earth and the cycle of life as a self-renewing movement. Regardless of where they reside, the bereaved express their loss according to local tradition, though the style varies between rural and urban communities and reflects the different expectations of different social levels. Yet there is an agreement among Moroccans—and all Muslims, for that matter—that death represents a bridge all must traverse in order to return to God. This thinking is not modern; rather, it has evolved since the times of early Muslim scholars, such as Jalaluddin Rumi and Abu'l-Qasim al-Junayd. These Muslim mystics focused their intellectual engagement on providing a spiritual meaning of death rather than a physical one, clarifying it as a return to the origin. God himself expresses it in the Qur'an: "Verily, we belong to Allah and unto Him we are returning."[28]

The understanding of death in the Muslim world transcends physical reality and social experience, as the family of the deceased goes from the preparation of the body for burial to the funeral to the funeral repast; then, the rituals performed appropriately, the family can focus on its grief. Leor Halevi offers a much-needed understanding of the Islamic traditions and the meaning of death. "Halevi provides new approaches to the treatment of a Muslim corpse and associated everyday urban practices. He explores the corpse from its deathbed, its preparation for burial to the grave to reflect on different layers of human interaction. All corpses are washed, wrapped, prayed for, and buried. For those who mourn, this helps them defy the definitiveness of death by providing the initial steps towards continuation after death."[29]

The Moroccan funeral feast must then be considered within the context of a much larger concept: how our presence on Earth is only temporary and portends a return to our creator, God. Our strength is limited, our knowledge is minimal, and our acceptance of our own mortality is a must. Stated differently, death provides the Muslim family and the community at large the opportunity to care for and support one another. The importance of the funeral repast lies in that desire for comfort and community. In Morocco the use of couscous during funerals emphasizes empathy and harmonic existence while symbolizing our common human bonds. Couscous as an everyday staple serves as the common foodstuff that underscores mortality and makes clear the fragility of life. Like Islam's emphasis on the need for all Muslims to care for one another through charity, the plainness of the mourning meal illustrates Islam's emphasis on humans as subject always to God—their mortality is made clearly apparent in contrast to God's omnipotent power.

To Moroccans—and all Muslims, for that matter—the funeral repast is an integral part of the concept of death and the afterlife. It also reveals the close relationship of life, creation, and resurrection—concepts derived from the holy Qur'an, the final revealed message from God. Whatever the case may be, scholars agree that the influence of religion, whether Christianity, Islam, Judaism, or any other, plays a pivotal role in defining the concept of death and framing the link between food and death within a cultural and religious context.

Notes

1. Christine Schirrmacher, "They Are Not All Martyrs: Islam on the Topics of Dying, Death, and Salvation in the Afterlife," *Evangelical Review of Theology* 36, no. 3 (2012): 251.

2. A. R. Gatrad, "Muslim Customs Surrounding Death, Bereavement, Postmortem Examinations, and Organ Transplants," *British Medical Journal,* 309, no. 6953 (1994): 521–523, www.jstor.org/stable/29724563, accessed December 29, 2016.

3. Mislav Popovic, "Chinese Funeral." traditionscustoms.com, www.chinaculture .org/gb/en_chinaway/2004-03/03/content_46092.htm, accessed May 1, 2017.

4. Jarmo Houtsonen, "Traditional Quranic Education in a Southern Moroccan Village," *International Journal of Middle East Studies* 26, no. 3 (1994): 489–500, www.researchgate.net/publication/231998156_Traditional_Quranic_Education_in_a_Southern_Moroccan_Village, accessed December 24, 2016.

5. Ibid.

6. Yann le Polain de Waroux and Eric F. Lambin, "Niche Commodities and Rural Poverty Alleviation: Contextualizing the Contribution of Argan Oil to Rural Livelihoods in Morocco," *Annals of the Association of American Geographers* 103, no. 3 (2013): 589–607.

7. Hassan Al-Ashraf, "Moroccan Ministers' High Salaries Causes Alarm," *Al Arabiya News Outlet,* June 6, 2012, http://english.alarabiya.net/articles/2012/06/06/218972.html, accessed December 24, 2016.

8. Hsain Ilahiane and John Sherry, "Economic and Social Effect of Mobile Phone Use in Morocco," *Ethnology* 48, no. 2 (2009): 85–98.

9. Ibid.

10. "France and Spain in Morocco," *Colonization of Morocco,* http://

colonizationofmorocco.weebly.com/life-under-imperialist-power.html, accessed December 30, 2016.

11. Daniel J. Schroeter, "Old Texts, New Practices: Islamic Reform in Modern Morocco," *American Historical Review* 120, no. 5 (2015): 2001–2002.

12. Hend Yasien-Esmael and Simon Shimshon Rubin. "The Meaning Structure of Muslim Bereavements in Israel: Religious Traditions, Mourning Practices, and Human Experience," *Death Studies* 29, no. 6 (2005): 495–518.

13. Julian C. York, "The Revolutionary Force of Facebook and Twitter," *Nieman Report* 65, no. 3 (2011): 49.

14. Sarah Digregorio, "Mind Your Manners: Eat with Your Hands," *New York Times,* January 17, 2012, www.nytimes.com/2012/01/18/dining/mind-your-manners-eat-with-your-hands.html, accessed April 3, 2017.

15. The Quranic Arabic Corpus, Sahih International, http://corpus.quran.com/translation.jsp?chapter=76&verse=9, accessed October 4, 2015.

16. "Who Are Funerals Really For? Funerals Are to Respect the Last Wishes of the Dead," *Two Views,* March 16, 2015, www.two-views.com/article_funerals.html, accessed April 3, 2017.

17. Seyyed Hossein Nasr, ed., *Islamic Spirituality: Foundations* (New York: Crossroad Publishing, 1987), 394.

18. Tony Walter, "La Scena degli Addii. Farewell Scene: Death and Funeral Rituals in Contemporary Western Society," *Mortality* 5, no. 1 (March 2000): 117–118.

19. Thomas Quartier, Chris A. M. Hermans, and Anton H. M. Scheer, "Remembrance and Hope in Roman Catholic Funeral Rites: Attitudes of Participants towards Past and Future of the Deceased," *Journal of Empirical Theology* 17, no. 2 (2004): 255.

20. Paul Giblin and Andrea Hug, "The Psychology of Funeral Rituals." *Liturgy* 21, no. 1 (2006): 11–19, www.tandfonline.com/doi/full/10.1080/04580630500285956?scroll=top&needAccess=true, accessed December 30, 2016.

21. L. A. Gamino, L. W. Easterling, L. S. Stirman, and K. W. Sewell, "Grief Adjustment as Influenced by Funeral Participation and Occurrence of Adverse Funeral Events," *Omega* 41 (2000): 91.

22. This practice, if I may add, is not limited to Moroccan culture or Native American customs. Rather, it is incorporated in other religions such as Christianity and Judaism. Of interest in this conversation is how within Christianity and its different denominations, the approach to funeral rituals and grieving, though varying, serves to unite the members of the community. Giblin and Hug write: "Judaism has much to say about mourning. Christianity has less to say about mourning and more about death and resurrection. Hope in the resurrection is based on the life and death of Jesus Christ and is symbolized in the cross. Christianity has, at times, been accused of 'spiritual bypassing,' that is, encouraging survivors to jump from the unfinished business of mourning to the deceased's spiritual journey to the next world. Within Christianity there are also interesting, if nuanced,

denominational differences to be noted. Catholics emphasize prayer as assisting the movement of the deceased into the new life while Protestants emphasize the bereavement function of ritual for survivors." Gary Giblin and Andrea Hug, "The Psychology of Funeral Rituals," *Liturgy* 21, no. 1 (2006): 11–19, www.tandfonline.com/doi/full/10.1080/04580630500285956?scroll=top&needAccess=true, accessed December 30, 2016, 17.

23. Andrea C. Walker and David E. Balk, "Bereavement Rituals in the Muscogee Creek Tribe," *Death Studies* 31, no. 7 (2007): 633–652.

24. For more on this, see Mohani Abdul, Hashanah Ismail, Haslina Hashim, and Juliana Johari, "Consumer Decision Making Process in Shopping for Halal Food in Malaysia," *China-USA Business Review* 8, no. 9 (2009): 40–47, www.academia.edu/1379711/Consumer_decision_making_process_in_shopping_for_halal_food_in_Malaysia, accessed September 15, 2016.

25. Robert Goss and Dennis Klass, *Dead but Not Lost: Grief Narratives in Religious Traditions* (Walnut Creek, Calif: AltaMira Press, 2005).

26. Walker and Balk, "Bereavement Rituals in the Muscogee Creek Tribe."

27. Gabeba Baderoon, "Everybody's Mother Was a Good Cook: Meanings of Food in Muslim Cooking," *Agenda* 17, no. 51 (2002): 4–15.

28. *The Holy Qur'an*, trans. Abdullah Yusuf Ali, 5th ed. (Birmingham, U.K.: Wordsworth, 2001), 156.

29. Janet Starkey, "Death, Paradise and the Arabian Nights," *Mortality* 14, no. 3 (2009): 286–302. She cites Leor Halevi, *Muhammad's Grave: Death Rites and the Making of Islamic Society.* (New York: Columbia University Press, 2007).

Bibliography

Abdul, Mohani, Hashanah Ismail, Haslina Hashim, and Juliana Johari. "Consumer Decision Making Process in Shopping for Halal Food in Malaysia." *China-USA Business Review* 8, no. 9 (2009): 40–47. www.academia.edu/1379711/Consumer_decision_making_process_in_shopping_for_halal_food_in_Malaysia, accessed September 15, 2016.

Al-Ashraf, Hassan. "Moroccan Ministers' High Salaries Causes Alarm," *Al Arabiya News Outlet,* June 6, 2012. http://english.alarabiya.net/articles/2012/06/06/218972.html, accessed December 24, 2016.

Baderoon, Gabeba. "Everybody's Mother Was a Good Cook: Meanings of Food in Muslim Cooking." *Agenda* 17, no. 51 (2002): 4–15.

Bahammam, Fahd Salem. *Food and Dress in Islam* (e-book). Modern Guide, 2012.

Bodo, M. K. *Halal Comfort Food: The New Muslim's Guide to Going Halal* (e-book). Amazon Digital Services, 2014.

"The Difference between a Sunni Muslim and a Shiite Muslim." http://teachersites.schoolworld.com/webpages/GHurst/files/difference%20between%20a%20 sunni%20muslim%20and%20a%20shiite%20muslim.pdf, accessed October 4, 2015.

Digregorio, Sarah. "Mind Your Manners: Eat with Your Hands," *New York Times,* January 17, 2012. www.nytimes.com/2012/01/18/dining/mind-your-manners-eat-with-your-hands.html, accessed April 3, 2017.

"Food—Food and Culture." JRank Articles. http://family.jrank.org/pages/639/Food-Food-Culture.html#ixzz3mIxzPfdE, accessed October 14, 2015.

"France and Spain in Morocco." *Colonization of Morocco.* http://colonizationofmorocco.weebly.com/life-under-imperialist-power.html, accessed December 30, 2016.

Gatrad, A. R. "Muslim Customs Surrounding Death, Bereavement, Postmortem Examinations, and Organ Transplants." *British Medical Journal* 309, no. 6953 (1994): 521–523. www.jstor.org/stable/29724563, accessed December 29, 2016.

Giblin, Paul, and Andrea Hug. "The Psychology of Funeral Rituals." *Liturgy* 21, no. 1 (2006): 11–19. www.tandfonline.com/doi/full/10.1080/04580630500285956?scroll=top&needAccess=true, accessed December 30, 2016.

Goss, Robert E., and Dennis E. Klass. *Dead but Not Lost: Grief Narratives in Religious Traditions.* Walnut Creek, Calif.: AltaMira Press, 2005.

The Holy Qur'an. Translated by Abdullah Yusuf Ali. 5th edition. Birmingham, U.K.: Wordsworth Editions, 2001.

Houtsonen, Jarmo. "Traditional Quranic Education in a Southern Moroccan Village." *International Journal of Middle East Studies* 26, no. 3 (1994): 489–500. www.researchgate.net/publication/231998156_Traditional_Quranic_Education_in_a_Southern_Moroccan_Village, accessed December 24, 2016.

Ilahiane, Hsain, and John Sherry. "Economic and Social Effect of Mobile Phone Use in Morocco." *Ethnology* 48, no. 2 (2009): 85–98.

Johnson, Marilyn. *The Dead Beat: Lost Souls, Lucky Stiffs, and the Perverse Pleasures of Obituaries.* New York: HarperCollins, 2006.

Le Polain de Waroux, Yann, and Eric F. Lambin. "Niche Commodities and Rural Poverty Alleviation: Contextualizing the Contribution of Argan Oil to Rural Livelihoods in Morocco." *Annals of the Association of American Geographers* 103, no. 3 (2013): 589–607.

Marshall, David, and Lucinda Mosher, eds. *Death, Resurrection, and Human Destiny: Christian and Muslim Perspectives.* Washington, D.C.: Georgetown University Press, 2014.

Nasr, Seyyed Hossein, ed. *Islamic Spirituality: Foundations.* New York: Crossroad Publishing, 1987.

Popovic, Mislav. "Chinese Funeral." traditionscustoms.com. www.chinaculture.org/gb/en_chinaway/2004-03/03/content_46092.htm, accessed May 1, 2017.

Quartier, Thomas, Chris A. M. Hermans, and Anton H. M. Scheer. "Remembrance and Hope in Roman Catholic Funeral Rites: Attitudes of Participants towards Past and Future of the Deceased." *Journal of Empirical Theology* 17, no. 2 (2004): 252–280.

Quranic Arabic Corpus. Sahih International. http://corpus.quran.com/ translation.jsp?chapter=76&verse=9, accessed: October 4, 2015.

Schirrmacher, Christine. "They Are Not All Martyrs: Islam on the Topics of Dying, Death, and Salvation in the Afterlife." *Evangelical Review of Theology* 36, no. 3 (2012): 250–265.

Schroeter, Daniel J. "Old Texts, New Practices: Islamic Reform in Modern Morocco." *American Historical Review* 120, no. 5 (2015): 2001–2002.

Smith, Jane Idelman, and Yvonne Yazbeck Haddad. *The Islamic Understanding of Death and Resurrection.* New York: Oxford University Press, 2002.

Starkey, Janet. "Death, Paradise and the Arabian Nights." *Mortality* 14, no. 3 (2009): 286–302.

Walker, Andrea C., and David E. Balk. "Bereavement Rituals in the Muscogee Creek Tribe." *Death Studies* 31, no. 7 (2007): 633–652.

Walter, Tony. "La Scena Degli Addii. Farewell Scene: Death and Funeral Rituals in Contemporary Western Society." *Mortality* 5, no. 1 (March 2000): 117–118.

"Who Are Funerals Really For? Funerals Are to Respect the Last Wishes of the Dead." *Two Views,* March 16, 2015. www.two-views.com/article_funerals .html, accessed April 3, 2017.

Yasien-Esmael, Hend, and Simon Shimshon Rubin. "The Meaning Structure of Muslim Bereavements in Israel: Religious Traditions, Mourning Practices, and Human Experience." *Death Studies* 29, no. 6 (2005): 495–518.

York, Julian C. "The Revolutionary Force of Facebook and Twitter." *Nieman Report* 65, no. 3 (2011): 49–50.

7

Alcohol Consumption, Transgression, and Death

Christa Shusko

A Cremation on the Banks of Lake Michigan

A strange scene it must have been: the crowd of black-robed men gathered around an enormous funeral pyre constructed on a desolate stretch of ground on the shore of Lake Michigan on July 16, 1892. The wooden coffin that had transported the body to this place was opened with the help of an ax. The dead man's body was placed on the pyre. After the mourners circled the pyre three times with their torches, the pyre was lit. Long funeral orations commenced. By turns the men read poetry, bits of philosophy, and eulogies to the man on the pyre. Somber songs were sung and played as the whiskey flowed freely. The pyre was of such a size that it burned for five hours, and the body that was on it was reduced to little more than ash. When the flames at last were extinguished, the ashes were collected and placed in an urn.

The men overseeing this mournful and elaborate ceremony were members of the short-lived Whitechapel Club, a social club founded in Chicago in the late 1880s.[1] While the club functioned primarily as a social and professional organization for young newspapermen (as well as others lucky enough to be admitted), its activities illustrate the ways in which the consumption of alcohol can, in the context of transgressive ritual, allow participants to confront death in meaningful ways. In the introduction to this volume, Candi K. Cann notes, "The ways in which food functions as symbol and operates as a material conduit between the living and the dead reveal much about our culture, our worldviews, and our understandings of the afterlife." An examination of the Whitechapel Club's ritual uses of

Twentieth Century Punch

1 can peaches
1 can pineapple
½ dozen oranges, cut in slices
½ dozen lemons, cut in slices
1¾ gallons Tokay wine (or sweet Catawba)
1 quart brandy
4 ounces Jamaica rum
4 ounces abricotine (Eagle Crème d'Abricot)

Put the above ingredients in a bowl and let the mixture stand for about 10 hours in a cool place, then filter it into a punch bowl with a nice piece of ice and dress the top of the ice with fruit and serve.*

*James C. Maloney, "Twentieth Century Punch," in *The 20th Century Guide for Mixing Fancy Drinks* (Chicago: James C. Maloney, 1900), 21.

alcohol thus reveals the ways in which its members sought to confront the uncertainties of death—and of life—in late nineteenth-century Chicago.

As Whitechapel member Wallace Rice recorded: "What we had done the night before in the way of punch was made of claret, port, Jamaica rum, brandy, and abricotine, a vivid red in color and so called 'blood punch,' fulfilling the prime conditions of being smooth and pleasant to taste going down and highly efficacious after absorption. What the Press Club did, stupid as usual, was to fill a large punch bowl with straight whisky, in which was a lump of ice and on which thin slices of lemon were floating, to be drunk from tin cups."[2] The closest recipe to this description that I have been able to locate is for "Twentieth Century Punch"—a much less impressive name than "Blood Punch," to be sure. And while I cannot imagine the Whitechapelers being overly concerned with fruit, it is the recipe I have included above.

General Considerations

In *Drink: A Cultural History of Alcohol,* Iain Gately notes that alcohol has been used in rituals pertaining to death for centuries, albeit in a variety of culturally specific ways. In ancient Greece, for example, "Wine was the drink of fighting men, the indispensable lubricant of death and honor, of sacking cities, of carrying off armor, cattle, and women. All their rituals were punctuated with libations of wine—the gods did not pay attention otherwise."[3] Drinking emboldened warriors as they faced death—as killers and as victims. In sixteenth-century Japan alcohol was an important component of ritual suicide: "Before committing *seppuku,* i.e., disemboweling themselves, Japanese suicides would take a farewell draft of sake and provide a cup for the second responsible for beheading them when the pain became too great."[4] In many cultural contexts, drinking alcohol punctuates mourning rituals, as it serves as a way to honor the dead and to console the living.[5]

By the late nineteenth century, the burgeoning field of psychology in Europe and America encouraged considerations of alcohol that increasingly interrogated its effects on consciousness. In his lectures published in *The Varieties of Religious Experience,* William James noted that intoxication, particularly alcoholic intoxication, is an important component of mystical experiences. James included alcohol as one easily identifiable (and too easily accessible, perhaps) psychoactive substance that might contribute to mystical experiences:

> The sway of alcohol over mankind is unquestionably due to its power to stimulate the mystical faculties of human nature, usually crushed to earth by the cold facts and dry criticisms of the sober hour. Sobriety diminishes, discriminates, and says no; drunkenness expands, unites, and says yes. It is in fact the great exciter of the Yes function in man. It brings its votary from the chill periphery of things to the radiant core. It makes him for the moment one with truth. . . . The drunken consciousness is one bit of the mystic consciousness, and our total opinion of it must find its place in our opinion of that larger whole.[6]

Though James would famously favor the metaphysical insights provided by nitrous oxide over those of the rather more plebian alcohol,[7] the "drunken consciousness" deserves closer examination, especially in regard to alcohol's use in mystical experiences and esoteric religious rituals. Georges Bataille similarly recognized the ways that alcohol could alter the emotions or consciousness, linking alcohol consumption to laughter as well as to truth. He wrote: "I offer a glass of alcohol to my thought: a return to sunny consciousness. . . . If I need alcohol, it is to be cleansed of the dust of others."[8] Thus, the consumption of alcohol functions as a means of both transformation and transgression.

This chapter examines the role of alcoholic beverages in the development of "mystical" or "sunny" consciousness, particularly as this consciousness developed in the context of the Whitechapel Club. I argue that alcohol was served in the club as a conduit to truth by means of transgression. The Whitechapel Club offers a fascinating perspective on drink and religion: its atheological practices help us consider the ways in which the consumption of alcohol may create religious identities, albeit unconventional ones. By uniting members in drunken consciousness, the club served as a place in which transgression served a purpose, that of leading men toward a truth that confronted death, rather than denying it. The scholar Hugh Urban writes, "For Bataille, the ultimate aim of transgression is not mere sensual pleasure, rather it is the transgression of the very boundaries of the self, the expenditure without hope of return, which shatters the limits of the finite human consciousness and merges it with the boundless continuity of the infinite."[9] Many might view the Whitechapel Club as supporting "mere sensual pleasure," but I argue that the club's particular and disciplined consumption of alcohol was in fact a more meaningful transgression. Though such excessive consumption of alcohol might not be a strategy that William James would favor, the drunken consciousness of the Whitechapel Club sought (and perhaps found) a Bataillian sunny consciousness, one that expanded, united, and said "yes" by surrounding itself with drink and with death.

While the Whitechapel Club's activities can be viewed as primarily social, the club's concerted intimacy with death, observable in the decor of its clubrooms and in the elaborate cremation ritual discussed earlier in this chapter, demonstrates that its consumption of alcohol was inextricably linked to death and was an attempt to confront the realities of death without recourse to more conventional religious models. Thus, I argue that the Whitechapel Club can be considered a meaningful religious community, even as it seemed at times to resist seriousness and to make fun of traditional religions. This model for understanding religion is drawn from David Chidester's *Authentic Fakes: Religion and American Popular Culture.* There Chidester writes that "even fake religions can be doing a kind of symbolic, cultural, and religious work that is real"[10] and further that "in my view, something is doing religious work if it is engaged in negotiating what it is to be human."[11] In examining these less formalized—and sometimes explicitly informal—"religions" of American popular culture, Chidester also notes popular American fascinations with death and sacrifice, which may further support a classification of the Whitechapel Club as "religious": "As an imaginative, imaginary realm, American popular culture is preoccupied with death, dying, and the dead, especially with heroic, redemptive sacrifice, which is a recurring motif of popular films, television, and other media. Clearly, death pervades American popular culture; from blockbuster entertainment to the nightly news, the body count is high. As a 'cult of death,' American popular culture, like American religious nationalism, seeks redemption in sacrificial death."[12]

Though Chidester examines more recent "religions" than the Whitechapel Club, we may perhaps see a foundational form of the "cult of death" in its activities. The Whitechapel Club might not be a group that would typically be categorized as religious, but the club's activities demonstrate a religious development that can be contextualized within late nineteenth-century America. In broadening our understandings of what may count as religious, the club offers a unique perspective on a "religion of no religion"—one that may inform our thinking about the ways that American "religions" might continue to develop in the twenty-first century. While some might argue that labeling the Whitechapel Club and similar groups as "religious" might make the concept of "religion" so broad as to be meaningless, I would argue that in these movements we can observe religious elements that allow us to broaden our definition of religion without vacating it of all specificity. For the Whitechapel Club, their religion, even if it was sometimes explicitly counter- or antireligious, sought to create a more meaningful existence for its members, one that would be more satisfactory than the models provided by the more conventional religion of Christianity in late nineteenth-century Chicago.

The Whitechapel Club also provides insights into the ways that communal drinking might specifically function in the context of masculine communities. Rather than a formalized fraternal organization like Freemasonry, the Whitechapel Club was a social and professional organization, and it may have sought to poke fun at the seriousness of sober fraternal organizations. Despite this, the motivations underlying membership in fraternal organizations and in the Whitechapel Club may have had

some similarities, and it is those similarities that can also justify the categorization of the Whitechapel Club as religious. In *Secret Ritual and Manhood in Victorian America,* Mark C. Carnes notes that late nineteenth-
century professional and social organizations "became a source of stability
amidst the social chaos of modern life."[13] But Carnes notes that fraternal
organizations did something more than this by requiring participation in
a series of complex initiatory rituals. Carnes notes that Lynn Dumenil argues, "The solemn setting [of the lodge] intensified the bonds of friendship, and the eclectic religious motifs underscored the values common to
all members." Carnes himself contends, "Fraternal ritual provided solace
and psychological guidance during young men's troubled passage to manhood in Victorian America." The hypermasculinity of the Whitechapel
Club, as will be shown, may similarly indicate club members' attempts to
carve out meaningful existences despite increasing uncertainties about
their identities—and even life itself. In confronting these difficult realities, albeit in unconventional ways, members of the club attempted to develop a drunken consciousness that would allow them to say yes to life by
saying yes to death.

The Whitechapel Club

The Whitechapel Club was established in Chicago in 1889.[14] It began as
the project of Chicago journalists, eventually totaling around ninety
members over its five-year existence. Though established primarily as a
professional organization, modeled in part on the Clover Club of Philadelphia, the Whitechapel Club drew on macabre imagery and instituted formalized if fluid ritual practices and initiations. The reporters who founded
the club saw it as an alternative to the Press Club of Chicago, which was
composed of more well-established and well-off newspapermen and edi-
tors. Instead, the founders of the Whitechapel Club were young reporters,
working for the "dailies," scraping out a living by reporting on sports and
political stories, but also on executions, violent crime, and the Plains
Wars.[15] The club membership soon included a number of men outside the
newspaper world, though newspapermen would continue to constitute its
core membership. The club's name was taken from the area in London
notorious as the location of Jack the Ripper's murders, and Jack the Ripper
was, officially, named the club's president. In his persistent absence from

club meetings, however, the vice president oversaw club business. In one of the few scholarly examinations of the Whitechapel Club, Lawrence Lorenz, a historian of journalism, writes: "The official purpose of the Whitechapel Club, boldly written on its state-issued certificate of incorporation, was 'Social Reform.' But that was certainly tongue-in-cheek. The Whitechapelers were not 'in any sense reformers, or actuated by the smug and forbidding spirit which too often inspires that species,' [club member Brand] Whitlock would write. 'They were, indeed, wisely otherwise, and they were, I think, wholly right minded in their attitude toward what are called public questions, and of these they had a deep and perspicacious understanding.' They were rebels, dissatisfied with the political and business practices of the 1890s."[16]

The members of the Whitechapel Club challenged not only social norms but even social reform itself. The club's ritual activities were explicitly transgressive—they shouted insults at members who were speaking (a practice called sharpshooting), held elaborate lying competitions, and emphasized death and drinking at all times. Indeed, drinking did seem to be the club's unofficial if primary purpose. Yet this drinking was contained and controlled, at least ideally. The desire for controlled drinking, even when that drinking might be considered excessive, can be seen in the club's more routine practices. In the context of regular activities, the most frequent drinks were beer and whiskey. In 1936 one club member, Wallace Rice, wrote a series of letters to Charles Dennis as the latter was in the process of writing and publishing a thirty-six-part series on the Whitechapel Club in the *Chicago Daily News*. Dennis had not been a member of the club, but he had employed several club members, including its founder, Charles Seymour. Seeking to correct assumptions of overly excessive drinking within the club, Rice wrote: "I wonder if I can persuade you that, although there was a great deal of drink consumed in Whitechapel, there was little or no drunkenness acquired within its walls. I recall a mild awe that was felt when the wagon man from Lemp's brewery told us one day that we were his best customers, though we knew that we did drink beer. There were always kegs of it at the symposia. We learnt that drink gets the empty stomach, and we ate a great deal when we drank."[17]

Here eating was combined with drinking in order to avoid, or at least control, drunkenness. On special occasions—such as when entertaining outsiders—punch was typically consumed. Thus, on these occasions, rather than individual drinks or cocktails, all members drank the same substance from the same bowl, further intensifying the communal components of its alcohol consumption. In some accounts the punch bowl was decorated with snakes and was "the largest ever cast in America," and one of the favored concoctions was reputedly known as "wild cow's milk," though these accounts may have been exaggerations, as one former member recalled a much simpler punch bowl and did not remember a punch of this name being made.[18]

One of the primary requirements for membership in the Whitechapel Club was the ability to "hold one's liquor," and in this we can see another way in which drunkenness was regulated in the club. Rice recalled, "During probation each man was expected not only to come to the club but to drink hearty with its members. His conduct during and after drinking was studied with care. He had to keep his liquor and his temper. If he didn'nt [sic] he was done."[19] The club had clearly devised methods for appropriate drinking within its walls, the goal being a well-balanced intoxication. Rice recalled a particularly disciplined period of drinking when the Clover Club of Philadelphia visited Chicago:

> Its [the Clover Club's] members, much more numerous than ours, were told off in relays to lead us to it [their whiskey "punch"]. Now it is a principle in heavy drinking to accustom the system to alcohol by copious draughts the night before a bout. We began on Thursday when the chestnut song was rehearsed. We drank the Clover Club into cheerful ebriety and stayed to finish after they had been carried away, and we were seasoned. Not one of our men succumbed that Sunday morning. We followed our cheerful custom of singing "Free as a Bird" over more than a score of Press Club innocents. We provided our own stunts through the evening and at 4 o'clock Charley Perkins arose in his place and asked Henry Heinemann about it, saying, "Mr. President, as we understand it, we were invited here to an entertainment. May we ask when your entertainment begins?"[20]

Here the club demonstrated the importance of preparation for alcoholic consumption. Drinking was undertaken with an almost athletic discipline, as livers were "seasoned" in preparation for the most intense bouts of drinking. The club's tastes for alcohol were also on display. The Blood Punch of the Whitechapel Club, which possessed a pleasant taste and was efficaciously absorbed, is contrasted with the Press Club's "punch," which was basically straight whiskey. With proper preparations, however, even a bad drink could be made to go down easily, though it is clear that such drinking was not considered ideal. Joseph Gustefeld writes: "While drinking can promote fellow-feeling it can also be a catalyst to angry words, denunciations and the exposure of those secrets by which social organization is held in place. *In vino veritas* but social order cannot stand too much *veritas.* In enhancing disorder and unpredictability there is also risk and danger. That in itself suggests the meaning of alcohol in developing the frame of anti-structure; of passage from serious to the playful; from predictable order to risky role-release."[21]

For the Whitechapel Club, it was precisely the unpredictability of alcohol that made it such an important ritual substance. Alcohol embodied the uncertainties of late nineteenth-century masculinity. The ritualized consumption of alcohol allowed the members of the Whitechapel Club to create a meaningful antistructure, one that engaged more fully with the truth that conventional society wished to ignore. It might have been "too much *veritas,*" to be sure, but such excess allows for our consideration of the Whitechapel Club's drinking as transgressive and meaningful in a Bataillian sense. In *Guilty,* which was written at the start of World War II, Bataille writes: "Drinking, debauchery, or struggle will be the only outlets that remain for me at the moment of this dark impossibility. Everything contracts in my depths: the horror must be endured without succumbing to vertigo."[22] In the "dark impossibility" of life in the midst of cultural crises, drinking helped club members face that impossibility. By linking drinking to death, the club's activities embodied a kind of Bataillian eroticism, one that confronts the terrifying realities of human frailty and individuality.

In addition to drinking, the club's other central activities focused on the collecting of images and artifacts of death. The club's emblem depicted a raven on a skull, and the club eventually acquired a "beautifully stuffed raven" for display in the club rooms. Members of the club famously gathered around a coffin-shaped table (in some accounts this was described as an actual coffin) in a room decorated with nooses, human skeletons, murder weapons, and Indian blankets allegedly stained with blood from the Plains Wars. One particularly generous member of the group—a medical doctor who oversaw an insane asylum—had donated his phrenological collection of skulls to the club after he had concluded his study of them; another handy member known as "Grizzly" Adams converted these skulls into shades for gas lamps as well as, possibly, drinking vessels.[23] The majority of the morbid items decorating the club were linked, at least within club members' memories, to violent deaths and executions. Rice noted that he could recall "nothing on the walls until we began getting hangman's ropes."[24] In decorating for the Clover Club's visit, the Blood Room, so called because of its red wall coverings, was decorated with the pelvic bones of horses that were "filled with red clover blossoms."[25] While striking, such a decor of death was not unique in its time. In *Wonder Shows: Performing Science, Magic, and Religion in America,* Fred Nadis writes: "In the 1890s, the Cabaret du Néant (or Tavern of the Dead) first opened its production in Paris and later in New York City. After entering the Cabaret, spectators followed a 'monk' down a blackened hall to a café with candles on coffin-shaped tables where they could order refreshments from waiters in funeral garb."[26] Other similar "death-themed drinking establishments" existed in Paris in this period.[27] Though there is no evidence of a tangible link between these establishments and the Whitechapel Club, the existence of these death-themed establishments points to particular fascinations with death in this period. Yet whereas the Paris and New York public establishments seem to have engaged with the dead as mere entertainment, the Whitechapel Club demonstrated a much more sustained and serious—if not less boisterous— engagement with death.

Many of the macabre artifacts collected by the club were used in the club's varied ritual activities. Some of the human remains even seem to have become honorary club members themselves: "Grinning at everything and everybody were several articulated skeletons, one or two of which always had places of honor at the main dining table."[28] In later reminiscences, club members recalled a Knights Templar sword that was used in a murder in Louisville, though accounts of the sword's specific role differed slightly; the club used this sword in a specific and important club ritual. Rice noted: "On state occasions the Knight Templar sword was taken down from the wall, placed on the coffin table and every guest was called upon to tell a lie. It was mandatory and the guest who, by common consent, told the biggest lie had the honor of wearing the sword during the remainder of the evening. Twice Chauncey M. Depew wore the sword. And the [*sic*] was the only man who ever had that signal honor twice."[29]

In this case, the transgressive practice of lying was linked with death and specifically with the act of murder. Worn as an honor, this sword marked off the individual who best breached the bounds of polite—or even truthful—speech. One of the club's favorite drinking songs, based on Bartholomew Dowling's poem "The Revel," included the following lyrics, fusing drinking with a celebration of death:

> We meet 'neath the sounding rafter,
> And the walls around us are bare;
> As they shout to our peals of laughter,
> It seems that the dead are there.
> But stand to your glasses, steady!
> We drink to our comrades' eyes,
> Quaff a cup to the dead already,
> And hurrah for the next that dies![30]

Death and drinking were thus inextricably linked in the club's regular and special events. And perhaps in no other club ritual can the connections among drinking, death, and transgression be seen as clearly as in the club's most elaborate and newsworthy undertaking—the ritual cremation of a deceased club visitor on the banks of Lake Michigan in 1892.

The Ritual Cremation of Morris Collins

The cremation took place in a complex ceremony on July 16, 1892. Joseph Jaxon, a close friend and honoree of the club,[31] had taken his friend Morris Collins to the Whitechapel Club earlier that year. In signing the club's register, Collins identified himself as "President of the Dallas (Texas) Suicide Club."[32] Collins had been an outspoken advocate for suicide rights, arguing in a fascinating article (which was republished in the account of his cremation) for the construction of death chambers in which the destitute, sick, and hopeless might voluntarily and mercifully bring an end to their own lives.[33] In some accounts, it was after receiving a goading from a Whitechapler that Collins should live up to the charge of his own club, that is, that he should commit suicide, that Collins finally ended his life, though in other accounts this was a long process—and one that Collins was forced to attempt several times before success was achieved. Collins had "left a note to Jaxon asking that his body be dissected for scientific purposes and the remains burned." Collins's sister "agreed to cremation but not dissection," and Jaxon asked the Whitechapel Club to assist in organizing the cremation.[34] Club members discussed the cremation of the poet Percy Shelley, and this seems to have served as the model for the cremation that took place in a remote area to the southeast of Chicago on the shores of Lake Michigan. The fact that former club members gathered to "re-create" the cremation twenty-five years later, long after the club's dissolution in 1894, demonstrated that this ritual, though singular in the club's history, had a lasting influence on the imaginations of Whitechaplers.[35]

The first cremation in America had occurred in 1876, but the practice remained unusual and controversial in 1892. Certainly the open-air cremation undertaken by the club would not have been the sort of cremation advocated for by most cremation proponents of this period.[36] The accounts of Collins's cremation note that some onlookers from the neighboring town had gathered, the construction of the funeral pyre having alerted them to the event in advance, though the club had attempted secrecy, and the bystanders were clearly frightened by the ritual: "On the knoll in front of which the pyre was built stood nearly two score of farmers. They viewed the ceremonies first with curiosity and then with awe and finally stood stricken with superstitious fear."[37] The account of the club members' responses differed from these more "common" responses. Through speeches, poetry recitations, and the solemn consumption of alcohol, Whitechaplers engaged most intimately with death, solemnizing a tragic life in a transgressive ritual.

Explaining his fascination with torture, death, and sacrifice, Georges Bataille wrote, "It is mad to want to avoid the horror of loss. At the limit of intolerance, desire calls the horror possible. It is a question of coming as close as you can to death. Without flinching, or, if necessary, even flinching."[38] And for Bataille, drinking can help us face some of these horrors: "An excess of work tires me. I have shattered nerves. I get drunk often. I feel I am faithful to life if I drink and eat what pleases me. Life is always enchanting, a feast, a party: an oppressing, unintelligible dream enriched nonetheless by a charm I enjoy. The feeling of chance demands that I face a difficult fate."[39] The Whitechaplers engaged in drunken feasts for pre-cisely these reasons. Grappling with life and death meant that they needed to face death fully, and to face up to what Bataille might call our discon-tinuity. In *Erotism,* Bataille writes: "We are discontinuous beings, indi-viduals who perish in isolation in the midst of an incomprehensible adventure, but we yearn for our lost continuity. We find the state of affairs that binds us to our random and ephemeral individuality hard to bear."[40] In seeking to confront that discontinuity and to feel, for a time, a continu-ity with others, the Whitechapel Club engaged in transgressive rituals that confronted death. In Bataille's view, death stands as a terrifying reminder of our eventual reentry into continuity. The club's activities thus allowed its members to face the difficult realities of death, and to temporarily ex-perience a kind of continuity in drunken consciousness.

Though club members had certainly encountered death before, in the case of the cremation of Morris Collins, they developed a ritual that al-lowed them to come as close as possible to death, without turning away from it, ultimately witnessing the dissolution of the human body within the flames. In *Erotism,* Bataille writes: "For each man who regards it with awe, the corpse is the image of his own destiny. It bears witness to a vio-lence which destroys not one man alone but all men in the end. The taboo which lays hold on the others at the sight of a corpse is the distance they put between themselves and violence, by which they cut themselves off from violence."[41]

Morris Collins thus functioned as a kind of Bataillian sacrifice, but one in which the sacrificial victim was his own executioner. For Bataille, sacrifice reestablishes truth. The act of sacrifice is one in which an object (or a person) is destroyed, but such destruction is not without value. In *The Theory of Religion,* Bataille writes: "The principle of sacrifice is destruction, but though it sometimes goes so far as to destroy completely (as in a holo-caust), the destruction that sacrifice is intended to bring about is not an-nihilation. The thing—only the thing—is what sacrifice means to destroy in the victim. Sacrifice destroys an object's real ties of subordination; it draws the victim out of the world of utility and restores it to that of unin-telligible caprice."[42]

The realm of unintelligible caprice is *real* reality; restoring the victim to that realm marks off the sacrificers' confrontation with truth. Bataille continues: "The power that death generally has illuminates the meaning of sacrifice, which functions like death in that it restores a lost value through a relinquishment of value. But death is not necessarily linked to it, and the most solemn sacrifice may not be bloody. To sacrifice is not to kill but to relinquish and to give."[43]

Collins's suicide was a gift to the Whitechapel Club, and his gift of his corpse for the club's ritual purposes marked the suicide as an attempt to restore "lost value" to the men of the Whitechapel Club. The integration of drinking with sacrifice underscored and intensified the club's attempts to create a sunny consciousness. And the truth of the sun for both Bataille and the Whitechaplers is that it warms and illuminates even as it blinds and burns.

Conclusions

Ultimately, the club's emphasis on death was, I think, the result of these journalists' encounters with actual death and with the uncertainties of their own positions in the world. Reporting on death, on the increased and new forms of violence that were proliferating in Chicago in the late nineteenth century, the men of the Whitechapel Club had become intimately familiar with violent death. Drinking might assuage some of these horrors, but it was only drinking in community and in the context of ritual activity that might give death meaning; alcohol and ritual allowed men to say "yes" to life, even in the face of death. Drinking within the club underscored both community solidarity and solitude. When these men were drinking in community, some truths concerning the human condition might be explicitly voiced, but many others might be observed silently by individual members. Individual Whitechaplers could grapple with their own demons, yet even those solitary thoughts occurred in the midst of cacophonous collectivity. And within that death-obsessed community, both life *and* death could be taken seriously. The unusual cremation of Morris Collins, as well as the club's more "regular" activities, importantly incorporated the consumption of alcohol with imagery of and rituals concerning death. While transgressing conventional late nineteenth-century social norms, the club actively sought to challenge these norms to create a more meaningful (if no less terrifying) existence. As Mary Douglas has argued, drinking is "a medium for constructing the actual world. The drinks are in the world. They are not a commentary upon it, nor a surface nor a deep structure model of its relations. They are as real as bricks and mortar. . . . Sampling a drink is sampling what is happening to a whole category of social life."[44] Thus, rather than simply being a strange if fascinating moment of history, the Whitechapel Club allows us to sample "a whole category of social life," to consider the important roles played by alcohol in transgressive religious ritual practices. In the case of the Whitechapel Club, a serious consideration of its drinking can help us consider the ways in which the consumption of food and drink can allow for significant transformations—physical, emotional, and spiritual—within the human subject.

Notes

1. Lawrence Lorenz, "Whitechapel Club: Defining Chicago's Newspapermen in the 1890s," *American Journalism* 15, no. 1 (1998): 83.
2. Wallace Rice to Charles Dennis, August 17, 1936, Wallace Rice Papers, Newberry Library, Chicago (hereafter cited as NL).
3. Iain Gately, *Drink: A Cultural History of Alcohol* (New York: Gotham Books, 2008), 12.
4. Ibid., 103.
5. For example, ibid., 148–149, discusses drinking rituals and mourning among slave communities in seventeenth-century Martinique; Sarah H. Meachum discusses the prevalence of drinking in colonial America, noting the regularity of drinking, especially at funerals, in *Every Home a Distillery: Alcohol, Gender, and Technology in the Colonial Chesapeake* (Baltimore: Johns Hopkins University Press, 2013); Patricia Lysaght notes alcohol as one important component of mortuary customs in Ireland in "Hospitality at Wakes and Funerals in Ireland from the Seventeenth to the Nineteenth Century: Some Evidence from the Written Record," *Folklore* 114, no 3 (2003): 403–420.
6. William James, *The Varieties of Religious Experience: A Study in Human Nature, Being the Gifford Lectures on Natural Religion Delivered at Edinburgh in 1901–1902* (New York: Modern Library, 2004), 421.
7. Dmitri Tymoczko, "The Nitrous Oxide Philosopher," *Atlantic,* May 1996, 93–101.
8. Georges Bataille, *Guilty,* trans. Stuart Kendall (Albany: State University of New York Press, 2011), 39.
9. Hugh Urban, "The Power of the Impure: Transgression, Violence, and Secrecy in Bengali Sakti Tantra and Modern Western Magic," *Numen* 50, no. 3 (2003): 301.
10. David Chidester, *Authentic Fakes: Religion and American Popular Culture* (Berkeley: University of California Press, 2005), 9.

11. Ibid., 18.

12. Ibid., 7.

13. Mark C. Carnes, *Secret Ritual and Manhood in Victorian America* (New Haven: Yale University Press, 1989), 2.

14. The Whitechapel Club applied for and received a Certificate of Incorporation from the secretary of state, Illinois, October 19, 1889. See Lorenz, "Whitechapel Club," 83, 100n5.

15. The Whitechapel Club was active during the time of the Columbian Exposition, which was also contemporary with the grisly murders of the serial killer that Eric Larson discusses in *The Devil in the White City: Murder, Magic, and Madness at the Fair That Changed America* (New York: Crown, 2003). Larson briefly discusses the Whitechapel Club on pages 31–32.

16. Lorenz, "Whitechapel Club," 87.

17. Wallace Rice to Charles Dennis, August 19, 1936, Charles Dennis Papers, NL.

18. Wallace Rice to Charles Dennis, August 11, 1936, Charles Dennis Papers, NL.

19. Ibid. I should note here that the Whitechapel Club was a decidedly fraternal organization. Though I do not have the time to enter into a discussion of gender issues here, I think that the intense (perhaps aggressive) masculinity of both Bataille and the Whitechapel Club is important to note. Wallace Rice reminisced many years later that "we had no woman inside the club rooms ever," though this prohibition does not seem to have extended to *dead* women, as the club kept the preserved head of an "Indian girl" in its rooms—and many of the skulls decorating the club were reputed to be those of women.

20. Wallace Rice to Charles Dennis, August 11, 1936, Charles Dennis Papers, NL.

21. Joseph R. Gusfield, "Passage to Play: Rituals of Drinking Time in American Society," in *Constructive Drinking: Perspectives on Drink from Anthropology*, ed. Mary Douglas (Cambridge: Cambridge University Press, 1991), 83.

22. Bataille, *Guilty*, 12. On the contexts for *Guilty*, see the translator Stuart Kendall's introduction, ix–xxxi.

23. Unless otherwise noted, information on the Whitechapel Club is drawn from research conducted at the Newberry Library and the Chicago Historical Museum. When using specific documents taken from those collections, I will cite those accordingly. Another example of the popularity of criminal skulls as drinking vessels in the nineteenth century appears in Gately, *Drink*, 145. Gately writes that the American pirate Blackbeard "was beheaded after death, and his skull continued in service as a receptacle for alcohol. It was converted into a very large punch bowl, called The Infant, 'which was used until 1903 as a drinking vessel at the Raleigh Tavern in Williamsburg.'"

24. Wallace Rice to Charles Dennis, August 17, 1936, Charles Dennis Papers, NL.

25. Ibid.

26. Fred Nadis, *Wonder Shows: Performing Science, Magic, and Religion in America* (New Brunswick: Rutgers University Press, 2005), 15.

27. "Café or Cabaret de L'Enfer (Hell's Café), Paris, France, Late 19th Century," Morbid Anatomy: Surveying the Intersticies of Art and Medicine, Death and Culture, May 16, 2012, http://morbidanatomy.blogspot.com/2012/05/cafe-or-cabaret-de-lenfer-hells-cafe.html, accessed May 15, 2015. This blog also notes similar trends somewhat later, in the 1950s, from which I have taken the phrase "death themed drinking establishments": "Death Themed Drinking Establishments of the Near and Distant Past: 'Cafe le Macabre,' London and 'The Conclave,' New Orleans," August 9, 2013, http://morbidanatomy.blogspot.com/2013/08/death-themed-drinking-establishments-of.html, accessed May 15, 2015.

28. Wallace Rice to Charles Dennis, August 17, 1936, Charles Dennis Papers, NL.

29. Ibid.

30. Typescript of "Our Last Toast" in Wallace Rice's Scrapbook of the Activities of the Whitechapel Club, Research Center, Chicago History Museum, Chicago.

31. Jaxon's own story is a fascinating one; he was half Blackfoot and had supported Louis Riel's resistance movement in Canada. Jaxon himself was arrested along with Riel, and he avoided execution only through an escape from prison, later fleeing to the United States. See Charles Dennis, "Whitechapel Nights, part 8," *Chicago Daily News,* August 3, 1936. Clippings of the thirty-six-part story appear in Wallace Rice's Scrapbook of the Activities of the Whitechapel Club.

32. For historical context on suicide clubs in America in the 1880s and 1890s, see Kathleen M. Brian, "The Suicideites: Morbid Masculinities in an Era of Selective Death," paper presented at the American Historical Association conference, Washington, D.C., January 2014.

33. In his own suicide note, published along with the *Sunday Herald* account, he stated: "When such a person has set himself resolutely against the practices of fraud and chicanery, upon which all business must lie, and has grown too sensitive to endure the tortures which wage slavery inflicts, there is no resting place upon the earth. When they die—and death must come soon to this class, whether from disease, or by their own hand, or at the end of the hangman's rope—society should at least render justice by giving them a decent burial and inscribe on their tombs words like these: 'Murdered by society,' 'Crowded off the earth by the competitive system.'" *Chicago Sunday Herald,* July 17, 1892, clipping in Wallace Rice's Scrapbook of the Activities of the Whitechapel Club.

34. Lorenz, "Whitechapel Club," 96.

35. "Heathen Mortuary Rites Followed by Eccentric Club for Suicide Member," *Harrisburg Telegraph,* July 23, 1917. Accounts of the commemoration of the cremation on the twenty-fifth anniversary appeared in a number of newspapers at this time.

36. See Stephen Prothero, *Purified by Fire: A History of Cremation in America* (Berkeley: University of California Press, 2001). Charles Dennis noted: "One of the club members who participated in the affair, Dr. Hugh Blake Williams, was so impressed by the night adventure, and particularly by his own emotions at the time, that he gave instructions then and there that after his death his body should be burned. Those instructions were carried out after his demise in 1911. By that time cremation of the dead had become almost a commonplace and Chicago had a properly equipped crematory." "Whitechapel Nights, part 30," *Chicago Daily News*, August 31, 1936, clipping in Wallace Rice's Scrapbook of the Activities of the Whitechapel Club.

37. *Chicago Sunday Herald*, July 17, 1892, clipping in Wallace Rice's Scrapbook of the Activities of the Whitechapel Club.

38. Bataille, *Guilty*, 83.

39. Ibid., 9.

40. Georges Bataille, *Erotism: Death and Sensuality*, trans. Mary Dalwood (San Francisco: City Lights Books, 1986), 15.

41. Ibid., 44.

42. Georges Bataille, *Theory of Religion,* trans. Robert Hurley (New York: Zone Books, 1992), 43.

43. Ibid., 48–49.

44. Douglas, *Constructive Drinking,* 9.

Bibliography

Bataille, George. *Erotism: Death and Sensuality.* Translated by Mary Dalwood. San Francisco: City Light Books, 1986.

————. *Guilty.* Translated by Stuart Kendall. New York: State University of New York Press, 2011.

————. *Theory of Religion.* Translated by Robert Hurley. New York: Zone Books, 1992.

Brian, Kathleen M. "The Suicideites: Morbid Masculinities in an Era of Selective Death." Paper presented at the American Historical Association conference, Washington, D.C., January 2014.

Carnes, Mark C. *Secret Ritual and Manhood in Victorian America.* New Haven: Yale University Press, 1989.

Chidester, David. *Authentic Fakes: Religion and American Popular Culture.* Berkeley: University of California Press, 2005.

Douglas, Mary, ed. *Constructive Drinking: Perspectives on Drink from Anthropology.* Cambridge: Cambridge University Press, 1987.

Gately, Iain. *Drink: A Cultural History of Alcohol.* New York: Gotham Books, 2008.

Gusfield, Joseph R. "Passage to Play: Rituals of Drinking Time in American Society." In *Constructive Drinking: Perspectives on Drink from Anthropology*, edited by Mary Douglas, 73–90. Cambridge: Cambridge University Press, 1991.

James, William. *The Varieties of Religious Experience: A Study in Human Nature, Being the Gifford Lectures on Natural Religion Delivered at Edinburgh in 1901– 1902*. New York: Modern Library, 2004.

Larson, Erik. *The Devil in the White City: Murder, Magic, and Madness at the Fair That Changed America*. New York: Crown, 2003.

Lorenz, Lawrence. "Whitechapel Club: Defining Chicago's Newspapermen in the 1890s." *American Journalism* 15, no. 1 (1998): 83–102.

Lysaght, Patricia. "Hospitality at Wakes and Funerals in Ireland from the Seventeenth to the Nineteenth Century: Some Evidence from the Written Record," *Folklore* 114, no. 3 (2003): 403–420.

Maloney, James C. *The 20th Century Guide for Mixing Fancy Cocktails*. Chicago: James C. Maloney, 1900.

McGovern, Patrick. *Uncorking the Past: The Quest for Wine, Beer, and Other Alcoholic Beverages*. Berkeley: University of California Press, 2009.

Meachum, Sarah H. *Every Home a Distillery: Alcohol, Gender, and Technology in the Colonial Chesapeake*. Baltimore: Johns Hopkins University Press, 2013.

Nadis, Fred. *Wonder Shows: Performing Science, Magic, and Religion in America*. New Brunswick: Rutgers University Press, 2005.

Prothero, Stephen. *Purified by Fire: A History of Cremation in America*. Berkeley: University of California Press, 2001.

Tymoczko, Dmitri. "The Nitrous Oxide Philosopher." *Atlantic*, May 1996, 93– 101.

Urban, Hugh. "The Power of the Impure: Transgression, Violence, and Secrecy in Bengali Sakti Tantra and Modern Western Magic." *Numen* 50, no. 3 (2003): 269–308.

8

Eating and Drinking with the Dead in South Africa

Radikobo Ntsimane

Introduction

Historically, it is impossible to pinpoint the origin of South African hospitality customs involving eating and drinking in connection with the death of a person. It is a traditional South African household custom to feed anyone who comes to visit, especially strangers. Some people call this *Ubuntu,* or African hospitality. This chapter examines the meaning of eating and drinking customs surrounding death, particularly when the host family has sufficient food in times when food is otherwise scarce. I confine myself to the South African environment, emphasizing particularly the Tswana and the Zulu people, whom I have lived among and had a chance to study. Both the Tswana and the Zulu people venerate their dead ancestors, and during their lives, the living are in constant communication with ancestral spirits. This is especially true of the traditional Zulus.

Before turning to contemporary practices, I look briefly at the historical traditions regarding death rituals connected to food. I am particularly interested in changes that have occurred regarding eating and drinking customs between the death and burial of a person, as well as after burial, when the deceased is sent into the realm of the ancestors through a series of rituals. This chapter also seeks to reveal the meanings behind the eating and drinking that take place in connection with the death and burial of a loved one.

Historical Background and Development

The Tswana people, found largely in the northwest and northern Cape provinces of South Africa and the neighboring Republic of Botswana,

UJEQE (Steamed Bread)

10 cups bread flour
1 packet yeast
1 tsp salt
¼ cup sugar
1 cup fresh milk
½ cup cooking oil, plus additional oil for the bowl
2 cups lukewarm water, plus additional water as needed

Pour flour into a bowl. Add yeast, salt, and sugar. In a separate bowl, mix milk, cooking oil, and 2 cups lukewarm water. In a bowl large enough to hold all the ingredients, mix dry ingredients with wet ingredients and add lukewarm water for consistency. Knead the dough on a floured surface until it reaches a smooth texture. Cover the dough in warm place for couple of hours, until it has risen. Fill a pot large enough to hold the bowl in which the bread will steam one-third with water and bring to a boil. Oil the interior of an enamel bowl that you will use to steam the bread. Put the dough in the oiled enamel bowl and place the bowl gently in the boiling pot. Monitor the water level in the pot and add water as needed. Boil furiously for a while. Stick a clean knife into the boiling *ujeqe*. When it comes out clean, the bread is ready. Remove the *ujeqe* from the pot. Cover it with a cotton cloth until it is cool and serve.*

---

*The basic recipe was provided by my colleagues Sinegugu Zwane and Thembeka Ngcemu.

have a word, *mogoga*, that refers to the meal one eats immediately after the burial of a person. The food is often a sour porridge called *ting*, which consists of *mabele* (sorghum) or *samp* (maize; called *stampa*), both of which used to be considered staple foods. Along with *ting* or *stampa*, meat from a specially slaughtered cow was also traditionally served. In the past, neighbors and relatives would bring supplies such as vegetables, ground sorghum powder (*bupe jwa mabele*), and *stampa* to supplement the meal, which relieved the bereaved family of the burden of finding extra food for the people coming to the funeral. The *mogoga* meal was prepared largely by boiling without the addition of any spices; it was generally expected to be a bland meal, without even a pinch of salt.

The tradition of the Zulu people, who come mainly from today's KwaZulu-Natal, may have varied from area to area but was not very dissimilar to that of the Tswana people. Unlike the Tswanas, however, the Zulus would invariably slaughter a goat, which is believed to assist in the communication with the departed ancestors in any ritual. The meat of a goat would be eaten along with steamed bread called *ujeqe*. Often the immediate family would consume the goat meat, while the other mourners would be fed beef. In the preparation of the meat for the funeral meal, the cow was usually slaughtered after the goat, which often occurred the day before the burial. The bland foodstuffs of *ujeqe* and *samp*, like those in the Tswana tradition, were served alongside the meat without any flavor enhancer. The exclusion of spices by both the Tswanas and the Zulus was intended to emphasize that eating occurred as a necessity, not as a joy. Serving a tasty meal would be misinterpreted as a joyous celebration; by emphasizing the blandness of the food and excluding any spices, Tswanas and Zulus underscored the function of eating over and above any incidental enjoyment. Sorghum beer called *umqombothi* would also be consumed in large quantities, mainly by the men who would have dug the grave and slaughtered and prepared the cow for boiling. An alternative, nonalcoholic drink called *amahewu,* its main ingredient being fermented maize, would be consumed by the teetotalers.

The anthropologist Axel-Ivar Berglund, who did intensive research on the Zulus, wrote that the Zulus understood death as the opposite of life, and a funeral operated as preparation for the recently deceased person to enter the life of the dead. In his book *Zulu Thought-Patterns and Symbolism,* Berglund showed how before and during the funeral the bereaved and the people coming to comfort and support them would behave as if they themselves were in the world of the departed. The funeral attendants were symbolically the (living) dead, and because of this, they would invert their traditional roles in life as though they were themselves deceased. They would use their left hand rather than their right, they would enter the house by reverse, they would eat only unsalted food, and they would sometimes go so far as to put their clothes on inside out. They would even open a hole in the wall directly opposite the doorway through which the corpse would be carried out.[1]

The strong belief that is still prevalent today among the Zulus is that the slaughtering of a goat is indispensable, as the noise it makes causes the ancestors to take notice and give the necessary blessings for the event taking place. Therefore, traditional Zulu homesteads will always slaughter a goat and eat its meat when someone has passed away. A piece of raw goat meat and a calabash of foaming beer is placed on the altar of the ancestors, called *umsamo,* in a special circular hut. This particular Zulu hut used to look like a beehive built out of branches and thatch; its small entrance required all to bend when entering it. After entering, men would sit on the right and women on the left, the eldest of both sexes sitting closest to the entrance and the youngest sitting farthest away. Today, though such huts are built with bricks and mortar and stand taller than the smaller historical ones, some are still thatched and others have corrugated iron roofs. The farthest place from the door, *umsamo,* is still a sacred place serving as an altar or seat of the ancestors. The beer and food offerings are placed there for the ancestors to lick them in appreciation of the ritual. For any ancestor ritual, the Tswana people would use a lamb instead. The geographical landscape of the Tswana people cannot be overlooked in these traditions, and it is possible that the Tswanas have more sheep as a result of their less mountainous areas; the Zulus, on the other hand, live in territory that is perfect for rearing goats.

The Eating and Drinking Phases of a Funeral

Eating and drinking happen in several stages after the death of a person. These stages can be divided into four periods: prefuneral, funeral, postfuneral and post-postfuneral. The amount and sophistication of the food served to those coming to comfort the bereaved differ from family to family, depending on their funds. Each community, however, has general assumptions regarding what to expect as far as food is concerned at different times after the announcement of a death.

Prefuneral Phase

The prefuneral eating and drinking happen when friends, relatives, and neighbors come to visit the bereaved family to seek confirmation of the death and comfort the grieving family.[2] Traditional hospitality customs dictate that regardless of the occasion, when a guest comes to one's house, one offers something to eat or drink before the guest leaves. It is rude not to do so. Out of kindness, from the announcement of death to the day before the funeral, the bereaved family offers food and drink to those who visit, whether they come as groups or as individuals and regardless of the time of day. The food and drink are often home-baked scones and tea or coffee.

Depending on the kind of death a person has suffered, some households have an exclusive meal for immediate family members. Among the Zulus, a goat is traditionally slaughtered and its chime (the chewed contents found in the stomach) and bile are used in a ritual. If the death was the result of an accident from machinery, the ritual would be performed as a way of attempting to prevent the repetition of that kind of death. If it was caused deliberately by means of a weapon, the ritual would be performed in an attempt to redirect such a death back to the person who is suspected by the diviners to have caused it.[3]

The Funeral Phase

People who could not come to comfort the family before the burial make it a point to come on the burial day to give a final send-off to the dead person. Saturday is now the preferred day for burial since the South African work week begins on Monday and ends on Friday. From the graveyard, mourners go back to the home of the deceased. There, after a ritual washing of hands in water with or without ritually cleansing herbs like crushed aloe, they will almost always stand in line to be served a meal from one of several serving points.

Beef, which is expensive, is traditionally a featured part of the meal. Though in the past an animal—a cow, a sheep, or a goat—was slaughtered to be consumed during this phase, bereaved families now procure meat from a butcher. *Samp,* rice, *ujeqe* (among the Zulus), *ting,* and one or two types of vegetables are also generally served. Fruit juice or a soft drink is served as well. In most cases, close family members and those who officiated at the burial, usually church leaders, are served separately in a tent and do not stand in line with the regular mourners. This is probably a way of acknowledging their hard work during the funeral ceremony.

Although people may be separated by rank and relations, the funeral meal is also a meal that restores family ties. It has potential therapeutic qualities in the sense that those family members who were estranged are

Ujeqe: the steamed bread is cut to speed the cooling off. (Photo by the author)

forced by death to eat around the same table, or at least under the same roof. Although no particular ritual is performed, the aura of the death forces people to bury the hatchet, lest they call upon themselves the wrath of the departed.

Because so much food is served freely, households that have shown in the prefuneral phase a potential for a good meal will attract a larger crowd than those that have demonstrated they are less well financially endowed. In extreme levels of poverty, especially among the economically disadvantaged South African black population, funerals serve as an opportunity to get a balanced meal. For some, that meal could be the only one in days.

It is important to note that among the Zulus and Tswanas, people who are not known to the bereaved family come to funerals. Anyone who wishes to attend a funeral is free to do so. In modern-day South Africa, it is customary for adults and children ten years of age and up to attend funerals. In such cases one can see that members of the community come together to lend support by their presence. The meal that the individual members of the community partake of demonstrates how eating at the funeral brings people together who may not necessarily come together in everyday life. The rich socialize with the people of their class in suburbs previously reserved for white people in the formerly racially segregated living areas.[4] The rich see themselves as materially better off, but in the event of the funeral, the class divide is temporarily obliterated. The funeral meal brings together people in a social gathering that would otherwise not have happened; for some of them the possibility of receiving a balanced meal is the attraction. If poverty levels among blacks were not so high, people would come purely for the sake of supporting the bereaved family and not, as it happens often nowadays, for the possibility of receiving a free meal.

POSTFUNERAL

After the funeral there is sometimes additional social feasting. I use the word *feasting* deliberately because what happens in such postfuneral gatherings can be viewed as inordinate. The postfuneral gatherings consist largely of young people who have changed from mourning attire to party clothes, which signifies a shift in the function of the feast. The post-burial feasting has been criticized in some quarters as excessive, especially by religious leaders; it is a somewhat new phenomenon that is manifested mainly in the emerging middle class, which has access to disposable cash. The cash is generated from funeral insurance policies that give a large payout at the death of an insured individual. The feasting is referred to as "after tears" because people shed tears until the body is interred and are then free to feast, allegedly in honor of the departed loved one. Around Pretoria, in Gauteng Province, such feasting is referred to as *visnons,* a corruption of Afrikaans *Wie sien ons?* (literally translated as "Who can see us?" but more colloquially understood as "Can you see how we indulge?").

Post-Postfuneral Phase

Because of the influence of the Zionist-Pentecostal, or so-called Spiritual, churches (*Dikereke tsa Moya*), there is usually a gathering at the home of the deceased after the burial. The gathering is named Ten Days, as this is the amount of time between the burial and this event, at which those gathered pray for the family and then share a meal. With almost no variation, the meal consists of scones and is accompanied by juice or tea. On rare occasions, families may include a smaller animal, such as a sheep or a goat.

Some families perform what is called *Bojalwa-jwa-digarawe* immediately after the burial, sometimes after the Ten Days ritual, to comfort the bereaved family. *Bojalwa* is sorghum beer, and *jwa-digarawe* means "of the shovels," and, as the name suggests, the ritual consists of using home-brewed sorghum beer to cleanse the tools (shovels, spades, and picks) used for digging the grave. Traditionally, people use water mixed with herbs to sprinkle on the digging tools to drive off bad luck; sorghum beer is sprinkled on the tools for the same reasons. The remaining beer is then consumed, mainly by the men who were involved in digging the grave. The grave diggers generally come from the surrounding community, and the family of the deceased will also prepare something for them to eat. This event is attended by only a few people, mostly the grave diggers, and it culminates in drunken singing by the men. All told, there are seldom more than fifty attendants, since most of those who came to the funeral have gone back to their villages and places of employment. No person will be turned away when meals and drinks are served, even if he did not participate in digging the grave.

One Year Later

It is the belief that traditional Zulu people have in the power of the deceased ancestors that is responsible for the ritual of *ukubuyisa* (specifically

The black calabash contains the remains of the *umqombothi*, whose foam the living dead has "licked." The jawbone of a goat and a plastic bag of unused *impepho*, incense, are to the left of the calabash. (Photo by the author)

translated as retrieval or reconciliation, its more colloquial meaning is homecoming), in which the spirit of the deceased is fetched from the grave and brought back home. The number of people attending this ritual is greater than those at the previous one. In writing about the interventions of the community to reconcile the formally feuding groups of the Mpophomeni community in the KwaZulu-Natal Province, Jone Salomonsen gives a brief description of the *ukubuyisa* ritual: "The cows were slaughtered by the male heads of the seven main clans living in Mpophomeni on the afternoon of the day before the big celebration. The blood and parts of the meat were placed in front of the memorial wall during the night as an offering to the invisible ancestors who were invited to accept and partake and thus help reconciliation take place. The meat was then cooked and shared with the community as part of the feast."[5]

Depending on the standing the deceased had in the family and his or her level of affluence, an animal will be slaughtered and sorghum beer and other beer will be prepared. Since a goat is favored because of the noise it makes when slaughtered, it is invariably used during the *ukubuyisa*. The goat chime and bile are mixed with some herbs and water and used to cleanse the relatives of any lingering bad luck. An elder or designated person will cleanse the family, from the eldest to the youngest, by rubbing the arms and feet with the mixture without wiping it off. After this, the goatskin is cut into strips that are then worn around the wrists of the family members as a sign that they participated in the ritual. Should a family neglect or ignore this ritual, it is believed that the dead person may haunt the family members and bring calamities on them. Because of poverty, however, some families will observe this ritual long after one year has passed. That being said, it is commonly believed that the ancestors (and the living) will still eat and drink even when the ritual happens long after the twelve-month period has passed.

In the Time of AIDS

As a result of the changed political climate in post-1994 South Africa, new access to wealth was not the only thing that brought about change to the funerals of the black population.[6] The money of the emerging middle class brought gluttony and drunkenness to funerals,[7] but the HIV/AIDS pandemic brought a different reality. Soon after the democratic government came into being at the end of President Mandela's term in 1998, South Africa, especially KwaZulu-Natal Province, had the highest prevalence of HIV infections in Africa. President Thabo Mbeki's regime (1999–2008)

furthered the prevalence of AIDS in the region through his failure to provide antiretroviral drugs (ARVs) to infected people.[8] Failing to provide
these drugs to slow or halt the spread of AIDS affected South Africa's funeral culture. Deaths were many and frequent. When the family bread-
winner was ill with HIV or AIDS, money was spent in trying to restore
his or her health. In addition to the loss of the primary source of family
revenue, such a death brought stigma: AIDS was generally connected to
sexual immorality. Finally, the family was humiliated by the lack of means
to provide enough food to feed all who came to comfort and help the family with the burial.

In a study done with Nokhaya Makiwane on how to help orphans to
remember, Philippe Denis wrote about AIDS-devastated families: "The
orphans suffer double loss. They miss their mother (or their father). But
they also miss the good life that was associated with the deceased parent.
The quality of lives has deteriorated. For example, they do no longer go to
the beach or to the restaurant as they used to do when their mother was
still alive. Or they no longer go to school because the school fees are too
high. Everything has become more difficult. The family battles financially. The grandmother, who takes care of the children, is tired. With AIDS
the world has turned upside down."[9]

Deaths as a result of the AIDS pandemic affected many households
negatively, and community members naturally preferred to go to a funeral
where food would be served. The normal rituals that accompany death
had to be either postponed or abandoned because they demanded the
presence of food that the bereaved family could not afford. It is ironic that
the practice that was meant to assist a bereaved family to grieve and process the loss of a loved one is now the source of shame because a family is
unable to give a dignified funeral for its deceased member because of the
inability to provide a meal. Thomas Cannel, who researched funerals in
Pietermaritzburg, KwaZulu-Natal, noted: "Many families go deeply into
debt to provide what they see as a suitable funeral for their dead. A common criticism by community leaders is that what cannot be spared for the
dying, great as their need may be, is given to the dead."[10] In a study that
clearly quantifies the costs of funerals in the time of AIDS, Darryl Collins
and Murray Leibbrandt demonstrated that the bulk of funeral funds went
to the provision of food; more than half of funeral expenses was earmarked
for food alone.[11] Although it was not originally a research subject in their

study, their research revealed the central and essential role food played in the average South African funeral.

One Death, Many Feasts

One would assume that after a series of prefuneral and postfuneral feasts, the bereaved family would need a long time to replenish its coffers in preparation for the next period. The reality is that after the dead person has been brought back home through the *ukubuyisa* ritual, the demand for more food, and this time by the ancestors, increases. As mentioned earlier, the life of a Zulu person is permeated by the ancestors' presence from birth to death. Axel-Ivar Berglund has argued that even sexual intercourse is accompanied by the presence of an ancestral spirit during the heat of copulation. In a discussion with an informant about the role of ancestors in eating *ujeqe* and drinking *umqombothi*, Berglund quoted his informant: "That is what I am saying. A man cannot eat these things alone, by himself. They are there, just very close (*eduze imphela*) when he is eating. When he is eating these things they are working there with him. That is why the thing of men (sexual intercourse) is the same as the eating of beer and meat. They all involve heat."[12]

All the rituals that are connected by rites of passage of an individual are intrinsically connected to ancestor veneration. At irregular intervals any ancestor from the clan can indicate in one way or the other that he or she is hungry and expects to be fed.

The ancestors are known as *amadlozi* or *abaphansi* (those of the ground level) in Zulu language and *badimo* (those above) in Setswana language; they are assumed to be alive in their spiritual world, engaged in activities that are similar to those of the living. In African religion they are also known as the living dead. It is not surprising, therefore, to a Zulu person or to a Tswana person to receive visits from a departed ancestor indicating a need to be fed. They initially appear in a number of dreams and later, if such dreams are ignored, they bring on the chosen feeder some disturbances, which may range from minor illnesses to major ones. When the chosen person worries about the disturbances, he or she is advised to confirm his or her suspicions about the communication from the ancestor. A diviner often confirms that a relative is hungry, and blood from either a goat or a fowl is then spilled and *umqombothi* brewed. A small clay pot with foaming *umqombothi* and a piece of raw meat is placed at the altar of the ancestors (*umsamo*) for the ancestor to come at night and lick to show approval of the ritual. After such appeasement and apologies for delays in responding to the demand for a meal are made, relatives (and sometimes neighbors) are invited to feast on the remaining food and drink. *Ujeqe* is served as the starch to accompany the meat.

There are instances when, without any provocation, the living person wishes to slaughter a beast and prepare a small feast for friends and relatives in order to thank the living dead for the success in his or her life. Such unprovoked initiatives tend to be on a grand scale because the host has had enough time to plan. As in other ancestor-related rituals, a goat and *umqombothi,* prepared in the traditional way, are served. Men are served boiled meat and *ujeqe* in a wooden tray, called *uqgoko.* There are cases in some households where men are served the food on a piece of corrugated iron sheet. *Umqombothi* is served in a clay calabash, *ukhamba,* which is slightly bigger than the one used at *umsamo.*

A Shift in Practice

Most of the rituals of eating relating to death that have been discussed above can be said to be older than the introduction of Christianity among the Zulus and Tswanas. With increased formal education and the imitation of dietary practices of white people, new ways of eating in connection to death have been adopted. Either to accommodate the black Christians whose faith can be viewed as synonymous with whites', or to show their ability to include the traditional world of ancestors who serve boiled meat and steamed bread, Zulus and Tswanas sometimes also serve food of Western origin, alongside Western utensils—spoons, forks, and knives. In situations in which traditional people and Christians and educated people are attending the same funeral together, a meal of rice, curry, or stew may be served separately. This meal is called *ukudla kwe-spoon* (literally, food eaten with a spoon) because Western cutlery is used. The *ukudla-kwe-spoon* is sometimes prepared by a special catering company that charges a lot of money. For hygienic and health reasons the food is prepared in a clean environment and includes a variety of vegetables. This is in strong contrast to the meal centered on a home-slaughtered beast and the resulting fat-saturated meat.

Although such meals are served separately, some people like to move from one kind of food to another—except, of course, the church leaders, who have moved away from their peoples' cultural practices. No one would be denied space to have what he or she wishes to eat or drink. But the main table is reserved for respectable members of society and the close family members. This gesture is meant to decrease the time such people have to wait for the meal rather than to serve them a better meal than the mourners waiting in line.

Conclusions

This chapter examines eating and drinking practices that occur, primarily among the Zulu people, after the death of a family member. The different phases, before, during, and after the burial, involve an expensive series of rituals that must be followed because of the fear of and hope regarding the departed ancestors' influence on the living. Though changes in these rituals have occurred over the years, continuity with the traditional past remains. Those who have more money or large funeral insurance payouts are able to provide sumptuous meals to the mourners during various phases of the funeral. Because no formal invitations to the funeral go out to specific persons, even those with no close relationship to the deceased will come and partake of the funeral meal. While the family of the deceased is comforted by the big numbers that help them give a decent send-off to their dead, those enduring poverty and hunger have the opportunity to eat a good meal. The funeral meal, and the bereavement rituals that follow, thus sustains not only the dead in their afterlife, but the living in this one.

Notes

1. Berglund dedicated an entire chapter to funerary reversals in *Zulu Thought-Patterns and Symbolism* (Cape Town: David Philip, 1976), 363–381.

2. See Langalibalele Mathenjwa, "The Resourcefulness of Elders and Their Strategic Intelligence in Dealing with Culture, Memory and Trauma: An African Perspective," in *Culture, Memory and Trauma: Proceedings of the Third Annual National Oral History Conference,* ed. Patricia Opondo and Christina Landman (Pretoria, South Africa: Research Institute for Theology and Religion, University of South Africa, 2013), 8. Also, in her response to a presentation by Jill Olivier

during the conference on HIV and AIDS, Bongi Zengele refers to this practice and explains it in an endnote: "This is a direct translation from *isiZulu* [language] and is related to the fact that you live for other people in community: when you suffer we all suffer with you, we identify with you and your pain." See Bongi Zengele, "A Practitioner's Response," in *Religion and HIV and AIDS: Charting the Terrain*, ed. Beverley Haddad (Pietermaritzburg: University of KwaZulu-Natal Press, 2011), 105–107.

3. The ritual is called *ukucupha* in Zulu, which means "to trap."

4. The Group Areas Act separated whites, blacks, Indians, and colored people and designated different living areas for these groups. Whites were assigned to better-developed areas that are still preferred by other racial groups today.

5. Jone Salomonsen, "Shielding Girls at Risk of AIDS by Weaving Zulu and Christian Heritage," in *Broken Bodies and Healing Communities: The Challenge of HIV and AIDS in the South African Context*, ed. Neville Richardson (Pietermaritzburg, South Africa: Cluster Publications, 2009).

6. The pre-1994 era was a period of racial discrimination in all spheres of life, particularly the economic one. Black Africans were excluded by law from going to school to train for well-paying jobs, and salaries were skewed to vastly favor both the hiring and the promotion of whites. The post-1994 democratic era has seen many blacks holding high-salaried jobs, and the Affirmative Action policy has opened opportunities for blacks to holds jobs previously reserved for whites.

7. Daniela Gennrich has shown in her research how some households have too little to spend on funerals, whereas others have far more than enough. First, more than 50 percent of the households she surveyed bore the total funeral costs, 33 percent bore some of the costs, and 14 percent had insurance policies that paid the entire cost. Second, on average, four times the total household income was spent on a single funeral (R5,000–R40,000). See Daniela Gennrich, *The Church in an HIV+ World: A Practical Handbook* (Pietermaritzburg, South Africa: Cluster Publications, 2004), 15.

8. A deeper discussion of Mbeki's refusal to provide ARVs can be found ibid, 34–35.

9. See Philippe Denis, "Memory Boxes: Helping AIDS Orphans to Remember," *Bulletin for Contextual Theology in Africa* 7, no. 1 (2000): 34–36.

10. See Thomas Cannel, "Funerals and AIDS, Resilience and Decline in Kwa-Zulu-Natal," *Journal of Theology for Southern Africa* 125 (July 2006): 21–37.

11. Collins and Leibbrandt write that of the total costs of the average funeral, $1,414, $750 was spent on food. This calculation is based on an exchange rate of R6.5 per U.S. dollar. Darryl L. Collins and Murray Leibbrandt, "The Financial Impact of HIV/AIDS on Poor Households in South Africa," *AIDS* 21 (suppl. 7) (2007): 75–81, www.ncbi.nlm.nih.gov/pubmed/18040168.

12. See Berglund, *Zulu Thought-Patterns and Symbolism*, 225. Berglund is more explicit on this matter on pages 117 and 118.

Bibliography

Berglund, Axel-Ivar. *Zulu Thought-Patterns and Symbolism.* Cape Town: David Philip, 1976.

Cannel, Thomas. "Funerals and AIDS, Resilience and Decline in KwaZulu-Natal." *Journal of Theology for Southern Africa* 125 (July 2006): 21–37.

Collins, Darryl L., and Murray Leibbrandt. "The Financial Impact of HIV/AIDS on Poor Households in South Africa." *AIDS* 21 (suppl. 7) (2007): 75–81.

Denis, Philippe. "Memory Boxes: Helping AIDS Orphans to Remember." *Bulletin for Contextual Theology in Africa* 7, no. 1 (2000): 34–36.

Gennrich, Daniela. *The Church in an HIV+ World: A Practical Handbook.* Pietermaritzburg, South Africa: Cluster Publications, 2004.

Mathenjwa, Langalibalele. "The Resourcefulness of Elders and Their Strategic Intelligence in Dealing with Culture, Memory and Trauma: An African Perspective." In *Culture, Memory and Trauma: Proceedings of the Third Annual National Oral History Conference, Richards Bay, 7–10 November 2006,* edited by Patricia Opondo and Christina Landman, 1–10. Pretoria, South Africa: Research Institute for Theology and Religion, University of South Africa, 2013.

Richardson, Neville. *Broken Bodies and Healing Communities: The Challenge of HIV and AIDS in the South African Context.* Pietermaritzburg, South Africa: Cluster Publications, 2009.

Salomonsen, Jone. "Shielding Girls at Risk of AIDS by Weaving Zulu and Christian Heritage." In *Broken Bodies and Healing Communities: The Challenge of HIV and AIDS in the South African Context,* edited by Neville Richardson, 17–38. Pietermaritzburg, South Africa: Cluster Publications, 2009.

Zengele, Bongi. "A Practitioner's Response." In *Religion and HIV and AIDS: Charting the Terrain,* edited by Beverley Haddad, 105–107. Pietermaritzburg, South Africa: University of KwaZulu-Natal Press, 2011.

Digestifs

Acknowledgments

Just as a chef needs people to taste, test, and try her food, this book also has had many people involved in its production. First, I want to thank Emily S. Wu for her thoughtful feedback during many of the early stages of the book. Her insights were invaluable and helped produce a tighter, more cohesive, and better book. I am thankful to call her friend. Next, I want to thank the various contributors to this book, as it was their chapters and perspectives that really allowed this book to come together and be realized. Without them, there would be no book. Ashley Runyon provided initial assistance in the various stages of this book; Patrick O'Dowd finished the project with me. Thank you, Ashley and Patrick—this is the second project I have worked on with you, and you are both simply amazing.

I was able to work on this project because of several grants. Baylor University's Honors College provided me with a semester sabbatical that gave me time to work on this project. Thank you, Tom Hibbs and Anne-Marie Schultz for granting me the sabbatical. Baylor's Religion Department provided me with three graduate assistants whose eyes and minds were essential to the development and editing of the various chapters; Greg Barnfield, Tim Orr, Yvette Garcia, and Nick Werse, thank you for your help and many hours you put in on this book. Thank you, Bill Bellinger and Jim Nogalski, for continuing to give me staff support; it has been priceless.

Princeton University's Center for the Study of Religion (CSR) awarded me a visiting fellowship and an office, and Princeton Theological University gave me a visiting scholarship and housing for the fall of 2015, during the initial manuscript process, and I am indebted to both of them for providing the lovely and enriching environment in which this book was written. I will forever associate food and death with my little office at 5 Ivy Lane and my view of the trees at Payne Hall. Thank you for granting me an opportunity to grow and thrive as a scholar.

Also, I am grateful to Charles Mathewes and Kurtis Schaeffer for inviting me to participate in the 2016 University of Virginia NEH seminar on the Problems in the Study of Religion. I received valuable feedback from wonderful seminar participants on the first drafts of this manuscript, but more than that, I simply enjoyed their fellowship and the chance to reflect on my path as a scholar.

This book is dedicated to my mother, J. Arden Griffin, who first taught me to cook as a little girl. My mother loved to cook; every recipe came with a story, and every dish was an act of love. Visiting my mother as an adult meant finding the cookie jar filled with chocolate crinkle cookies and the refrigerator stuffed with my favorite foods. Food was my mother's language of love, and this book idea came out of that realization. Mom—I miss you, and I thank you for all those meals, snacks, and deserts you made to show you how much you loved us. I am grateful, and hope to pass on your legacy in the kitchen to my daughter. Finally, Maia, my beautiful girl, thanks for making me a mother. It has been fun growing and learning with you.

Contributor Biographies

Candi K. Cann is associate professor of religion and the Baylor Interdisciplinary Core at Baylor University. She is the author of *Virtual Afterlives: Grieving the Dead in the Twenty-first Century* (University Press of Kentucky, 2014), a textbook, *The World Religions: Essential Readings and Handbook,* and numerous articles and book chapters examining death from a cross-cultural and comparative perspective. She is also a certified thanatologist, writes course modules for the Funeral Service Academy, is a regular reviewer for *Mortality* and the Association of Death Education and Counseling (ADEC), and is on the panel of Death, Dying and Beyond for the American Academy of Religion.

Lacy K. Crocker is a Ph.D. candidate in religion at Baylor University. She focuses on ancient Near Eastern temple architecture and symbolism. Additionally, she has an interest in the relationship of death and dying and religious architecture and practices.

Rabbi Gordon Fuller is a native midwesterner, originally from Detroit. He has a bachelor's degree in human development from Northwestern University and a master's degree in social work from the University of Chicago. He has spent the last twenty-five years in Texas, most recently as the rabbi at Agudath Jacob in Waco, but he has just moved to Maryland, where he is now rabbi of Congregation Shirat HaNefesh. He is coauthor, with Dr. Joel Roffman, of the book *Coping with Adversity: Judaism's Response to Illness and Other Life Struggles* (2008).

Joshua Graham has his M.Sc. in social anthropology from the University of Edinburgh and is a Ph.D. candidate at the University of Bath, U.K. His research focuses on the cultural significance of foodstuffs and funeral food traditions.

Radikobo Ntsimane is an honorary lecturer in the School of Religion, Philosophy and Classics at the University of KwaZulu-Natal. He holds a Ph.D. in the history of Christianity. He is also a deputy director in the Provincial Department of Arts and Culture, responsible for museums' collections and research. His publications are grounded largely in the use of the oral history methodology of research.

David Oualaalou is a global affairs analyst, blogger, author, and professor. A former international security analyst in Washington, D.C., he is currently a visiting professor of government at Texas A&M Commerce and an international security guest lecturer at Baylor University. He holds a Ph.D. in public policy: homeland/international security from Walden University and an M.A. degree in international relations: security policy from St. Mary's University in San Antonio. His analyses of global affairs have appeared in many newspapers and online journals, including the *Huffington Post, South China Morning Post, New York Times, Defense Alert Journal, MSN News, Al-Jazeera, Security News Wire,* and *Freedom,* and he is the author of two forthcoming books: *The Ambiguous Foreign Policy of the United States toward the Muslim World: More Than a Handshake* (Lexington Books, 2016) and *Volatile State: Iran in the Nuclear Age* (Bloomington: Indiana University Press, 2018).

Jung Eun Sophia Park is assistant professor in the Religious Studies and Philosophy Department at Holy Names University in California. She earned her Ph.D. in Christian spirituality at the Graduate Theological Union, and she has published numerous articles, including "Jesus of *Minjung* on the Road to Emmaus (Luke: 24:13–32): Envisioning a Post-*minjung* Theology," in *Jesus of Galilee: Contextual Christology for the 21st Century,* edited by Robert Lassalle-Klein (Orbis, 2011), "Religious Life in the U.S.: A Vocation of Border Crossing," *New Theology Review* 27, no. 1 (2014), and "The Galilean Jesus: Creating a Borderland at the Foot of the Cross (Jn. 19:23–30)," *Theological Studies* 70, no. 2 (2009). She is also the author of *A Hermeneutic on Dislocation as Experience: Creating a Borderland, Constructing a Hybrid Identity* (Peter Lang, 2011). She has published various writings, including a spiritual essay book, *Beauty of the Broken,* in Korean. Her research interest is border-crossing spirituality, with an emphasis on Eastern religions in the global context.

Christa Shusko is assistant professor of religious studies at York College of Pennsylvania. Her research focuses on the history of religions in America, particularly communal societies and other "new" religious movements in the late nineteenth century. She recently contributed a chapter on spiritualism and the Oneida Community to the *Handbook of Spiritualism and Channeling,* edited by Cathy Gutierrez (Brill, 2015).

Emily S. Wu is an instructor in the Religion Department and Service-Learning Program at Dominican University of California. Her primary research interest is in the healing rituals, practices, and narratives in Chinese and Chinese American contexts, and she is the author of *Traditional Chinese Medicine in the United States: In Search of Spiritual Meaning and Ultimate Health* (Lexington Books, 2013). She is currently a cochair of the Steering Committee of the Religions, Medicines, and Healing Group of the American Academy of Religion. Wu's teaching and community work also deeply explore diasporic, transnational, and cross-cultural Asian experiences.

CONDIMENTS

Index

James, William, 153, 154
Jannah, 129. *See also* heaven; West
Land; "world to come"
Japan, 4, 153
Jesus, 23, 39, 43, 66, 70, 146n22. *See
also* Christianity; church;
Eucharist; Jesus; Mary, Mother
jing, 28
Judaism, 6–7, 107–24, 145, 146n22.
See also Gehenna; *kaddish;*
Talmud; Torah; *Sheol;* "world to
come"; Yom Kippur
juice, 175, 178

kaddish, 118–20. *See also* Judaism
karma, 30, 45
Kimchi (Fermented Cabbage), 40
Koran (Qur'an), 127, 130–31, 137,
144–45. *See also* Islam;
Muhammad, prophet; Shi'ite;
Sunni
Korea, 4, 32n14, 37–54

last meal, 2–3
Last Supper (Communion). *See*
Eucharist
liquor. *See under* alcohol

Malaysia, 20
Mary, Mother, 23. *See also* Catholics;
Christianity; church; Jesus
Mass, Catholic. *See* Catholicism
material-semiotic method, 89, 95, 101
Maw Maw Wallace's Chess Pie, 90
meal, funeral. *See* funeral meal
meat, 17, 22, 24–25, 46, 49, 66, 72,
109–10, 112, 138, 172–75, 180,
182–83. *See also* beef; chicken;
pork
Memorial Day, 42, 74
memorialization practices, 3–6, 23,
55, 58, 60, 65, 68, 76–78, 79n11,
80n13, 80n15, 81n23, 89, 93, 95,

100, 107, 110–11, 116, 120, 180.
See also memory
memory, 23, 61, 63, 76, 89, 93, 94,
160. *See also* memorialization
practices
Methodists, 60, 93, 98. *See also*
Christianity; church; Protestants
Mexico, 5–6, 55, 58, 60, 67–69, 74,
76, 78, 80n13, 80n18
Mictecacihuatl (Lady of the Dead), 68
milk, 60, 62, 109, 158
mogoga, 172
money, 3, 24–25, 29, 38, 41, 45, 48,
53n27, 72, 74, 77, 81n28, 96,
180–84; coins, 44
Mongolia, 39
Moroccan Couscous, 126–27
Morocco, 7, 125, 128–34, 136–39,
141–44
Mount Young Chi, 44, 47, 48, 49
mourning, 4, 7, 59, 61–62, 81n23, 96,
113–15, 117–20, 125, 133, 138,
143, 145, 146n22, 153, 165n5, 177
Muerte, Santa (Saint Death). *See*
saints
Muhammad, prophet, 137. *See also*
Islam; Koran (Qur'an); Shi'ite;
Sunni
Mulian, 26–29, 33n23
murder, 26, 112, 156, 159, 160–61,
166n15
music, 45, 48, 64, 120–21; song, 43,
81n28, 151, 158, 161
Muslim. *See* Islam

Native Americans, 141–42, 146n22
New Year's, 62, 74; New Year's Day
(*sul*), 40, 51
Nirvana, 42–44, 47, 51, 53n17
nuts, 24, 27–28, 46, 158

offerings to the dead: food, 3–4, 5–6,
9n7, 17, 19, 21–30, 33n17, 38–39,

Material Worlds

Books in this series explore worlds of our own making. Emphasizing interdisciplinary perspectives on material culture, authors interpret the ways in which individuals and communities create environments, traditions, and symbols from art, architecture, furnishing, food, and dress. In addition to interpreting the cultural values that artifacts and environments reveal, the series sheds light on the diversity of material worlds across the social landscape. Whether remote or close to home, the worlds uncovered by this series reflect the ways that "material" and "culture" come together in everyday lives.

Series Editor
Simon J. Bronner

Dying to Eat: Cross-Cultural Perspectives on Food, Death, and the Afterlife
Edited by Candi K. Cann

Virtual Afterlives: Grieving the Dead in the Twenty-First Century
Candi K. Cann

Designing the Centennial: A History of the 1876 International Exhibition in Philadelphia
Bruno Giberti

Culinary Tourism
Edited by Lucy M. Long

Funeral Festivals in America: Rituals for the Living
Jacqueline S. Thursby

www.ingramcontent.com/pod-product-compliance
Lightning Source LLC
Chambersburg PA
CBHW031133270326
41929CB00011B/1610